TOURING
THE
WESTERN
NORTH CAROLINA
BACKROADS

▲▲▲▲

# TOURING THE WESTERN NORTH CAROLINA BACKROADS

▲▲▲▲

BY

CAROLYN SAKOWSKI

JOHN F. BLAIR, PUBLISHER

WINSTON-SALEM, NORTH CAROLINA

Cover photographs, counter clockwise from top:
*Church near Kona, Roan Mountain Tour*
*Scenic Byway, Cradle of Forestry Tour*
*Former location of the Markle Handicraft School, Burnsville to Mars Hill Tour*
*The top of Hawksbill Mountain, Table Rock Tour*
*Pearson's Falls, Hunting Country Tour*
*Mountain Laurel, Table Rock Tour*

Manufactured by Eerdmans Printing Company
Composed by The Composing Room of Michigan
Book design by Debra L. Hampton

This book is printed on acid-free paper.

Library of Congress Cataloging in Publication Data

Sakowski, Carolyn, 1948-
    Touring the western North Carolina backroads / by Carolyn
Sakowski.
        p.    cm.
    Includes bibliographical references.
    ISBN 0-89587-077-0
    1. North Carolina—Description and travel—1981- —Tours.
2. Historic sites—North Carolina—Guide books. 3. Automobiles-
Road guides—North Carolina. 4. North Carolina—History,
Local.
    I. Title.
F252.3.S25 1990                                        90-484
917.5604'43—dc20                                        CIP

*To my parents, Arthur and Alice Sakowski, and my husband, Alton Franklin, for their love and support.*

# Table of Contents

# Key to Road Classifications

I-40            Interstate highway.

U.S. 421          Federal route, usually well traveled and well maintained. Road signs show the highway number inside a shield.

N.C. 181          Primary state highway, also well traveled and maintained. Road signs show the highway number in a white diamond inside a black square.

*State Road numbers are located on the posts holding the stop signs*

S.R. 1501        Secondary state road. These vary greatly in quality. Some are paved and others gravel, though plans are underway to pave them all. Road numbers are on the posts holding the stop signs at the entrance to the roads (see photograph).

*Forest Road numbers are found on short brown posts*

F.R. 451         Forest road maintained by the United States Forest Service. Usually an old logging road, so travelers can expect washboard conditions. Road numbers can be found on short brown posts near the entrance to the roads (see photograph).

# Preface

After living in or near the mountains of western North Carolina for most of my life, I have watched them undergo a rapid and startling transformation in a very few years.

Statistics from the North Carolina Department of Travel and Tourism state that over 60,000,000 tourists visited North Carolina during 1988. The Blue Ridge Parkway counted 25,566,863 travelers, while Great Smoky Mountains National Park was visited by 8,786,147 people. Since the Blue Ridge Parkway and Great Smoky Mountains National Park are two of the most popular destinations for tourists in western North Carolina, it is obvious that tourism in the mountains is now big business.

With increased traffic and the appearance of retail outlets and tourist attractions that cater to such crowds, much of the area's isolated beauty, as well as many of its unblemished landscapes and quaint communities, have disappeared. Tourists in the mountains who once cursed the endless hours of driving on narrow, two-lane roads with hairpin curves and switchbacks can now be whisked from one major tourist center to the next on four-lane superhighways.

To those who knew the mountains as they once were, the convenience of the new highways is welcome, but there is also a sense of loss for the slower pace that the old roads mandated. This book seeks to recapture some of that past flavor. Although it is growing difficult to trace a route that doesn't cross a well-traveled, commercialized segment of highway, it is still possible to travel backroads through areas reminiscent of bygone eras.

In order to avoid the most publicized of the tourist areas, I have tried to steer clear of interstates and four-lane highways. Since the Blue Ridge Parkway and Great Smoky Mountains National Park have been the subjects of numerous guidebooks, I have also omitted them, except for a few recommended side trips.

Sometimes I found it necessary to travel on dirt or gravel roads to stay on the "backroads," but I have tried to alert readers when rough roads may be anticipated. Travelers should also be forewarned that forest roads (designated F.R.) are usually old logging roads that are not as well maintained as the state highway system. State highways (designated N.C.) are usually paved and well maintained. State roads (designated S.R.) vary greatly in quality. Some are paved and some are gravel, but most of them can be negotiated even by a Winnebago, unless otherwise noted in the text. The state of North Carolina has recently announced plans to pave most of its remaining secondary roads, so their condition should improve in the next few years.

But this book is not meant to be a mere listing of directions for scenic routes. To gain a true feeling for the mountains as they once were, it is necessary to learn something about the history of the region. Because most of the North Carolina mountains were isolated and developed slowly, the history of the area has been neglected. Frequently, there are only one or two sources for a county's history, usually self-published books written by people in the community with enough foresight to realize that there would someday be a need to preserve a history that was quickly being forgotten. Because such sources are difficult to track down, I have tried to select highlights from as many sources as possible to turn this book into something that is as much a history of western North Carolina as it is a tourist guidebook.

In choosing the twenty-one tours, I tried to select routes that combined rich historical tradition, amusing stories about local characters, and tidbits of folklore and legend, as well as exceptional scenery. I know I have not included all the routes that meet those criteria, but I hope I have at least made a good start.

Each tour includes a map and photographs to give travelers some idea of what may be seen along the route. There is also a Bibliography for those who would like to read more about western North Carolina. An Appendix lists agencies that can supply more detailed maps and information.

I'm sure many of us have had occasion to ask, "I wonder where that road goes?" This guide is designed to supply the answer, as well as the impetus to follow that road. Whether you are traveling through the area for a few days, vacationing for a longer period, looking for new experiences off the main highways during your frequent visits, or merely satisfying your curiosity about the area in which you live, I hope that your backroads journeys bring you a little closer to the history, people, and beauty of western North Carolina.

# Acknowledgments

This book greatly benefited from helpful suggestions made by the following people: George Ellison of Bryson City; Alice White of the Cherokee County Historical Museum; Cynthia and Wayne Modlin of Macon County; Gert McIntosh of Highlands; Georgia Paxton and John Wesley Jones of Flat Rock; Clarice Weaver of Ashe County; Shirley Wayland of Watauga County; and Mrs. Douglas Barnett of Morganton.

Several professionals from the United States Forest Service also offered recommendations. They included Charles Miller of the Tusquitee Ranger District; Don Fisher of the Pisgah Ranger District; Michael Cook of the French Broad Ranger District; Gary Bennett of the Highlands Ranger District; and Bill Lee of the Wayah Ranger District.

Others to whom I am indebted for their time or assistance include Bob Greene of Brown Mountain Beach; Jennifer Wilson of Roan Mountain State Park; Linda Deyton and Grant Ward of Yancey County; Phyllis Burroughs of Avery County; Karen Doll of Lenoir; Rita Bond of Cashiers; Lucile Roberts of Madison County; Jo Greene of Ashe County; Beverly Means of Bryson City; the staff of the Toecane Ranger District; Michael Anderson of the Grandfather Ranger District; Frank Roth of the French Broad Ranger District; Judy Green of the Highlands Ranger District; and Joe Barnett of the Cheoah Ranger District.

This book would not have been possible without the help and support of the wonderful staff of John F. Blair, Publisher—Margaret Couch, Lisa Wagoner, Susan Cheshire, Steve Kirk, and Debbie Hampton.

Special thanks must also go to the staff at the North Carolina Room of the Forsyth County Public Library in Winston-Salem. Their fine collection proved extremely helpful.

Finally, thanks go to my mother- and father-in-law, Mary and Charles Franklin, for providing a home base during many weekends spent driving the mountain backroads.

TOURING
THE
WESTERN
NORTH CAROLINA
BACKROADS

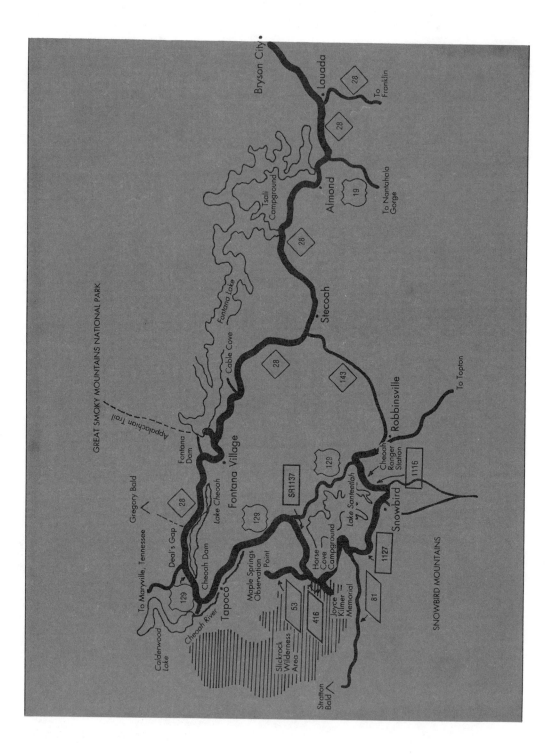

This tour begins in Bryson City, the county seat of Swain County. It follows Fontana Lake to Lake Cheoah and the village of Tapoco. Next, it follows the Cheoah River to Lake Santeetlah, then heads toward the Joyce Kilmer Memorial Forest and the Slickrock Wilderness Area. It continues around Lake Santeetlah to the Snowbird Mountains before reaching Robbinsville, the county seat of Graham County. Total mileage: approximately 80 miles.

▲▲▲▲▲▲▲▲▲▲▲▲▲▲▲▲▲▲▲▲▲▲ *The Tour of the Lakes*

The tour begins at the Swain County Courthouse in Bryson City, a town built in a bowl-like depression formed by the Tuckasegee River in the Cowee Mountain range, which connects the Smokies to the north with the Balsams to the southeast. The surrounding area was once an important Cherokee village called Bear's Town or Big Bear Farm, the home of the Cherokee Chief Big Bear. An important leader in the late 1700s and early 1800s, Big Bear was granted a reservation of 640 acres in the treaty of 1819 because he was "believed to be a person of industry and capable of managing his property with discretion," in the language of the treaty itself.

*Big Bear Farm*

*Yonaguska*

Another important Cherokee chief, Yonaguska, or Drowning Bear, lived 3 miles northeast of Bryson City on U.S. 19. An historical marker indicates that the land known as Governor's Island or Ferguson Fields was the approximate site of Yonaguska's home. It is also the site of an ancient mound, and it may have been the mother-town of the early Cherokees.

At the age of sixty, Yonaguska suffered a severe illness that caused him to go into a coma. Thinking he was dead, his people began mourning. Twenty-four hours later, Yonaguska regained consciousness and announced that he had visited the spirit world.

Yonaguska had been known to use alcohol to excess. Upon his recovery from the coma, he called a council. According to James Mooney, "In an eloquent speech that moved some of his audience to tears, [Yonaguska] declared that God had permitted him to return to earth especially that he might thus warn his people and banish whisky from among them." The chief asked his adopted son, Will Thomas—later an important leader of the Cherokees himself—to write an abstinence pledge. The rest of the council was convinced to sign it. From that moment until Yonaguska's death in 1839—less than a year after the Cherokee Removal—whiskey was "unknown among the East Cherokee," according to Mooney.

Though he counseled friendship with the white man, Yonaguska was always suspicious of missionaries. When the Bible was translated into Cherokee, he would not allow it to be read to his people until he had heard it first. After listening to several chapters, Yonaguska remarked, "Well, it seems to be a good book—strange that the white people are not better, after having had it so long."

Near the Swain County Courthouse is an historical marker honoring Horace Kephart. As a young librarian in St. Louis, Kephart was captivated by Francis Parkman's accounts of life in the West, but he was disappointed that few others wrote as well as Parkman. "It is most unfortunate that there exists in American literature no intimate and vivid account of the western hunters and trappers," Kephart noted. "It is one thing to describe events; it is another to make the actors in those events live and speak in the reader's presence."

By 1904, Kephart was feeling hemmed in by obligations to his wife and family. He also had a serious problem with alcohol. Rather than heading to his beloved West, he came east to the Smokies to recuperate his health and "to enjoy the thrills of singlehanded adventure in a wild country." He later wrote, "Knowing nobody who had ever been here, I took a topographic map and picked out on it, by means of the contour lines

*Horace Kephart*

and the blank spaces showing no settlement, what seemed to be the wildest part of this region; and there I went." His destination was the Smoky Mountains in North Carolina.

Kephart also noted before leaving St. Louis that "the most diligent research failed to discover so much as a magazine article, written within this generation, that described the land [around Bryson City] and its people. . . . Had I been going to Teneriffe or Timbuctu [*sic*], the libraries would have furnished information a-plenty; but about this housetop of eastern America they were strangely silent; it was terra incognita."

For three years, he lived on the site of an abandoned copper mine on the Little Fork of the Sugar Fork of Hazel Creek. He stayed comparatively sober and made himself a part of the community. Kephart then moved to the main hotel in Bryson City, the Cooper House. There, he established himself as such a celebrity among timbermen, salesmen, tourists, and traveling merchants that the structure was called the Kephart Tavern.

He lived in Bryson City until 1931, when he was killed in a taxicab accident while returning from a bootlegger's with a visiting writer. Kephart left his legacy in two books. He became known as "the dean of american campers" or "the grand old man of the campfire and long trail" for his classic work, *Camping and Woodcraft*, published in 1906 and still in print. With its historical references to explorers, its trivia about everything from tepee building to cave exploring, and its practical information about survival in the wilderness, the book still makes wonderful reading. His second book, *Our Southern Highlanders*, published in 1913, is filled with anecdotes and folklore about the way of life in the Appalachians. Kephart neither satirized nor exploited the people he came to know so well. He is credited with preserving much that would otherwise have been lost.

Kephart's greatest contribution was probably the vision and energy he devoted to the formation of a national park in land that he saw being destroyed by lumber interests. He was one of the principal forces behind Great Smoky Mountains National Park; 138,843 acres of land were officially dedicated the autumn after his death.

In the town cemetery that overlooks Bryson City, a ten-ton granite boulder marks Kephart's grave. It is said that from a groove in the top of the boulder, you can see Mount Kephart, one of the highest peaks in the Smokies, 30 miles to the north.

From Bryson City, follow U.S. 19/74 South for 5.6 miles to Lauada. Continue straight on U.S. 19/74 for another 3.1 miles, then turn right onto N.C. 28, heading north toward the community of Almond. It is another 3.4 miles to the signs announcing Tsali Recreation Area, on the right. In addition to campsites, the recreation area provides a boat launch for Fontana Lake, stables, and an 18-mile horse trail that follows the shoreline.

## Tsali

The story of Tsali has come to symbolize the Cherokees' treatment during the Removal of 1838 along the Trail of Tears. Over the years, many sources have distorted the facts about Tsali, but he remains a hero—the myth that has evolved represents Cherokee resistance to a brutal and inhumane policy. As detailed more fully in the Cherokee County Tour and the Trail of Tears Tour, the American government ordered the forcible removal of the Cherokees from their lands in the East to territory set aside for them in Oklahoma. When the Cherokees stubbornly refused to move, General Winfield Scott and a group of seven thousand men were dispatched to enforce the evacuation.

In late 1838, during one roundup of the reluctant Cherokees, an old man named Tsali (sometimes anglicized to Charley), his wife, his brother, his three sons, and their families were seized. According to Mooney, while the group was being taken to Fort Lindsay, a stockade near the junction of the Tuckasegee and Little Tennessee rivers, they plotted an escape, with the women hiding weapons in their clothing. Other sources maintain that the escape was a spontaneous reaction when soldiers prodded Tsali's wife with their bayonets in an effort to get her to move faster. Tsali and his group attacked the soldiers, killing anywhere from one to four, again depending upon the source. Official military reports say that two soldiers were killed and one was seriously wounded. Tsali's band fled to a cave in the Smokies located on the Left Fork of Deep Creek.

At this point, the versions of the story split dramatically. The version that is usually told says that a group of rebel Cherokees led by Utsala (or Oochella) was quartered at the head of the Oconaluftee River. When Tsali and his group escaped, General Scott seized upon the incident as an opportunity for compromise. He approached Will Thomas—Yonaguska's adopted son, "a trader who for more than twenty years had been closely identified with the Cherokee and possessed their full confidence," according to Mooney—and made his proposal. If Tsali and his followers would agree to turn themselves in, the other fugitives hiding in the Smokies would be "allowed to stay unmolested until an effort could be made to secure permission from the general government for them to remain," again as recorded by Mooney.

*Will Thomas*

Thomas approached Utsala with the proposal. Utsala realized it was futile for his small band of starving men to continue resisting Scott's seven thousand, but he was also bitter because his own wife and son had starved to death while hiding out. He finally consented, rationalizing that it was better that a few should be sacrificed than that all should die.

Thomas then rejected General Scott's offer of an escort and rode off to find Tsali. Tsali listened to Thomas in silence before answering, "I will come in. I don't want to be hunted down by my own people." Tsali, his brother, and his two oldest sons surrendered. They were executed by a Cherokee firing squad near the mouth of the Tuckasegee. Wasituna, Tsali's fourteen-year-old son, was spared because Scott insisted, "We do not shoot children."

Several historians have rejected this version after examining the official military documents.

Will Thomas did indeed play an important role, but one quite different from the romantic version above. The band of Cherokees living in Quallatown had received permission to stay in western North Carolina. Fearing that the Cherokees who evaded the roundup might jeopardize that permission, Thomas had been helping the soldiers from the start.

*Utsala*

Utsala had successfully defended the rights to his reservation in the state supreme court fifteen years before, but he did not trust the soldiers to adhere to legalities. He fled into the mountains with a small group, and his wife and son died of starvation while in hiding. After the Tsali incident, Thomas did convince Utsala to assist in capturing Tsali's band in exchange for permission to stay in the area. Utsala's men did capture Tsali and his group, but there is no evidence that Will Thomas journeyed to Tsali's hideout and convinced him to surrender. There is also no evidence that Tsali came in voluntarily to sacrifice his life for his people. Military documents also indicate that Tsali was not the primary target of the army's search. His two sons and a son-in-law were captured by Utsala's men. They were executed by Utsala's Indians on November 23. On the following day, Colonel William S. Foster and the Fourth Infantry left the area. It was not General Scott but Colonel Foster who issued a proclamation exempting Utsala and his band from removal, in consideration for their assistance in the search for the murderers. Foster announced to Utsala and his warriors that the Removal was officially ended and that they should notify any Indians still in hiding to join their brothers at Quallatown. Since he noted in his report that he considered his orders completed, Foster apparently did not think Tsali had played a major role in the murder of the soldiers. Utsala's band captured Tsali on the day the soldiers left and executed him the following day near present-day Bryson City. Regardless of the historical accuracy of the legend that persists, the Tsali Recreation Area survives as a tribute to the spirit of the Cherokees, as well as to a single man. A highly dramatized version of Tsali's sad story is retold at the Mountainside

Theatre in the community of Cherokee every night during the summer, when the outdoor drama *Unto These Hills* is performed. The drama may be factually inaccurate, but sometimes tearjerkers can produce positive results.

## Will Thomas

Will Thomas continued to be instrumental in pleading the Cherokee cause to Congress. In 1842, the Cherokees still living in the Appalachian Mountains were granted permission to remain. In 1846, the Eastern Band of the Cherokees was officially recognized. Since North Carolina refused to grant Indians rights as landowners, Thomas became their authorized agent, purchasing land in present-day Swain, Jackson, and Graham counties for them. When the War Between the States broke out, Thomas organized two hundred Cherokees and formed the Thomas Legion, which fought on the side of the Confederacy.

By 1867, Thomas's mental state had deteriorated to the point that he was declared *non compos mentis* and committed to the state asylum for the first time. His finances were in shambles, and the status of the Cherokee lands had to be unraveled through a series of lawsuits. In 1874, the courts ruled that the lands in question could only be held as security for the Cherokees' debts. It was also ruled that the remainder of the Removal and Subsistence Fund—set aside for the Indians in 1838 and made contingent upon their move to Oklahoma—should be released to them. From 1877 until his death in 1893, Thomas lived in and out of state mental institutions. However, Mooney's conclusion that "the East Cherokee of today owe their existence as a people" to Will Thomas is still valid.

## Tsali Recreation Area

At the Tsali Recreation Area, N.C. 28 crosses from Swain County into Graham County. Formed in 1872, Graham County has been characterized as some of the most rugged, isolated, and inaccessible land in the eastern United States. The Snowbird, Unicoi, Cheoah, and Yellow Creek mountains virtually enclose the entire 299-square-mile county. The first white settlers didn't arrive until the 1830s. The first road in the area appeared in 1838, constructed for the purpose of

*Fontana Dam*

*Fontana Dam with Great Smoky Mountains National Park in background*
Courtesy of Lance Holland

removing the Cherokees. Today, almost 60 percent of the county is located in national forests.

It is 7 miles from the Tsali Recreation Area to Stecoah, a picturesque farming community. It is approximately 1 mile from the Stecoah School to a junction with N.C. 143, then another 6 miles on N.C. 28 to the Cable Cove Recreation Area, on the right. This recreation area offers camping, hiking, and boating access to Fontana Lake. It is only 4 miles from Fontana Dam, the Appalachian Trail, and Great Smoky Mountains National Park. A 1-mile nature trail helps hikers identify trees, shrubs, and historical features.

It is 3.6 miles farther to an intersection with a fork leading to Fontana Dam; follow the right fork to the highest dam in the eastern United States. The massive structure is 480 feet high and 376 feet wide at its base. It holds back the 29-mile-long, 10,640-acre Fontana Lake. Visitors can drive across the dam. A cable car transports spectators from the visitors' center at the top to the power station below. Fontana Lake, created by the dam, has a 240-mile shoreline at an elevation of 1,727 feet.

After the bombing of Pearl Harbor on December 7, 1941, the federal government ordered the construction of a gigantic hydroelectric dam on the Little Tennessee River for aid in the production of atomic energy. By January 1942, more than six thousand workers had converged on the site, and twenty-four-hour, seven-day workweeks began. By January 1945, the first production unit was in operation, and the world's fourth largest hydroelectric dam was completed shortly thereafter.

After viewing the dam, return to the intersection with N.C. 28. Turn right, continuing on N.C. 28. It is 2.5 miles to the entrance to Fontana Village, on the left. The village served as a lumber camp in 1890, when the Montvale Lumber Company logged this side of the Little Tennessee. Mrs. George Leidy Wood, the wife of a lumber-company executive, spent a great deal of time in the camp and fell in love with the area. She suggested the name Fontana, and it stuck.

A second village called Fontana was con-

*Cottage at Fontana Village*
Courtesy of Lance Holland

*Fontana Village*

*Lake Cheoah*

structed farther up Eagle Creek in 1902 by the Montvale Lumber Company. It was more than just a tent camp, boasting the Fontana Hotel and the first Fontana post office. When Great Smoky Mountains National Park was established, the federal government drastically cut the amount of forest available for logging. At that point, Fontana became a mining town.

The copper mines near Fontana operated three shifts daily and employed more than a hundred miners. The Southern Railroad spur hauled carloads of ore to smelters in Copper Town, Tennessee, just over the state line. With the bombing of Pearl Harbor, the government ordered the mining terminated immediately, and the miners were directed to vacate their homes.

The six thousand workers who came to build Fontana Dam lived across the river at a spot called Welch Cove. They built a completely new and modern Fontana, with large community and recreation buildings, cafeterias, a hospital, a school, a theater, churches, and modern houses. When the work on the dam was completed in 1945, the Tennessee Valley Authority, overseeing the project, asked that some "agency, public or private, assume the operation of the townsite of Fontana Village." There were no takers for a year. Finally, Government Services, Inc.—a private business with no connection to the government—turned it into a vacation resort.

Today, there are over 250 rustic cottages and an inn to house vacationers. Fontana Village operates its own water and sewage treatment facilities and boasts a cafeteria, a laundry, a supermarket, a post office, and a service station. A recreation hall, game rooms, a swimming pool, and tennis courts are also available for guests at the resort. The village offers organized activities during the summer that include concerts, movies, talent shows, and square dancing, in addition to boating, horseback riding, hiking, swimming, and fishing.

It is 2.3 miles from the entrance to Fontana Village to the lower-level observation area for Fontana Dam. N.C. 28 follows the shoreline of

*Gregory Bald*

*Cheoah Dam*

Lake Cheoah, which was created by the damming of the Little Tennessee farther downriver. On the right is Great Smoky Mountains National Park. After 7.9 miles, you will reach an intersection with U.S. 129 at Deal's Gap, on the Tennessee–North Carolina border; this is the western end of the national park. A junction with Gregory Bald Trail is nearby. A 6.6-mile hike on the trail leads to Gregory Bald, which the Cherokees called Tsistuyi, the Rabbit Place. It was there that rabbits had their "town houses." Tsistuyi was also the home of the Great Rabbit—this chief of the rabbits was supposedly as large as a deer. Today, Gregory Bald, devoid of large trees, offers a spectacular view of the area.

Turn left onto U.S. 129. After 2 miles, the highway passes below Cheoah Dam and in front of its power plant. Around 1910, the Aluminum Company of America investigated the possibility of damming the Little Tennessee for the production of power to be used in the manufacture of aluminum. As war spread across Europe in 1915, the demand for aluminum increased. Concrete was poured for Cheoah Dam in March 1917, and the powerhouse began operation on April 6, 1919. At the time, the 225-foot structure was the highest overflow dam in the world, and its turbines were the world's largest. No other dam could exceed Cheoah Dam's 150,000-volt transmission line or its 5,010-foot span across the river. The nearby community of Tapoco grew up to accommodate the two thousand workers brought in to build the dam. The town was first called Cheoah, but it was changed because there was already a community by that name on Sweetwater Creek. The name Tapoco was drawn from the Tallassee Power Company.

In 1930, that same power company completed Calderwood Dam farther downriver, across the Tennessee line. Part of the railroad between Tapoco and Calderwood was covered by newly formed Calderwood Lake. The railroad bridge across the Little Tennessee below the mouth of the Cheoah River was transferred to the jurisdiction of the North Carolina Highway Commission.

*Tapoco Lodge*

*Maple Springs Observation Point*

Along with the useable portions of the old railroad bed, it is now part of the road you are traveling. When the highway was finished in 1931, Tapoco began to develop as a tourist attraction.

Completed in 1930, the Tapoco Lodge served as Andrew Mellon's private lodge while his aluminum company's power projects were under construction. Several cottages were added later, and it wasn't long before tour buses began to make the journey from Asheville. After the construction subsided, the town shrank to twenty-five or thirty residences. Driving across the bridge below the dam, you will see Calderwood Lake on the right. It is less than 1 mile to Tapoco. The brick Tapoco Lodge is on the right.

U.S. 129 now enters the gorge of the Cheoah River, which falls over a rocky bed for the next 7 miles downstream. You will pass under a huge pipe that is part of the aqueduct from Lake Santeetlah to Lake Cheoah. There is a sign on the right 7 miles from Tapoco directing you to Horse Cove Campground and the Joyce Kilmer Memorial Forest. Turn right onto Old U.S. 129 (S.R. 1147). After 0.5 mile, the road merges with Santeetlah Road (S.R. 1134) which is paved for a little over 2 miles. You will pass under the aqueduct tunnel again. The road then becomes F.R. 416. It is 5.5 miles from U.S. 129 to Horse Cove Campground, located on Little Santeetlah Creek. Just past the campground is an intersection. If you turn right onto F.R. 53, it is a side trip of 4.5 miles to the Maple Springs Observation Point. Designed for the handicapped, the 0.5-mile loop trail provides a panorama of Lake Santeetlah and much of the Nantahala National Forest. Great Smoky Mountains National Park can be seen in the distance.

It is 1 mile on F.R. 416 past the intersection near Horse Cove Campground to the parking area at the Joyce Kilmer Memorial Forest, one of the few remnants of virgin forest on the east coast. The forest is left completely to nature's control; no plants or trees, living or dead, may be cut or removed. The forest contains magnificent examples of more than a hundred species of trees, many of them over three hundred years old. Some trees exceed a hundred feet in height and twenty feet in circumference. The 3,800-acre forest was set aside in 1936 as a memorial to Joyce Kilmer, a soldier-poet who was killed in France during World War I and whose best-known poem is "Trees."

The parking lot provides access to a 2-mile recreation trail that loops through the forest and passes through Poplar Cove, where there is a plaque dedicated to Kilmer at the foot of a hemlock. There are over 60 miles of hiking trails in the Joyce Kilmer Memorial Forest and the adjoining 14,000-acre Slickrock Wilderness Area, offering a true wilderness experience. Maps are available at the Cheoah Ranger Station, which you will pass later in the tour.

Return to the intersection near Horse Cove Campground. Turn right onto S.R. 1127. It is almost 2 miles to a turnoff on the right leading to Stratton Meadows and Tellico Plains. Stratton Bald was the home of John Stratton, who came to present-day Graham County from Tennessee in the 1830s and was probably one of the first white settlers in the vicinity. Stratton earned the nickname Bacon John, the story goes, for catching nineteen panthers—or "painters," as they were called in the mountains—and making their shoulders and hams into painter bacon. It is said that he arrived on Stratton Bald with nothing but his rifle, blanket, cooking utensils, and ammunition. In the ten years he lived in the area, he made enough money from herding cattle and selling deer, bear hams, and hides to buy a farm in Tennessee.

It is 0.2 mile to the turnoff for the Snowbird Mountain Lodge, on the right. This is a rustic mountain inn built of chestnut logs and native stone. There is an excellent view of the Snowbird range from its flagstone terrace.

A few miles farther down S.R. 1127 is the Blue Boar Lodge, on the left. More modern looking than the Snowbird Mountain Lodge, the Blue Boar was built by Fred Bruckmann, who organized and promoted boar hunts in the Snowbird Mountains, a tradition that continues today. The

*Joyce Kilmer Memorial Forest*

*John Stratton*

wild boars are part of an interesting segment of local history.

In 1908, the Whiting Manufacturing Company of England purchased an extensive tract of land for logging purposes. George Gordon Moore of St. Clair, Michigan, was hired by the company to establish a European-style shooting preserve for the entertainment of wealthy clients on sixteen hundred acres on Hooper Bald, elevation 5,429 feet. Three years were spent in preparing the preserve. A ten-bedroom clubhouse and a four-room caretaker's cottage were built, a horse trail laid out, and telephone lines strung from the village of Marble, in Cherokee County. A road was constructed to Hooper Bald, and twenty-five tons of barbed wire were hauled by wagon to fence in the game lots. A six-hundred-acre enclosure with huge chestnut rails arranged nine high was built for wild boars. The buffalo enclosure was over 1 mile in circumference.

In 1912, animals began to arrive in Murphy and Andrews in wooden crates shipped by rail. Some were hauled to the bald by wagons pulled by oxen; later, the logging railroad from Andrews was used. The final inventory included eight buffalo, fourteen young wild boars, fourteen elk, six Colorado mule deer, and thirty-four bears, including nine huge Russian brown bears. Two hundred wild turkeys and ten thousand English ring-necked pheasant eggs were also brought in.

The hunting preserve was ill-fated. The bears quickly learned to climb out of their enclosure, while the boars learned to dig out of theirs. The location was so remote that the anticipated visitors never materialized. Local poachers killed off the wild turkeys. The buffalo did not fare well in their new environment, so they were sold; likewise, the elk were sold to start a herd at Mount Mitchell. By the 1920s, only the caretaker, Cotton McGuire, remained. The Whiting Manufacturing Company finally gave him full ownership and forgot their dream of a hunting lodge.

Of all the animals, only the wild boars flourished. They are supposedly descended from Russian wild boars—hence the nickname by which

*Hooper Bald Hunting Preserve*

they are known locally, Rooshians—but their physical traits bear a stronger resemblance to the *wildschwein* (wild pigs) of the Harz Mountains of Germany. It is said that they can jump twenty-foot obstacles and hit the ground running at full speed. They stand three feet high and weigh between two and four hundred pounds. Hunters love them for their fighting spirit, speed, and stamina. Hunting dogs are probably less enthralled when they come into contact with the razor-sharp tusks. Naturalists don't care much for the wild boars either, since the boars' rooting leaves a path of destruction.

The wild boars' reputation as game animals spread. Hunts were held year-round, many of them organized out of the Blue Boar Lodge. There are still boar hunts today, though the season is regulated to insure the survival of the population.

After a short distance, you will pass a turnoff on the right leading to the community of Snowbird, the heart of the settlement of the Snowbird Cherokees, who are descendants of the refugees allowed to stay after Tsali's surrender. It was Will Thomas who purchased land in the Little Snowbird Mountain area for the Snowbird Cherokees. The land remains in their hands today.

As you continue to follow S.R. 1127, the road skirts the shoreline of Lake Santeetlah. Begun in 1926, Santeetlah Dam first generated power in 1928. The lake covers more than three thousand acres and enjoys a reputation as one of the best bass-fishing lakes in the area.

A little less than 3 miles from the Blue Boar Lodge, turn left onto S.R. 1116, which skirts the lake and leads to the Cheoah Ranger Station after 2.3 miles. The ranger station was built on what was once the location of Camp Santeetlah, a Civilian Conservation Corps (CCC) camp. The CCC was formed to provide employment for men during the Depression. Enrollees had to be physically fit, unemployed, and unmarried, and they had to make allotments for their families. Each man received thirty dollars per month, twenty-five of which were sent to his family; if he had no family, the sum was held until his retirement. The CCC built bridges, fire towers, and trails, planted trees, fought fires, cleared land, stocked streams, and did just about any kind of public work connected with conserving and developing natural resources. Camp Santeetlah housed over two hundred men in 1935, but it was closed upon America's entrance into World War II. A twenty-minute interpretive trail takes visitors around the site of the former camp.

Follow S.R. 1116 to its intersection with U.S. 129. Turn right to reach Robbinsville. If you would like to continue past Robbinsville, take U.S. 129 to Topton; from there, you can turn left and take U.S. 19 back to Bryson City or turn right and follow U.S. 129/19 into Andrews.

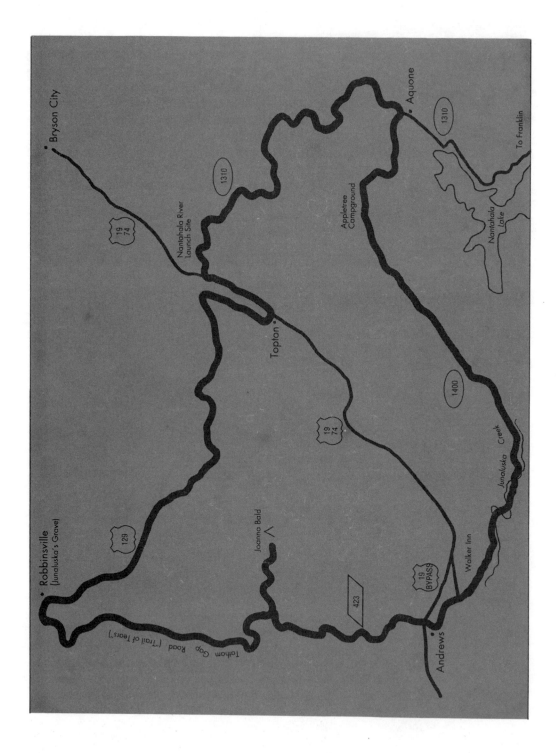

This tour begins in Robbinsville, the county seat of Graham County, at the gravesite of one of the greatest Cherokee chiefs, Junaluska. It then proceeds to Topton, where it swings through the Nantahala Gorge to Aquone. The tour turns toward Andrews, following Junaluska Creek, then picks up a segment of the historic Trail of Tears, leading back to Robbinsville. Total mileage: approximately 45 miles.

# ▲▲▲▲▲▲▲▲▲▲▲▲▲▲▲▲▲▲▲▲▲▲▲▲▲▲▲▲▲▲▲▲▲▲▲▲▲▲▲▲▲▲The Chief Junaluska Tour

*Chief Junaluska*

On a tour that includes part of the site of the Cherokee nation's most sorrowful tragedy, it seems fitting to begin at the memorial to one of the Cherokees' greatest chiefs, Junaluska. Drive past the Graham County Courthouse on Main Street in Robbinsville to a ninety-degree right turn. There is a sign indicating that Junaluska's grave is 150 yards on the left. It is well worth the effort to park on the side of the road and walk to the hilltop, where two large boulders surrounded by an iron fence mark the gravesites of Junaluska and his wife, Nicie.

In the War of 1812, the eloquent Shawnee Chief Tecumseh forged an Indian confederacy to fight the white settlers along the frontier. According to Cherokee tradition, there was much support for Tecumseh and his cause among their tribe. Tecumseh supposedly journeyed to a Cherokee gathering at the Soco town house, near present-day Soco Gap, where he captivated the gathered chiefs until Junaluska, one of the influential patriarchs, convinced the Cherokees to remain neutral in Great Britain's fight against the Americans.

The Cherokees did not side with Tecumseh—who soon formed a pact with the British—but rather joined the American troops led by General

Andrew Jackson. On the banks of the Tallapoosa River in Alabama in the Battle of Horseshoe Bend on March 27, 1814, it was the Cherokees who saved the day.

Jackson's troops were held at bay, unable to approach the fortress held by the Creek Indians because of the heavy cross fire. Junaluska led a Cherokee force that swam silently across the river to the enemy's rear, captured Creek canoes, and established a beachhead. Upon leaving to fight the Creeks, Junaluska had boasted that he would exterminate them; he returned a war hero, but he was forced to admit that some Creeks still lived. It was then that his friends awarded him the nickname Junaluska, which meant "He tried repeatedly, but failed."

In 1910, the Daughters of the American Revolution unveiled the memorial that marks the graves of Junaluska and his wife. It supposedly took sixteen oxen to transport the boulder marking Junaluska's grave to its present site. The inscription reads, "Here lie the bodies of the Cherokee chief Junaluska, and Nicie, his wife. Together with his warriors, he saved the life of General Jackson, at the Battle of Horseshoe Bend, and for his bravery and faithfulness North Carolina made him a citizen and gave him land in Graham county. He died November 20, 1858, aged more than one hundred years."

Retrace Main Street through the center of Robbinsville and head south on U.S. 129 for 8.2 miles through a flat farming valley surrounded by mountains. As the mountains open to the left, you will be able to see the Nantahala River Gorge far below. At the community of Topton, also known as Red Marble Gap, U.S. 129 intersects U.S. 19/74. Turn left, heading toward Bryson City and into the gorge area on U.S. 19 North/74 East. It is 1.6 miles to S.R. 1310 and the Nantahala River Launch Site, one of the main public access areas for the hundreds of rafters and kayakers who shoot the rapids of the Nantahala Gorge. Turn right onto S.R. 1310 and travel past the launch site.

This part of the tour parallels the scenic Nan-

*Graves of Chief Junaluska and his wife, Nicie*

tahala River. In his *Letters from the Alleghany Mountains*, Charles Lanman wrote, "The river Nan-ti-ha-lah, or the 'Woman's Bosom,' was so named on account of its undulating and narrow valley, and its own intrinsic purity and loveliness." Whether Nantahala really does mean woman's bosom in Cherokee is debatable, but the fact that the Cherokees also called the river canyon Land of the Middle Sun seems perfectly logical. The gorge is so deep and its sides so sheer that the Indians believed only the noonday sun could penetrate its depths. The Cherokees had several legends about mythic creatures who dwelt in the isolated gorge; they are discussed in detail in the Nantahala Tour.

The drive alongside the Nantahala River is one of the most scenic in western North Carolina. There are cascades and small waterfalls all along the way. Approximately 2.8 miles past the launch site is a waterfall pouring from the top of the gorge on the left. It is partially hidden by trees, so you may be able to hear it before you see it. It is most easily spotted in the fall and early spring, when the foliage is sparse. You may have to look back upon reaching the bridge.

It is 9 miles from the launch site to the Aquone post office, then 0.7 mile farther to S.R. 1400. It is easy to miss this turn; look for the first paved road to the right. There is a small highway sign indicating that this is the route to Andrews, as well as a forest-service sign pointing toward Appletree Group Campground.

S.R. 1400 is an unexpectedly straight road for such mountainous terrain. You will pass Appletree Group Campground and signs indicating public boat-launch areas for Nantahala Lake. After crossing from Macon County into Cherokee County, the route parallels Junaluska Creek and is known locally as Junaluska Road.

There are conflicting views about the exact place of Junaluska's birth, but it has been established that he was living on a farm about 0.25 mile below the bridge crossing Junaluska Creek in 1838, when he and the rest of his tribe were forced to move to Oklahoma.

*Nantahala River*

Junaluska returned from the War of 1812 a hero for saving the life of Andrew Jackson, but his opinion of Jackson was considerably changed by the late 1830s. Old Hickory was by then president of the United States, and an instrumental man in the implementation of the Cherokee Removal treaty. Junaluska reportedly said, "If I had known that Jackson would drive us from our homes, I would have killed him that day at the Horseshoe." It is little wonder that Junaluska came to harbor such bitterness, for his wife and other members of his family died on the Trail of Tears. (He remarried. It is a later wife, Nicie, who is buried by his side.)

Around 1843, Junaluska returned from the West, walking the entire distance. He tried to reclaim his old home on Junaluska Creek, but the government would allow Indians to settle only in unoccupied places. He set up a new home in what is now Graham County. In 1847, the state made a tardy retribution by awarding Junaluska 337 acres of land, making him a citizen of North Carolina, and giving him the sum of one hundred dollars. Junaluska was reportedly seventy-one years old at the time, and his anger had changed into a resigned grace. He spoke a few words of appreciation before both houses of the state legislature: "If I had as many as I am years old to devote to the service of North Carolina, I could not repay her for this great gift she has given me."

*William Walker* _____

A little over 12 miles after the turn onto S.R. 1400, you will see the Walker Inn on the right. In 1839, immediately after the Cherokee Removal, William Walker and his partner, Colonel John Waugh, were granted a tract of 295 acres in an area known as Old Valleytown. They supposedly dismantled Junaluska's home and transported the logs to a site farther down the valley, where they erected the first store in the area. In 1846, the local post office was moved to their store as well. The logs were burned for fuel in 1926, so nothing remains of the historic structure today.

In 1844, William Walker married Margaret Scott and built a two-story log house that he soon expanded into the stately Colonial structure that

*Walker Inn*

survives as the Walker Inn. The inn became an important stopping place on the turnpike from Franklin to Murphy, serving many important visitors over the years. In 1845, Colonel Alan Davidson, a lawyer traveling the legal circuit, described it in this manner: "At Wm. Walkers at Old Valleytown, was one of the very best houses in Western North Carolina, the bill for man and horse was fifty cents." Another visitor, landscape architect Frederick Law Olmstead, described the inn in 1857 as "a house which the wealthy planters from the low country make a halting station on their journey to certain sulphur springs farther north and east."

But the Civil War brought trouble to the Walkers. As in all accounts of Civil War action in the mountains, the facts are obscured by the subjectivity of the narrators. Margaret Walker's version of her husband's capture by "bushwackers"—men called simply "Union soldiers" by other sources—is moving nonetheless. "On October 6, 1864," she wrote, "there came to my house at 11 A.M., twenty-seven drunken men. They had stopped at a still house and were nearly swearing drunk. Dinner was just set on the table, but they did not eat, as they were afraid they would be poisoned, but they broke dishes from the table, and went to my cupboards, and smashed my china and glassware." Despite his wife's pleadings, William Walker, ill at the time, was taken away. Margaret followed the next day on horseback, accompanied by her sister for the first 15 miles, then on her own for another 6 upon entering an area where her sister feared to go. Margaret's search was in vain. She returned home to find most of her belongings destroyed and to face the prospect of raising five sons alone. She continued to run the Walker Inn, winning the reputation for being the finest housekeeper in the mountains, but her search for her missing husband never ceased. She wrote, "I wept for three years and two pillows were so stiffened by salt tears that they crumbled to pieces." Margaret Walker deserves full credit for raising her sons and making the Walker Inn famous. She never found any trace of her husband. The Walker Inn is listed on the National Register of Historic Places.

It is approximately 0.5 mile past the inn to an intersection with U.S. 19 Business. Turn left and head toward the business district of the town of Andrews. In 1890, the local railroad bypassed Valleytown, which had until then been the focal point of the area. The undeveloped tract of land near the proposed depot was quickly surveyed, platted, and sold, inaugurating the new town of Andrews. William Pitt Walker—one of the Walkers' five sons—was among the first to see the writing on the wall and relocate. He began the town's original mercantile business in 1891.

In 1897, the railroad also brought the first major industry to the area. The Kanawha Hardwood Company prospered by hauling timber from as far away as Graham County, even building the Snowbird Valley Railway Company in 1905 for help in moving the wood down to Andrews. In 1899, a second industry—the F. P. Cover & Sons Tannery—came to town.

Andrews boomed in the early part of this century, but the indiscriminate use of timber resources soon proved disastrous. With the timber gone, the industries left. Andrews still survives as the second largest town in Cherokee County, but the beautiful homes built by the Walkers and the Covers attest to better days.

After 0.4 mile on U.S. 19 Business, there is a sign on the left in front of the Valleytown Motel designating the beginning of Tatham Gap Road (the first section of which is now called Robbinsville Road). The sign reads, "Tatham Gap Road: A part of the Trail of Tears originally built about 1838, to remove the Cherokee Indians to Oklahoma." Turn right and begin the route that constitutes 12 miles of the infamous Trail of Tears.

When elected president in 1828, Andrew Jackson put through Congress the Indian Removal Act, by which all Indians were to be led west of the Mississippi. The state of Georgia, spurred by the discovery of gold in the Dahlonega district in the Appalachians, passed a law confiscating all

*Marker for Tatham Gap Road*

Cherokee lands. The pressure for removal intensified, though votes in Congress were close and the Indians did have many white supporters. The 1835 Treaty of New Echota proved the final blow. With only five hundred Cherokee signatures on the treaty supposedly representing the tribe of more than sixteen thousand, preparations were made to move them westward. The Cherokees would receive five million dollars and land in present-day Oklahoma in exchange for their seven million acres of land in the East.

*Cherokee Removal of 1838*

By May 1838, only two thousand of the sixteen thousand Cherokees had moved voluntarily. General Winfield Scott and a force of seven thousand men were sent to evict the remaining Indians. The tragedy that transpired was poignantly described by James Mooney in his voluminous report to the Bureau of American Ethnology in 1898, reading in part,

> Under Scott's orders the troops were disposed at various points throughout the Cherokee country, where stockade forts were erected for gathering in and holding the Indians preparatory to removal. From these, squads of troops were sent out with rifle and bayonet to every small cabin hidden away in the coves or by the sides of the mountain streams, to seize and bring in as prisoners all the occupants, however or wherever they might be found. Families at dinner were startled by the sudden gleam of bayonets in the doorway and rose up to be driven with blows and oaths along the weary miles of trail that led to the stockade. Men were seized in their fields or going along the road, women were taken from their wheels and children from their play. In many cases, on turning for one last look as they crossed the ridge, they saw their homes in flames, fired by the lawless rabble that followed on the heels of the soldiers to loot and pillage. So keen were these outlaws on the scent that in some instances they were driving off the cattle and other stock of the Indians almost before the soldiers had fairly started the owners in the other direction. . . . A Georgia volunteer, afterwards a colonel in the Confederate service, said: "I fought through the Civil War and have seen men shot to pieces and slaughtered by thou-

sands, but the Cherokee removal was the cruelest work I ever knew."

To prevent escape the soldiers had been ordered to approach and surround each house, as far as possible, so as to come upon the occupants without warning. One old patriarch when thus surprised, calmly called his children and grandchildren around him, and kneeling down, bid them pray with him in their own language, while the astonished soldiers looked on in silence. A woman, on finding the house surrounded, went to the door and called up the chickens to be fed for the last time, after which, taking her infant on her back and her two other children by the hand, she followed her husband with the soldiers.

General Scott established his headquarters for the Removal at Fort Butler, in present-day Murphy. He also established a series of outlying stockades to hold the captured Indians until they began their journey westward. There was no direct way to bring the Cherokees held at Fort Montgomery, in present-day Robbinsville, across the Snowbird Mountains, so General Scott hired James Tatham, a Valleytown resident, to lay out a road from Robbinsville to Andrews. Tatham staked out the route without the aid of a compass, and soldiers hacked it out of the virgin wilderness. The route from present-day Robbinsville to Andrews became one of several trails used by the soldiers to evacuate the Indians.

By October 1838, the main procession of the Removal was set to begin. Michael Frome described the trek in his book *Strangers in High Places*:

> The young, the sick, and the small, 14,000 of them; having stowed blankets, cook pots, and trifling remembrances in their six hundred wagons, bid adieu to their ancestral land, and marched across the Tennessee, across the Ohio, across the Mississippi in the dead of winter, averaging ten miles a day over the frozen earth, stopping to bury their dead who perished of disease, starvation, and exhaustion and to conduct Sabbath worship to the Great Spirit . . . while the new President, Martin Van Buren, advised Congress before Christmas that all had gone well, the Indians

*Entrance to the site of
Chief Junaluska's grave*

*Joanna Bald*

having moved to their new homes unreluctantly. The whole movement was having the happiest effects, he so reported with sincere pleasure.

The 1,200-mile trek to Oklahoma took six months. Sources vary, but it is estimated that between 10 and 25 percent of the tribe died along the way. The route they took became universally known as the Trail of Tears.

The white settlers who moved in after the Removal called the route Tatham Gap Road in honor of the man who laid it out. It survives as a gravel forest-service road today. Though the road is frequently rough, its views are spectacular, and the dark history of this route remains eerily present—perhaps because the road has changed little since 1838.

Continue on Tatham Gap Road across the four-lane U.S. 19 Bypass. It is 0.4 mile past the bypass to a stop sign. Turn right onto S.R. 1390 (the sign reads Stewart Road). Turn left at the first road, S.R. 1391, and head toward the Snowbird Mountains. The road curves. Take the first right, F.R. 423. You have been following the original course of Tatham Gap Road ever since you left U.S. 19 Business, but it is only when you hit the gravel of F.R. 423 that you can begin to imagine the oppressiveness of the Cherokees' journey.

It is 4.4 miles to the sign indicating Joanna Bald, to the right. It is only a short drive to the bald, which offers an impressive view of Cherokee and Graham counties. The Cherokees called Joanna Bald the Lizard Place, after a great lizard with a glistening throat that was frequently seen sunning itself on the mountaintop.

From the intersection at Joanna Bald, F.R. 423 heads downhill for 5.8 miles to the outskirts of Robbinsville. The beginning of the original Tatham Gap Road is at the edge of the property that the state of North Carolina granted to Junaluska in his later years.

Turn right at the intersection and head into downtown Robbinsville. Junaluska's grave is to the right, bringing the tour full circle.

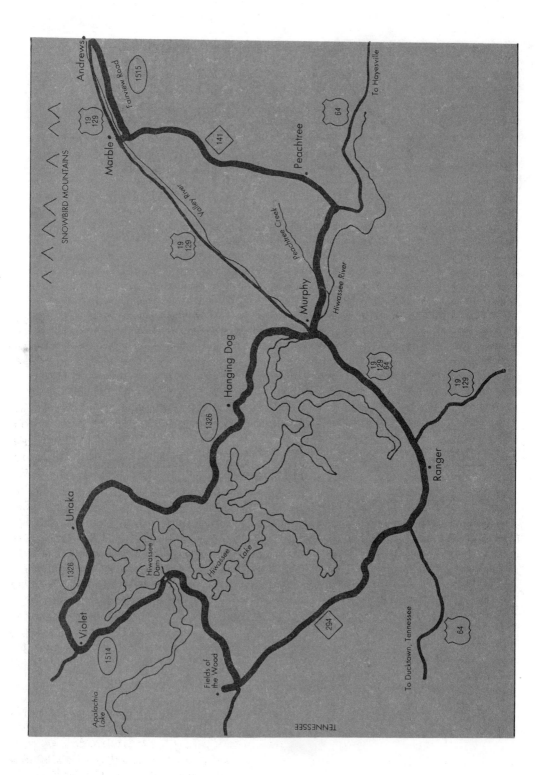

This tour travels through Cherokee County, the westernmost county in North Carolina. It begins in the town of Andrews and follows the Valley River to the once-prosperous community of Marble and the ancient Indian site at Peachtree. From there, it follows the Hiwassee River through Murphy, past Hanging Dog, and around Lake Hiwassee and its Tennessee Valley Authority (TVA) dam. The tour then goes to the Fields of the Wood before returning to Murphy. Total mileage: approximately 62 miles.

▲▲▲▲▲▲▲▲▲▲▲▲▲▲▲▲▲▲▲▲▲▲▲▲▲▲▲▲▲▲▲▲ *The Cherokee County Tour*

*Valley River Valley outside Andrews*

The tour begins at Fairview Road (S.R. 1515), at the Andrews city limits. If you turn off U.S. 19 Bypass onto U.S. 19 Business at the western edge of town, Fairview Road will be the third road on the right. Turn right and head out of town. Though it may be a little trouble to locate, this route is preferable to the four-lane highway that whisks most travelers from Andrews to Murphy. A beautiful river valley opens immediately; you are paralleling the Valley River, to your right. On old maps, the Valley River was identified by a variety of Indian names, including Gunahita (meaning long) and Konehete (meaning valley). As recently as the 1930s, maps were referring to the old flood plains, which had spread to a width of about 2 miles, as the Konnaheeta Valley. Today, those flood plains are known as the valley of the Valley River—a nice tongue twister, the Valley River Valley.

When George Featherstonhaugh recounted his trip through the area in his 1837 book, *A Canoe Trip up the Minnary Sotor*, he described the prosperous river country as "a valley enlarging to a mile of rich bottom land surrounded by lofty and picturesque hills covered with fine woods. This was the Paradise of the Cherokees, their wigwams built on graceful knolls rising above the level of the river bottoms, each of them having its patch of Indian corn with beans climbing to the top of each plant, and squashes and pumpkins growing on the ground."

Though the Cherokees were living in log cabins by Featherstonhaugh's day, the author was correct in his assessment of the area's fertility. Approximately 10 miles long, the valley offers the most level land in the entire county; the bottoms contain practically three-fourths of the cleared land in Cherokee County and are the heart of its agriculture. The valley is surrounded by the Snowbird Mountains on the right and the Valley River Mountains on the left.

In 1858, the editor of the *Asheville Spectator* described a scene similar to the one visible from Fairview Road today: "The valley . . . is one of the most beautiful I have ever seen; and, in fertility, it does not deceive its looks. Not only is the soil fertile, but there is, in the hillsides and valleys, a mineral wealth perfectly inexhaustible. . . . I could stand and gaze at it,—beautiful even in its not half cultivated state,—and my heart swells with pride, when I think that all this beauty is within my own glorious Carolina."

After 5.4 miles, Fairview Road ends at N.C. 141. Turn right. It is 1.5 miles to the Marble post office. Henry Moss, the first white settler in the area, arrived in 1842. Marble's period of prosperity started with the exploitation of its mineral resources. Iron ore was dug around 1845, and an English company opened a successful gold mine in 1861 that operated until 1896. But it took the most extensive marble deposits in the state of North Carolina to assure the area's economic success and supply the name for the resulting town.

The marble deposits were of very high quality, with an estimated thickness of five hundred feet. The Columbia Marble Company's product dominated the local mining industry—high-grade marble of regal blue and sterling gray, colors that lent themselves to intricate carving and pol-

*The community of Marble*

ishing. The regal marble is found only in this valley. Some 90 percent of the marble mined locally was used for monuments and building stone. Area people were especially proud when their marble was selected for use at Arlington National Cemetery.

Getting a block of marble out of the quarry required seven men. Once out, it was sawed into slabs with blades with diamond bits. It required from fifty-two to fifty-six man-hours to saw a single block into slabs.

The town of Marble hit its height in the early 1900s. Incorporated in 1914, it saw three of its iron-ore mines reopened during World War I. But the boom period was brief, and by 1940 the town was no longer incorporated. Unlike so many boom towns in the mountains, some of Marble's original one- and two-story commercial buildings can still be seen along the railroad tracks. They offer mute evidence of what the community once was.

*Evan Jones*

After viewing what remains of Marble, retrace your route, continuing south on N.C. 141 past the intersection with S.R. 1515. It is 3.6 miles to the volunteer fire department in the community of Peachtree. In 1735, the once-powerful Natchez Indian tribe was uprooted from its homeland in Mississippi by the French. The Natchez Indians established a village just above Peachtree Creek and eventually merged with the Cherokees. By 1820, the area that is now the Valley River Valley had been established as a center for Baptist missionary work among the Indians. The Natchez village above Peachtree Creek became the site of Reverend Evan Jones's Baptist mission, which contained several buildings, including a gristmill and a sawmill. Reverend Jones was the man responsible for translating the New Testament into the Cherokee language and for compiling a Cherokee spelling book. When the Cherokees were forced to move west, Jones chose to move his mission with them. The vicinity is still known locally as the Mission Area.

From Peachtree, it is almost 6 miles to an intersection with U.S. 64. Turn right, heading west

*Hiwassee River*

toward Murphy. The Hiwassee River is a scenic presence on the left. Some early maps gave the river's name as Owassa, which means main river in Cherokee. Others claim that Hiwassee means savannah or meadow. Whatever the translation, the name is Hiwassee today. In his 1849 account of his travels, Charles Lanman described the river in this manner: "The Owassa is a tributary of the noble Tennessee, and is as clear, beautiful, rapid and picturesque a mountain river as I have ever seen." Since Lanman's journey had taken him all over western North Carolina, that was quite a statement.

The area the tour is now passing through holds the beginnings of Cherokee County's long history of settlement. At the place where Peachtree Creek flows into the Hiwassee River from the right stand the remains of the Peachtree Mound and Village Site. The site has proven to be of considerable interest to both historians and archaeologists because of the information it has revealed about early settlement.*

*Peachtree Mound and Village Site*

There was an unscientific exploration of the Indian mound in 1885; considerable archaeological material was removed to Richmond, Virginia, where it is now housed in the Valentine Museum. In 1933, the Smithsonian Institution sponsored and organized a more thorough investigation, which arrived at several interesting conclusions. Smithsonian investigators placed the earliest occupation of the site during the Archaic period (8000 to 1000 B.C.) and agreed that it was continuously occupied until historic times. They came to believe that the site was the ancient Cherokee village of Guasili, mentioned by three chroniclers of Hernando De Soto's 1540 expedition, which searched for gold in the area. The chroniclers wrote that they were kindly received and hospitably entertained by the Indians in Guasili. Among other foodstuffs, the Spaniards were given three hundred dogs, which the Indians bred for eating purposes at that time. Corn was provided for the Spaniards' horses, and the officers of the expedition were lodged in the town house on top of the mound. De Soto left without finding gold. Another Spaniard, Juan Pardo, arrived in 1567, also searching for gold. It is believed that after Pardo's expedition, the Spaniards mined the area for more than a century.

The Smithsonian investigators described the mound in their report:

> It may be said that the Peachtree site consisted of an artifactually rich and extensive habitation site. . . . Upon this village site was built a hard packed area which later became the floor of a ceremonial structure of stone and wood. This was covered by a small round-topped mound, about 60 feet in diameter. Over this mound, and separated from it by a sand strata, was a larger secondary mound which underwent at least two major periods of construction and several minor additions. The secondary mound had upon it three ceremonial buildings, as evidenced by three superimposed floors.

The report also estimated that 250,000 pieces of Indian pottery had been found at the site, and it mentioned the discovery of sixty-eight burial sites, some enclosed in stone-lined graves.

*Murphy*

It is approximately 3.5 miles from the Peachtree Mound and Village Site to the intersection where U.S. 64 merges with U.S. 19/23 Bypass. Continue straight. The road you are traveling becomes known as Peachtree Street and passes into the center of Murphy, the county seat of Cherokee County. Ironically, Murphy is nearer to the capitals of seven other states (Kentucky, Georgia, Tennessee, Alabama, South Carolina, Florida, and West Virginia) than it is to its own.

During the Cherokee settlement of the area, the village where the Hiwassee and Valley rivers meet—the present site of Murphy—was called Tlanusiyi, the Leech Place. In his report to the Bureau of American Ethnology in 1898, James Mooney recorded the following legend:

> Just above the junction is a deep hole in Valley river, and above it is a ledge of rock running across the stream, over which people used to go as on a bridge. . . . One day some men going along the trail saw a great red object, full as large as a house, lying on the rock

ledge in the middle of the stream below them. As they stood wondering what it could be they saw it unroll—and then they knew it was alive—and stretch itself out along the rock until it looked like a great leech with red and white stripes along its body. It rolled up into a ball and again stretched out a full length, and at last crawled down the rock and was out of sight in the deep water. The water began to boil and foam, and a great column of white spray was thrown high in the air and came down like a waterspout upon the very spot where the men had been standing, and would have swept them all into the water but that they saw it in time and ran from the place.

Mooney reported that this was one of the best-known myths of the Cherokees, and he corrected an 1849 report by Charles Lanman, who had said that Tlanusiyi meant large turtle. Both men wrote of the Cherokee belief that, as Lanman put it, "there is a subterranean communication between this immense hole in Owassa and the river Notely [Nottely], which is some two miles distant. . . . The testimony adduced in proof of this theory is, that a certain log was once marked on the Notely, which log was subsequently found floating in the pool of the Deep Hole in the Owassa."

## Middle or Valley Cherokees

As white settlement proceeded westward and forced the Indians to spread out, the Cherokee tribe divided into distinct groups. While the factions living in South Carolina, Georgia, and Tennessee were quick to assimilate the white man's culture, those in certain villages west of the Blue Ridge tended to be more conservative and traditional. They became known as Middle or Valley Cherokees and their villages as Middle or Valley towns. The Peachtree-Murphy area came to be the center for those villages.

In 1813, giving in to pressure from their white neighbors, the Cherokees allowed part of a new road connecting Tennessee and Georgia to be built through their land. The Unicoi Pike passed alongside the Hiwassee River and spawned several inns, which were run by mixed-blood members of the Cherokee nation. Sometime around 1828, A. R. S. Hunter, the first white man to settle in the area, built an Indian trading post across the Hiwassee from the present site of Murphy. The small settlement was later called Huntington.

Not long before that time, gold had been discovered in Cherokee territory located in what is now Georgia. The Cherokees had adopted the white man's ways more readily than any other tribe, but the lure of gold made prejudice rear its ugly head. The whites began to pressure the Cherokees to accept land west of the Arkansas River in exchange for their eastern territory.

Though the Cherokees were divided over whether to accept the government's offer, the great majority opposed the Removal plan. The question grew so serious that by 1820 the Cherokee nation passed a law declaring that entering into any negotiation for the sale of tribal lands without the consent of the national council would be considered treason, punishable by death.

The Cherokees had already learned some hard lessons about the white man's democracy, and when they found their lands and rights threatened, they sent a delegation to Washington led by John Ross, the head of the upper house of the tribe's bicameral legislature. Ross's presentation to Congress, excerpted here, was an eloquent statement underscoring the hypocrisy of the federal government in its dealings with the Cherokees:

*John Ross*

> Happy under the parental guardianship of the United States, [the Cherokees] applied themselves assiduously and successfully to learn the lessons of civilization and peace, which, in the prosecution of a humane and Christian policy, the United States caused to be taught them. Of the advances they have made under the influence of this benevolent system, they might a few years ago have been tempted to speak with pride and satisfaction and with grateful hearts to those who have been their instructors. . . . But now each of these blessings has been made to them an instrument of the keenest torture. Cupidity has fastened its eye upon their lands and their homes, and is seeking by force and by every variety of oppression and wrong to expel

them from their lands and their homes and to tear them from all that has become endeared to them. . . . Having failed in their efforts to obtain relief elsewhere, [they] now appeal to Congress, and respectfully pray that your honorable bodies will look into their whole case, and that such measure may be adopted as will give them redress and security.

John Ross received his answer with a new treaty proposed in 1835. While an Indian council representing fewer than five hundred of a population of more than sixteen thousand Cherokees met at New Echota, Georgia, Ross was held prisoner in Washington without a charge against him. Signed that same year, the treaty was proclaimed in 1836. President Van Buren proposed a two-year extension to give the Cherokees time to move to Oklahoma.

*Fort Butler*

Fort Butler was built in Huntington, becoming one of six fortifications in North Carolina established for the purpose of gathering the Cherokees for removal. It soon became obvious, however, that the majority—especially the traditional Indians from the Valley Towns—had no intention of moving voluntarily. In the spring of 1838, a force under General Winfield Scott occupied Fort Butler as its headquarters, and the forced evacuation of the Cherokees began in earnest. In describing the Removal, James Mooney wrote that it "may well exceed in weight of grief and pathos any other passage in American history." Historical records seem to bear him out. More details on the Removal may be found in the Chief Junaluska and Tour of the Lakes tours.

The center of Murphy is the intersection of Peachtree and Hiwassee streets. Turn left onto Hiwassee Street and head downhill. You will see the historical marker for Fort Butler just past the bridge over the river, though nothing of the actual fort remains. There is a more detailed discussion of the Cherokee County Courthouse and other downtown Murphy buildings in the Standing Indian Tour.

Backtrack to Peachtree Street and head northwest out of town, in the opposite direction from which you came. It is 2.9 miles to the signs identifying the community of Hanging Dog and another 1.5 miles to the Hanging Dog Campground. Formerly referred to as the Old Mill when it was owned by Nathan Dockery, the campground property was condemned and purchased by the TVA during the time when it was planning the Hiwassee Dam; it is now part of Nantahala National Forest. Hanging Dog was the site of one of the last battles of the Civil War fought east of the Mississippi, on May 6, 1865. Confederate forces claimed that Union renegades raided and burned the Cherokee County Courthouse in an effort to destroy court claims against themselves. Confederate forces stationed in the community of Valleytown chased the raiders and caught up with them at Hanging Dog, precipitating the skirmish.

The tale that accounts for Hanging Dog's name is an excellent example of mountain folklore. Due to crop failure, a Cherokee village found itself facing starvation during one of the most bitterly cold winters in memory. A man called Deer Killer was the only Cherokee able to find game that year, thanks to his expert hunting dog. After a whole day of maneuvering a large buck for his master to kill, the dog was able to chase the quarry into range. When Deer Killer's arrow struck but failed to kill the prey, the deer broke for the nearby creek, closely followed by dog and master. While swimming the creek in pursuit, the dog became entangled in a mass of logs, vines, and debris. Seeing his beloved dog in danger of drowning, Deer Killer jumped into the icy water and freed him. The two then continued across the creek and resumed their chase. When they brought deer meat back to the village, there was enough to share with everyone. Deer Killer told of his dog's swipe with death. From that time, the Indians took to calling the creek where the dog had been hung up in debris Hanging Dog Creek.

Peachtree Road has now become S.R. 1326. You are winding among the coves of Hiwassee Lake. In 1935, Congress authorized the TVA to build a dam on the Hiwassee River for flood control and the generation of electricity. Over sixteen hundred men were employed. Hiwassee Lake is the reservoir created by the dam.

Your route now passes through the small communities of Grape Creek and Unaka. About 1.2 miles past the Unaka Volunteer Fire Department, it changes to gravel, still circling the lake for another 3.3 miles before reaching a fork in the road. Continue on S.R. 1326, which is the lower fork on the left, heading downhill. After 2 miles, you will reach a stop sign at the intersection with S.R. 1514. Turn left, heading toward the Violet Baptist Church. After 4.3 miles, you will pass the Naval Ordnance Laboratory, established in the 1940s, en route to the Hiwassee Dam visitors' overlook.

The overlook provides an excellent opportunity to see the top of the dam. There is a sidewalk paralleling the road along the top. Built of concrete, the dam is 307 feet high and more than 0.25 mile long. It is the highest overspill dam in the United States. In 1954–55, the first integrated pump-turbine used in an American power plant was installed here. Water flows from Hiwassee Lake to the dam, where the turbine generates power during peak hours of demand. Downriver to the west is Apalachia Dam and Lake, where the used water is dumped. During the night, when demand for power drops, the Hiwassee unit functions as a pump, drawing water out of Apalachia Lake, lifting it 205 feet, and putting it back in the Hiwassee Lake reservoir for use the next morning during peak hours. It is 0.6 mile from the Hiwassee Dam overlook to the visitors' reception center, on the right. There, the famous pump-turbine can be seen in action.

It is 4.8 miles from the dam to the junction of S.R. 1514 and N.C. 294. Turn right, following the signs for 0.7 mile to Fields of the Wood.

In *A Traveler's Guide to the Smoky Mountains Region*, Jeff Bradley characterized Fields of the Wood as "one of those things that future civilizations will ponder over." The official brochure available at the site describes it as a "Bible-theme park developed on more than 200 acres." After driving through the gates (and pleasantly discovering there is no admission charge), you will see

*Hiwassee Lake*

*Fields of the Wood*

dozens of religious monuments on the sides of two adjacent slopes. The park is owned and maintained by the Church of God of Prophecy, and many of the church's affiliates have donated monuments. Among the attractions are the world's largest cross (150 feet tall and 115 feet wide), a replica of Christ's sepulcher, prayer monuments along a giant stairway, an electric Star of Bethlehem, and the main attraction—the world's largest representation of the Ten Commandments. The grass "tablet," 300 feet square, is laid out on a mountainside, while the letters spelling out the Ten Commandments are 5 feet high and 4 feet wide. A 24-foot-tall, 34-foot-wide statue commemorating the New Testament stands at the top of the mountain, and visitors can walk to the platform on top of the statue for a panoramic view of the Ten Commandments below. Visitors are encouraged to take photographs. There is even a building with a lounge and a gift shop nearby. The area is billed as one of the "Biblical Wonders of the Twentieth Century," and there is little doubt that it probably is.

Leaving Fields of the Wood, turn left onto N.C. 294, heading toward Murphy. It is 13.5 miles to a junction with U.S. 64. Turn left and complete the tour by traveling the 5 miles into Murphy.

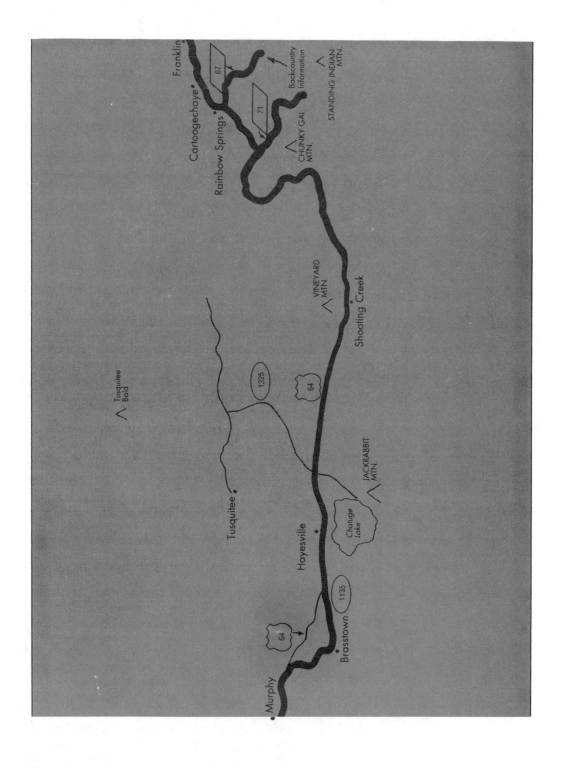

This tour begins in Murphy, the county seat of Cherokee County. It travels to Brasstown and the John C. Campbell Folk School, then to Hayesville, the county seat of Clay County. From there, it climbs through the Chunky Gal Mountains to Standing Indian Mountain, then through Winding Stair Gap and into Franklin, the county seat of Macon County. Total mileage: approximately 75 miles.

▲▲▲▲▲▲▲▲▲▲▲▲▲▲▲▲▲▲▲▲▲▲▲▲▲▲▲▲▲▲▲▲▲▲▲▲▲▲▲*The Standing Indian Tour*

*Murphy*

The center of downtown Murphy is the intersection of Peachtree and Hiwassee streets. If you were to head south, driving downhill on Hiwassee Street, you would see the historical marker for Fort Butler just past the bridge over the Hiwassee River. Fort Butler was one of the temporary stockades built to house captured Cherokees until they could be removed to Oklahoma in 1838. Fort Butler's role in Murphy's early history is discussed more thoroughly in the Cherokee County Tour. If you were to head north on Hiwassee Street, you would see the distinctive Murphy United Methodist Church, with its large central dome flanked by projecting gables. The church was built in 1922. However, to begin this tour, you should head east on Peachtree Street to the impressive Cherokee County Courthouse, located one block from the town square. The present structure is actually Cherokee County's fifth courthouse. It is listed on the National Register of Historic Places.

Soon after the Cherokee Indians were moved to Oklahoma, Cherokee County was created and opened for white settlement. Legislation was passed in 1838 designating a county seat and naming it after Archibald D. Murphey, whose efforts had resulted in the formation of North

*Cherokee County Courthouse in Murphy*

Carolina's public-school system. An error in spelling dropped the *e* in Murphey's name, and it was never restored. There was a petition to name the new county seat after Junaluska, a Cherokee chief who many believe was born here, but the movement never gained the necessary momentum.

By 1844, Murphy had its first permanent courthouse. The building remained standing until May 1865, when, shortly after the surrender at Appomattox, Union sympathizers raided Murphy and burned the courthouse. Confederates claimed that the courthouse was burned in an effort to destroy records, since most of the Union renegades responsible had cases pending against them, with papers on file inside the building. That may be a one-sided view, but it is no doubt the one that prevailed during the pursuit of the culprits. Confederate forces finally caught the Union renegades at Hanging Dog, and the May 6 encounter is believed to have been one of the last battles of the Civil War east of the Mississippi.

Owing to financial circumstances after the war, the community decided to rebuild the courthouse using the old bricks. A one-story structure was erected, but the builders discovered that they still had enough bricks for a second story, which was completed in 1868. The second courthouse was replaced in 1891 by a commodious building erected one block from the town square and its predecessor, at the site of the present courthouse.

That building burned in 1895. Murphy had to build again. The 1896 version was a Romanesque brick structure featuring two towers in front, the larger of which contained a belfry and an enormous clock. But Murphy seemed to have a problem with fires—the fourth building burned in 1926.

The present courthouse was completed in 1927. A neoclassical structure, it was built of beautiful, unpolished blue marble from the nearby regal marble works. Its tower, including the flagstaff, is 132 feet high. It contains a bell and clocks facing in each of the four directions. A bronze eagle with wings spread for flight is mounted atop the flagpole.

Next to the courthouse is the old Carnegie Library building, constructed in 1922. It now houses the Cherokee County Historical Museum, which contains one of the most eclectic collections in western North Carolina. The collection began with a man named Arthur Palmer—the owner and operator of a filling station in Marble—but it grew to encompass over two thousand relics gathered over a seventy-year period. The collection was donated to the local historical society in 1977 by Herman West. The exhibits include displays of native rocks and minerals; Indian artifacts such as pottery, war instruments, jewelry, baskets, tools, and toys; artifacts left by the Spanish explorers; old guns, powder horns, and swords; and even some stuffed animals. One display of particular interest features fairy crosses, which are framed and displayed on one of the museum's walls. The legend of the fairy crosses will be explained later in the tour, but previewing the crosses may make it more vivid.

Across the street from the museum is the Church of the Messiah, an Episcopal church built in 1896. Its stained glass window is from Tiffany's in New York. Miss Lucy Morgan is remembered for her work with the Penland School near Burnsville (see the Overmountain Victory Trail Tour). Her mother was one of the principal forces behind the movement to build the Church of the Messiah. Remembering how her mother canvassed the area for contributions by sending cards with holes the size of quarters stamped out of them, Miss Lucy speculated, "I imagine a great part of the church was built with the quarters returned in Mama's cards." Since there were only two Episcopal families in Murphy at the time, she was probably right.

Continue east on Peachtree Street, which becomes U.S. 64 when it leaves the business district. Approximately 3.7 miles after crossing the intersection with U.S. 19/74, you can see the confluence of the Hiwassee River, on the right, and Peachtree Creek, coming in from the left. This is the location of the Peachtree Mound and Village Site, described in the Cherokee County Tour.

*Fairy crosses*

About 1 mile farther on U.S. 64, just past Tri-County Community College and the Murphy Medical Center, is a fork in the road. Follow the right fork, S.R. 1548, which takes you to Brasstown.

You may have seen the exhibit of fairy crosses at the Cherokee County Historical Museum. At first glance, the tiny stone crosses appear to be man-made. They used to be abundant in certain fields near Brasstown. No one knows their exact origin, but the Cherokees offer a legendary explanation. Stories of the Yunwi Tsunsdi, or Little People, appear frequently in early Cherokee mythology. The Cherokees believed that there were several locations in the Appalachians occupied by Little People, tiny, fairylike spirits who were as kind and helpful as they were comely. They were noted for finding lost people—especially children—and guiding them home. They often lived underwater, and they were known to help local fishermen, but they were wary of people and usually made themselves invisible when human beings were around. The Little People should not be confused with the Nunnehi, another Cherokee race of spirits to be discussed later in this tour. Little People hardly reached a man's knee. The Cherokees tell that the Little People were gathered for singing and dancing near Brasstown one day when a messenger arrived from a distant land. When he spoke of Christ's death on the cross, the Little People wept, their tears falling upon the earth and turning into small crosses. They left without noticing that the ground was literally covered with the precious product of their grief. Most of the crosses have been collected over the centuries, but if you are lucky enough to find one, it will supposedly bring you good fortune.

Today, Brasstown is known for a different type of artistry, thanks to the John C. Campbell Folk School. When you reach the sign that says "Welcome to Brasstown," turn right onto S.R. 1564. It is 0.4 mile to the Keith House, on the left, which serves as the school's main building.

During his lifetime, John C. Campbell was considered the preeminent authority on economic and social conditions in the Appalachians. He and

*John C. Campbell Folk School*

his wife, Olive Dame Campbell, were intrigued by the possibility that Danish-style folk schools might serve as an alternative to the schools they saw in the mountains. Danish folk schools were free of traditional forms and methods, directing education toward preserving the integrity and developing the native intelligence of area people. Implicit in the folk-school theory was the use of "all that is native and fine" in local culture.

But John Campbell died in 1919, before his dream of a folk school in western North Carolina became a reality. In 1925, after returning from over a year's worth of study of folk schools in Denmark, Olive Campbell and her friend Marguerite Butler founded the John C. Campbell Folk School in Brasstown on twenty-five acres donated by a local family.

According to its current brochure, the school was inaugurated as "a progressive social experiment centered around adult education, cooperative agriculture, and community service." Young men learned modern farming and husbandry methods, while girls received instruction in home economics and revived mountain crafts, such as weaving. The folk school also aided the community in 1926 by founding a credit union and in 1938 by funding a loan system for helping local students buy their own homes and farms.

In 1930, Mrs. Campbell arranged the first woodcarving course to be taught at the folk school. By 1933, the school boasted thirty-six carvers, ranging from an eleven-year-old to grandfathers. They came to form the nucleus of the world-famous Brasstown Carvers, the best-known of the school's craftsmen. Though they began by carving animals they saw around them, the carvers grew equally famous for fashioning everything from museum crèches to napkin rings. They still come to the folk school every Friday to sell the work they have done in the past week and to pick up blocks for carving new figures. The school sands the figures and applies coats of preservative to them before selling them to customers from all over the country through the John C. Campbell Folk School Craft Shop.

Today, the school offers more than 350 weekend, week-long, and two-week-long courses such as pottery, quilting, weaving, blacksmithing, basketry, clogging, storytelling, gospel singing, and fiddling. Those courses and numerous others attract over three thousand students a year from all over the map.

The famous craft shop is located next to the Keith House. You can also find information about the school and its course offerings there. If you drive 0.4 mile past the Keith House, you will see the rest of the campus—now grown to 365 acres—spread on both sides of the road. Many of the unique stone buildings were designed and built in the late 1920s and the 1930s under the direction of Leon Deschamps, a Belgian engineer who worked for the school. A map of the entire campus is posted on the bulletin board in front of the Keith House.

After visiting the folk school, return to the "Welcome to Brasstown" sign and turn right onto S.R. 1135 for 2 miles to U.S. 64. Turn right, heading east. It is 5.7 miles to the town of Hayesville, the county seat of Clay County.

### Clay County and Hayesville

Clay County is the least populated of North Carolina's mountain counties, primarily because the Nantahala National Forest occupies 65,560 acres of land, or 50 percent of the entire county. Miles of trails in the national forest, including Appalachian, Rim, Fires Creek, and Chunky Gal trails, make this area a prime spot for hikers who are serious about escaping the crowds.

Clay County was formed as the result of a campaign promise made by George Hayes when he was running for the state legislature in 1860. Hayes was having an uphill fight in his home territory, Cherokee County, but he stumbled upon a lively issue when he traveled to the southeastern section of the county to campaign. Local constituents were angered by the fact that they could not travel to their county seat, Murphy, and return home in a day's journey. They favored the formation of a new county, with a seat of government closer to home.

Hayes knew a good thing when he saw it. His

*Chatuge Lake*

*Tusquitee*

promise to introduce legislation to form a new county became the focal point of his campaign. He captured the southeastern part of the county and won the election, then kept his promise in 1861. The seat of the new county was named Hayesville in his honor.

Due primarily to the disruption caused by the Civil War, the Clay County government was not organized until 1868. A courthouse was built in 1888, and the Old Jail was constructed in 1912. Turn left onto U.S. 64 Business. It is less than 1 mile to the courthouse square. A well-preserved example of vernacular Italianate architecture, the courthouse is listed on the National Register of Historic Places. The former jail houses the Clay County Historical and Arts Center. You will also notice a marker designating the location of Fort Hembree, another of the stockades used to hold the Cherokees before the Removal to Oklahoma in 1838.

Return to U.S. 64. Turn left, heading east. Chatuge Lake, billed as "the crown jewel of the TVA lakes," is ahead on the right. Constructed in 1941–42, it boasts over 130 miles of shoreline. The Chatuge Dam is 144 feet high. Extensive camping facilities are located nearby at Clay County Recreation Park and farther down the highway at the United States Forest Service's Jackrabbit Mountain Recreation Area.

It is 1.4 miles from the Chatuge Dam and Clay County Recreation Park to the turnoff for Tusquitee. A creek, a community, a chain of mountains, and a bald—all named Tusquitee—are in the general area on the left. In his report to the Bureau of American Ethnology in 1898, James Mooney recorded a curious legend about Tusquitee Bald. The Cherokee name for the area translates as "where the waterdogs laughed." Waterdogs, or mudpuppies, as they are often called, are salamanders noted for the way they muddy river waters. "A hunter once crossing over the mountain in a very dry season, heard voices," Mooney recorded, "and creeping silently toward the place from which the sound proceeded, peeped over a rock and saw two water-dogs walking together on their hind legs along the trail and talking as they went. Their pond had dried up and they were on the way over to Nantahala River. As he listened one said to the other, 'Where's the water? I'm so thirsty that my apron [gills] hangs down,' and then both water-dogs laughed." The tale may well have lost something in translation, but it obviously made an impression on the Cherokees, as they named the prominent bald after the incident.

*Jackrabbit Mountain Recreation Area*

After 3.8 miles, you will pass an intersection with N.C. 175 and a turnoff for Jackrabbit Mountain Recreation Area. This camping facility is located on a peninsula wooded with pines and surrounded by Chatuge Lake. It has over a hundred campsites, a swimming beach with shower facilities, hiking trails, picnic areas, and a launching ramp for boats. For camping information, contact the Tusquitee Ranger District's office in Murphy.

Stay on U.S. 64. The peak on the left is Vineyard Mountain. Local tradition says that an Englishman once set out a good many grapevines here, but he later gave up his enterprise and returned to his native land. The vineyard has been remembered, even if the man's name is forgotten.

*Shooting Creek*

Continuing another 2.2 miles, you will come to the community named Shooting Creek. If you happen to get out of your car within earshot of the creek, be sure to listen with the utmost attention—Shooting Creek is a babbling brook, taken quite literally. In *North Carolina: A Guide to the Old North State*, compiled by the Work Projects Administration in 1939, it was recorded that "the people of an Indian town on the Hiwassee River, near its confluence with Shooting Creek, prayed and fasted that they might see the Nunnehi [a race of supernatural beings]. At the end of seven days the Nunnehi came and took them under the water. There they still reside and on a warm summer day when the wind ripples the surface those who listen well can hear them talking below."

Past Shooting Creek on U.S. 64 is Glade Gap (elevation 3,679 feet), the route through the Chunky Gal Mountains. It is 7 miles to a scenic

*View from Chunky Gal Mountains*

*Standing Indian Mountain*

overlook on the left at the top of the gap. In *These Storied Mountains*, John Parris wrote that this range received its name when a buxom Cherokee maiden eloped with a Wayah brave. The girl's father caught up with the two as they paused to refresh themselves at the big spring in the gap in the mountains. The girl was forced to return home without her lover, and the other village maidens, envious of her well-endowed body, took to calling her Chunky Gal. It is doubtful that "chunky gal" was part of the Cherokee vocabulary in its exact translated form, but the name does seem to fit the high ridge that this route follows.

It is another 4.3 miles to a small sign on the right. Turn right onto F.R. 71. (It is easy to miss the sign, so begin looking as soon as you crest the hill. If you come to the Macon County line, you have gone too far. Turn around, go back 0.4 mile, and take a left.) When you come to a fork, stay on F.R. 71. The road changes to gravel. It will take twenty to thirty minutes to drive the 5 miles to the parking area at Deep Gap. There, you can gain access to an extensive series of hiking trails, including the Appalachian Trail. The parking area at Deep Gap is also the closest you can drive to Standing Indian Mountain. As you drive into the parking area, Kimsey Creek Trail, which runs conjunctively with the Appalachian Trail over this stretch, will be on your left. To get to Standing Indian Mountain, take the trail in the uphill direction. A 2-mile hike will bring you to the summit, from which you can view the remnants of the Standing Indian. You will pass the Standing Indian shelter on your way to the rocks.

Standing Indian Mountain, elevation 5,498 feet, has been called "the grandstand of the southern Appalachians." It dominates Standing Indian Basin, a horseshoe-shaped area formed by the Nantahala and Blue Ridge mountains and bisected by the Nantahala River. There are several prominent peaks over 5,000 feet along the rim. Though you may not be able to pick out anything that looks like a standing Indian in the jumble of rocks, you will undoubtedly enjoy the spectacular view from the treeless "bald."

*John Wasilik Memorial Poplar*


*Rainbow Springs* ————————————

The Cherokee name for Standing Indian Mountain translates as "where the man stands." According to legend, the area was once terrorized by a huge bird that would swoop out of the skies and carry off children. To defend against such raids, the Cherokees cleared the mountaintops to make them better lookout points, then posted sentries.

The beast's lair was finally discovered in the cliffs atop what is now Standing Indian Mountain. The cliffs were inaccessible to the Cherokees, so they prayed to the Great Spirit for assistance. Their prayers were answered—the Great Spirit sent lightning to destroy the bird and its home. The Indian sentry stationed nearby was so frightened by the lightning that he tried to flee the mountaintop. He was turned to rock for deserting his post, and his stone figure has kept vigil ever since. According to early accounts, the likeness used to be more easily recognizable, but erosion has taken its toll over the years. The cliffs where the great bird lived, however, are still very much in evidence.

Retrace F.R. 71 and turn right on U.S. 64. It is 2.7 miles to Rainbow Springs, which was the base of the Ritter Lumber Company's logging operations in the early 1900s. Practically all of Standing Indian Basin has been logged at least once. The Ritter Lumber Company used the selective-cut system, taking all good timber more than fifteen inches in diameter. They left small trees, large, defective trees, and poor lumber species. The United States Forest Service purchased the land in 1920, but the area's virgin timber has been lost forever.

Turn right onto F.R. 67. It is 1.2 miles to Rock Gap and the trailhead for an 0.7-mile hike through a stand of poplar and cherry trees to the John Wasilik Memorial Poplar, named for an early ranger in the Wayah district. The great tree is the second-largest yellow poplar in the United States, with a diameter of 8 feet and a circumference of 25 feet. It was 125 feet tall at one time, but its top was blown off by a storm. When the Ritter Lumber Company was logging the area, a sister tree of equal size was cut. The weight of the tree strained the oxen hauling it so badly that it was decided to leave the other big poplar.

It is another 1.4 miles to the Standing Indian Campground, Ritter's main logging camp at one point. If you continue on F.R. 67, it is a short distance to a bulletin board designated the Backcountry Information area. Information is posted about the complex system of hiking trails in the area; there is a hike to suit almost every type of visitor. The pavement ends at the Backcountry Information area. After another 6.5 miles on F.R. 67, you will pass the trailhead for Timber Ridge Trail, which crosses the Nantahala River and follows an old railroad grade left from logging days for 0.5 mile to the base of Big Laurel Falls. Another 0.5 mile on F.R. 67 will take you to a trailhead for a short hike of 0.1 mile to Mooney Falls. This trail is an especially popular one for photographers and for families that enjoy short hikes. There are also designated trails for horseback riders, as well as several longer and more difficult hikes that connect with the Appalachian Trail and the trails to Standing Indian Mountain.

Retrace F.R. 67 and turn right on U.S. 64, once again heading east. It is 2.6 miles to Winding Stair Gap, elevation 3,820 feet, where the highway was literally carved through a mountain. It is another 0.5 mile to a scenic overlook that provides a panoramic view of Macon County, the town of Franklin, and the Little Tennessee River Valley.

As U.S. 64 descends the Nantahala Mountains, the road enters the Cartoogechaye Creek area. In 1818, two white settlers, Jacob Siler and William Brittain, entered Indian territory and set about building a shelter for their horses. The Cherokee Chief Santeetlah suddenly appeared on their third morning in the area and told them, "Be gone to your own house." Siler, however, insisted that he had come to stay. He went on to become a great friend of the Cherokees. After Brittain moved on, Siler convinced his three brothers—William, Jesse, and John—to join him. They settled in the

*Backcountry Information Area*

*Cartoogechaye Creek*

valley. It was through the efforts of William Siler that the Sand Town branch of the Cherokees was allowed to remain in North Carolina during the Removal. Since the Sand Town Indians—or any other Indians, for that matter—were not permitted to own land, William Siler provided them with a tract on Cartoogechaye Creek near Muskrat Creek. Though isolated from the other Cherokees for years, they eventually merged with Indians in the Qualla area or joined their kinsmen in Oklahoma.

*Franklin*

It is approximately 7 miles through the valley to Franklin, the county seat of Macon County. The highway widens to four lanes. Turn left onto U.S. 441 at the stoplight and enter town. In 1849, Charles Lanman wrote, "The little village of Franklin is romantically situated on the little Tennessee. It is surrounded with mountains, and as quiet and pretty a hamlet as I have yet seen among the Alleghanies."

The town was established in 1855, though it had an historic tradition stretching for centuries before that. On the right next to a small group of stores after you cross the Little Tennessee River is a large mound of grass-covered earth. An historical marker identifies it as the Nikwasi Indian

*Nikwasi Indian Mound*

Mound. Nikwasi was one of the oldest Cherokee settlements and an important ceremonial center. It was one of the few towns in Cherokee country that possessed the "everlasting fire," which was important in religious ceremonies. Even in the 1890s, older Cherokees claimed that the sacred fire continued to burn in the Nikwasi Indian Mound. Destroyed and rebuilt twice, Nikwasi was continuously occupied until the land was sold in 1891. In 1947, residents of Macon County, including many schoolchildren, raised money to purchase the mound and save it from developers and entrepreneurs.

According to Cherokee tradition, the mound was the town house where the Nunnehi lived. In Cherokee, Nunnehi means "people who live anywhere." Some translations make it "people who live forever," which explains why the Nunnehi were also called the Immortals. Not to be confused with the Little People, who populated other areas of the mountains, the Nunnehi looked like average Cherokees—whenever they allowed themselves to be seen, that is. Usually, they remained invisible and reclusive. Like the Little People, the Nunnehi loved music and dancing, and their drums could often be heard echoing through the hills. Both groups were generally friendly, and both were noted for helping lost Cherokees find their way home.

*Nunnehi at Nikwasi*

James Mooney recorded one traditional Cherokee story about the Nunnehi at Nikwasi. Years before white men came to the area, local Indians faced certain defeat at the hands of an invading tribe that had just finished plundering Cherokee towns in South Carolina. The men of Nikwasi met the opposition on the town's outskirts, when, according to Mooney, "suddenly a stranger stood among them and shouted to the chief to call off his men and he himself would drive back the enemy." The Nikwasi warriors assumed the stranger to be a chief who had come with reinforcements from the Overhill settlements in Tennessee. They fell back as ordered, and it wasn't long before they saw a great company of warriors coming out of the side of the mound. "The Nunne'hi poured out by hundreds, armed and painted for the fight, and the most curious thing about it all was that they became invisible as soon as they were fairly outside of the settlement, so that although the enemy saw the glancing arrow or the rushing tomahawk, and felt the stroke, he could not see who sent it." Nikwasi was saved thanks to the Nunnehi, and the Cherokees then knew that the Immortals lived inside the mound.

Mooney also reported that the Cherokees believed the Nunnehi resided in the mound as late as the Civil War—a surprise attack on a Confederate stronghold at Franklin was canceled when Union soldiers saw a large contingent of soldiers, presumably Nunnehi, guarding the town as they approached.

After visiting the Nikwasi Indian Mound and the town of Franklin, you can continue on U.S. 441/23 to Dillsboro and Asheville, or you can return to the stoplight and follow U.S. 64 East/28 South to Highlands (see the Highlands Tour).

*Cherokee Historical Museum*

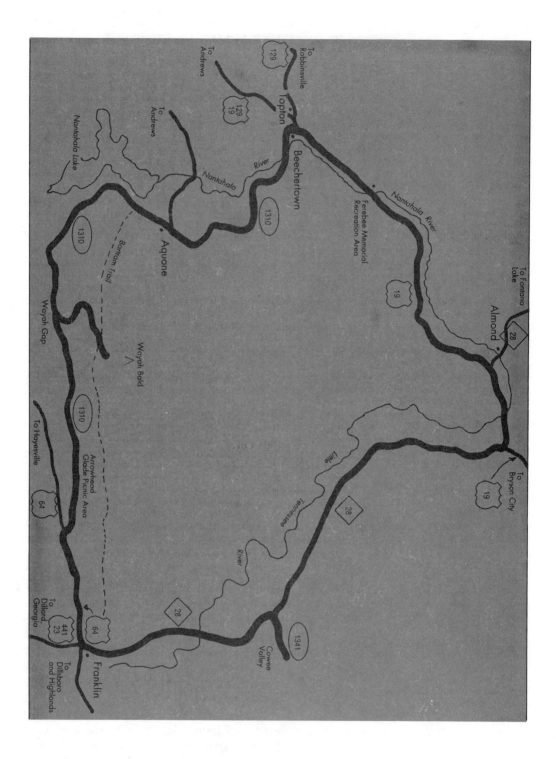

This tour begins in the town of Franklin and follows the Little Tennessee River to the ruby mines of Cowee Valley. It then follows the Nantahala River through its famous gorge, passing Nantahala Lake and Wayah Bald before returning to Franklin. Total mileage: approximately 85 miles.

# ▲▲▲▲▲▲▲▲▲▲▲▲▲▲▲▲▲▲▲▲▲▲▲▲*The Nantahala Tour*

*Nikwasi Indian Mound*

*Sir Alexander Cuming*

The tour begins at the Nikwasi Indian Mound in Franklin, which marks the site of an ancient Cherokee village. The Standing Indian Tour explains the Cherokee legends about the Nunnehi, or Immortals, who supposedly lived inside the mound and kept the sacred ceremonial fires burning. In later years, the same mound played an important role in the relations between Indians and white men.

In 1721, the British-appointed governor of South Carolina met with Cherokee chiefs representing thirty-seven towns to sign a treaty establishing the first boundary line between Indian lands and English settlements. Between 1721 and 1730, however, the French became increasingly influential among the various Indian tribes, and the Cherokees grew so disillusioned with the British and their promises that they, too, began to consider an alliance with the French.

It was in 1730 that Sir Alexander Cuming came to Nikwasi and pulled off one of the biggest diplomatic coups in frontier history. It appears that Cuming was something of a con man; upon his arrival in Charleston, he had established a reputation as a rich man on the strength of borrowed money and a lot of bravado. It is not quite clear whether anyone actually granted him the authority to negotiate with the Indians, but under the pretense of journeying to Cherokee territory for scientific exploration, he took it upon himself to conduct a secret mission to persuade the

Cherokees to maintain their alliance with the British.

The end result was that Cuming convinced the Cherokees to submit to all the concessions desired by the British. Some accounts attribute Cuming's success to a keg of rum and a call to the chiefs to drink to King George's health. Others say that he simply impressed them with his bold bearing. At any rate, he persuaded the Cherokees to select seven chiefs to accompany him back to England.

During their four months abroad, the Cherokee chiefs were the toast of London, going to the theater, inspecting ships, posing for a portrait by William Hogarth while wearing court costumes, and generally delighting the English with their painted faces and the feathers they wore in their hair. They presented the king with four scalps, five eagle tails, and a "crown." In return, they received a substantial quantity of guns, ammunition, and, most importantly, red paint. A treaty was signed in which the British pledged their friendship "as long as the mountains and rivers last, and the sun shines." The colonial governor of South Carolina reported that the Cherokee chiefs returned "in good health and mightily well satisfied with His Majesty's bounty to them."

After viewing the site of Cuming's historic encounter, proceed north through downtown Franklin, following the signs to N.C. 28. For years, an historical marker announcing a "Cherokee Defeat" has been located 2.4 miles north of Franklin on N.C. 28. A second marker designating "Cherokee Victory" is 1.2 miles farther up the road. Recently, it was discovered that the markers are located in the wrong sites, and plans have been made to move them. The "Cherokee Defeat" marker will be moved to the east side of U.S. 23/441 approximately 0.1 mile north of S.R. 1104 at Norton, which is 9 miles south of Franklin. The "Cherokee Victory" marker will move to the east side of U.S. 23/441 a few hundred yards south of S.R. 1632, approximately 2.6 miles north of the defeat marker.

Regardless of the confusion about the location of the two battles, the events that led up to them are important to an understanding of the disintegrating relationships between white settlers and the Cherokees who lived in this area.

By the time hostilities between the French and the British began around 1756, the Cherokees—despite Sir Alexander Cuming's earlier efforts—were growing dissatisfied with their treatment at the hands of the British. Several unfortunate incidents only served to escalate the bitterness, despite the pleas of the more level-headed of the leaders on both sides.

In February 1756, a group of Cherokees accompanied a British expedition against the Shawano tribe. Not only were the Cherokees treated with contempt by the British forces, but they had to endure a march through the snow, during which they lost all their provisions. On the journey home, they were forced to kill their own horses for food. Upon finding some horses running loose on the range, the Cherokees confiscated them. The white owners interpreted the act as horse stealing and killed a number of Indians, mutilating their bodies and taking the scalps to a local settlement to collect the regular price for French Indian scalps. Young Cherokee warriors were prepared to take revenge, but their elders convinced them to seek satisfaction through legal channels.

*Governor Lyttleton holds*
*Oconostota hostage*

Next, some men from Fort Prince George, located in present-day Pickens County, South Carolina, "committed an unpardonable outrage at the neighboring Indian town while most of the men were away hunting," according to James Mooney. The Cherokees retaliated by attacking back-country white settlements.

Several Cherokee chiefs seemed on the verge of bringing the situation under control again when South Carolina Governor William Henry Lyttleton demanded the surrender and execution of several Indians known to have killed colonists. The Cherokees sent a delegation headed by a chief named Oconostota to discuss a peace arrangement. Lyttleton ordered the entire delegation (some say twenty-five men, others say thirty-two) held as hostages until the Cherokee "murderers" were surrendered. The chiefs were imprisoned in a room hardly large enough for half their number. Atakullakulla, one of the best friends of the English, interceded and gained the release of Oconostota and several other chiefs.

Oconostota, however, wanted his disgrace revenged. He led a siege of Fort Prince George in February 1760, after Lyttleton had left thinking everything was under control. Oconostota summoned the commanding officer—saying he wanted to talk peace—then shot him. The soldiers inside the fort retaliated by killing the rest of the still-imprisoned chiefs.

*Archibald Montgomery's force attacks Cherokee Middle Towns*

Colonel Archibald Montgomery's British force of sixteen hundred men, fresh from Indian warfare in western Pennsylvania and New York, arrived to reinforce Fort Prince George. After burning five Indian towns in lower South Carolina by June 1, Montgomery decided to attack the Middle Towns farther north. On June 27, his men entered "a plain covered with wood and brush so thick that one could scarce see three yards distance with an ugly muddy river in the middle of it, overlooked on one side by a high mountain, and on the other by hilly uneven ground," according to one source. It was there that more than six hundred Cherokees lay in ambush. The British were forced to retreat to Fort Prince George. It is this Cherokee victory that is the subject of one of the controversial historical markers.

Montgomery's defeat sealed the fate of Fort Loudon, near present-day Knoxville, Tennessee. The forces there had held out under siege by eating horses and dogs, aided by the kindness of some Cherokee women who smuggled food to their sweethearts among the white soldiers. But by August 8, Captain Demeré and his men were forced to surrender. After the British left, the Indians discovered that ammunition had been buried or thrown into the river, counter to the surrender settlement. Enraged at this duplicity, the Cherokees attacked and killed Demeré and his men.

In June 1761, Colonel James Grant arrived with a large force. The Cherokees attacked on the tenth of that month at a site about 2 miles south of their battle with Montgomery. This time, they were unable to inflict heavy casualties. The British marched on to Nikwasi, and during the next two weeks Grant burned local Indian towns, not to mention the crops and orchards of all the Middle Towns of the Cherokees. The Indians quickly sued for peace, a peace that was to be short-lived, as we will see later in the tour.

Approximately 6 miles from Franklin (1.4 miles after crossing the Little Tennessee River), you will come to Cowee Baptist Church, Cowee Creek Road, and the community of West's Mill. Turn right onto Cowee Creek Road (S.R. 1341). For the next 4 miles, the road travels through the Cowee Valley, also known as the Valley of Rubies. Though people in the area had known about the red stones in the creek bed for years, it wasn't until Dr. George Frederick Kunz of Tiffany's in New York made an official report about the Cowee Valley rubies in 1893 that their value was realized. Alerted to the stones' worth, area landowners began to mail their stones to Tiffany's for cutting. Word got out, and in 1895 the American Prospecting and Mining Company of New York bought out old claims and began work under the supervision of W. E. Hidden. The company's main goal was to find the source of the rubies so abundant in the gravel creek beds.

The American Prospecting and Mining Company and others began to sink shafts and test holes. In 1912, Joseph H. Pratt and Joseph V. Lewis conducted a geological survey for the state of North Carolina. Their work revealed that there was indeed an occurrence of corundum in the Cowee Valley. Corundum is a gem species second in hardness only to diamonds. Its colored varieties are rubies and sapphires. It is valuable not only for its decorative qualities, but also for its use in watch movements, abrasives, and the manufacture of bearings for electrical equipment. Pratt and Lewis compared the Cowee Valley with the Mogok Valley in Burma, the world's premier ruby field.

It turned out that the percentage of marketable

stones, though consistent, was too low to cover the high labor costs. The main source was never discovered, and commercial mining was finally abandoned in 1914.

The work done by the mining companies was primarily exploratory, so the creek's gravel beds remain intact. The valley is enjoying another mining boom today—a boom of an entirely different nature. Situated along Cowee Creek Road are dozens of ruby mines open to the public. For a nominal fee, tourists and rock collectors can buy panning privileges in the nearby creek—as well as the use of screens and stools—to search for fabulous gems. Most of the mines have exhibits or posted records of gems found at the site to inspire rock hounds.

After touring Cowee Creek Road, retrace your route to N.C. 28. Turn right, heading north. It is 0.6 mile to an historical marker reading "Pottery Clay." It seems that this area was blessed with natural resources of all types. In the early 1760s, Andrew Duché, a potter from Savannah, Georgia, learned that clay similar to that used in Chinese porcelain could be found in Cherokee territory. He traveled into the wilderness, located a source of kaolin, and negotiated with the Cherokee chiefs for the right to mine their clay.

*Wedgwood Pottery*

In 1767, British pottery manufacturer Josiah Wedgwood sent South Carolina planter Thomas Griffiths to make similar arrangements. The Indians were quickly learning the game, and they set a high price for the clay that the white men wanted so badly. The traders who supplied the packhorses did likewise. Nonetheless, Griffiths managed to ship several tons of the white clay to England. It was made into the inaugural Queensware, for which Josiah Wedgwood and his company were to become famous. Even a dinner service fashioned for Catherine the Great came from Macon County clay. Wedgwood later found a more economical source for his clay, but those early place settings have now become museum pieces.

N.C. 28 is peppered with historical markers. It is 0.8 mile to the next one, which designates the site of Cowee, the chief town of the Middle Cherokees. In 1773, Dr. John Fothergill, one of London's leading physicians, commissioned William Bartram of Philadelphia to explore the South in order "to collect and send me all the curious plants and seeds and other natural productions." For four years, Bartram traveled all over the Southeast, gathering specimens and keeping a journal that has become an invaluable source of historical information and a classic work in its own right. In 1775, Bartram visited the Cowee area and recorded his observations:

*Cherokee Middle Town of Cowee*

> I arrived at Cowe [*sic*] about noon. This settlement is esteemed the capital town: it is situated on the bases of the hills on both sides of the river, near to its bank, and here terminates the great vale of Cowe, exhibiting one of the most charming mountainous landscapes perhaps anywhere to be seen; ridges of hills rising grand and sublimely one above and beyond another, some boldly and majestically advancing into the verdant plain, their feet bathed with the silver flood of the Tanase [the Little Tennessee], whilst others far distant, veiled in blue mists, sublimely mounting aloft with yet greater majesty lift up their pompous crests, and overlook vast regions.

Bartram went on to note that Cowee consisted of a hundred homes and was dominated by a great town house built on a twenty-foot mound. He described the town house as "a large rotunda" that could easily accommodate most of the town's residents.

A year after Bartram's visit, the town was destroyed in another series of confrontations between the Cherokees and white settlers. When the Revolutionary War began, the Cherokees sided with the British. The newly formed state governments of North Carolina, South Carolina, and Virginia decided to join in a concerted military effort to punish the Indians, who had been attacking settlements on their frontiers.

*Griffith Rutherford*

On September 1, 1776, General Griffith Rutherford and an army of twenty-five hundred left present-day Old Fort and crossed the Swannanoa Gap heading for the Cherokee Middle Towns, where they planned to rendezvous with Colonel Andrew Williamson and his South Carolina army.

Williamson reached the Little Tennessee and the Middle Town of Watauga on September 8 but found it deserted. Rutherford arrived the next day, but Williamson had gone. The general sent a detachment to look for Williamson. The rest of his army set about destroying the Cherokee towns along the Little Tennessee, including Nikwasi and Cowee. Rutherford then decided to leave some of his troops to wait for Williamson. He took twelve hundred men across Wallace Gap with the intention of destroying the Cherokee towns along the Hiwassee River in Clay and Cherokee counties.

Meanwhile, Williamson arrived in Nikwasi, only to learn that Rutherford had gone on to the Cherokee Valley Towns. He camped at Cowee on September 18, then headed across the mountains at Indian Grave Gap. A large force of Cherokees was gathered there, and the two groups fought for over two hours. Williamson's force was able to hold the field, and they continued their march through what is now Nantahala Gorge. Their trip was so arduous that it took them four days to march the approximately 20 miles to present-day Topton. Before meeting Rutherford in Murphy, they destroyed most of the Cherokee towns along the Valley River. Rutherford and Williamson succeeded in destroying most of the Middle and Valley towns during this campaign.

In more recent times, the Cowee Mound, once a Cherokee ceremonial center and part of the village destroyed in Rutherford's campaign, has been recognized as one of the most important archaeological sites in western North Carolina.

The tour continues along the Little Tennessee River for another 13.2 miles until N.C. 28 intersects U.S. 19 at Lauada. Turn left onto U.S. 19 South, which will become a two-lane highway after crossing the T. A. Sandlin Bridge. A little over 6 miles later, the route enters the steep Nantahala Gorge, following the Nantahala River. Ahead is one of the most impressive scenic drives in western North Carolina. The gorge is so deep and its sides so sheer that the Cherokees called it

*Nantahala River*

*Uktena*

the Land of the Middle Sun, referring to the fact that direct sunlight is shut out until nearly noon.

Naturally, such a place would figure to be inspiration for legends, and again the Cherokees have not let us down. They believed the gorge to be the home of Uktena, "a great snake as large around as a tree trunk with horns on its head and a bright, blazing crest like a diamond on its forehead, and scales glittering and flashing like sparks of fire," as transcribed by James Mooney. Uktena could not be wounded except by being shot "in the seventh spot from the head because under this spot are its heart and its life." The diamond on its forehead was called Ulunsuti, which translates as "transparent." If anyone could detach it, he would see the future. Many tried to capture the talisman, but those who looked upon Uktena were so dazed by the diamond's light that they were drawn toward it, to certain death. One hunter was finally able to shoot the serpent on the seventh spot while it slept. It is said the Cherokees still keep the large, transparent crystal with the blood-red streak through its center in a secret cave high in the mountains.

The 9-mile stretch of the Nantahala River you are following is widely recognized as world-class whitewater. Continuous rapids and moderately high water during the summer offer a challenge for whitewater enthusiasts; periodic releases by the Nantahala Power and Light Company's dam provide the fast water needed for rafting or paddling. An entire outfitting industry has developed along this stretch.

It is 8.3 miles from the sign announcing the entrance to the gorge to the Nantahala River Launch Site. All along the route, there are picnic tables and areas where you can pull over to watch adventurers running the river. The Ferebee Memorial Recreation Area is a particularly scenic spot.

At the launch site, turn left onto S.R. 1310. The small community centered around the power plant is known as Beechertown. You will also notice an historical marker indicating that William Bartram met the Cherokee Chief Atakullakulla

*Running Nantahala Falls on the Nantahala River*
Courtesy of Nantahala Outdoor Center

near this spot in May 1776.

After Bartram left the village of Cowee, he tried to convince his white guide to lead him over the Nantahala Mountains to the Overhill Towns. The guide refused because the area was not considered safe for white men at that time, and Bartram went on alone. When he arrived at present-day Beechertown, he met a band of Indians led by Atakullakulla, who was known among the Cherokees as "the wily savage" and "the Indian capable of enthusiasm for good and evil." Such designations would not seem to have been a good omen for Bartram. As a token of respect, he yielded the trail to the chief. "His highness with a gracious and cheerful smile came up to me," Bartram wrote, "and clapping his hand on his breast, offered it to me, saying, I am Ata-cul-culla; and heartily shook hands with me, and asked if I knew it." Bartram identified himself as a Quaker from Pennsylvania and then proceeded to stretch the truth in the interest of self-preservation by informing the chief that "the name Ata-cul-culla was dear to his white brothers of Pennsylvania." The two passed a few more pleasantries. Impressed that he was known so far away, Atakullakulla welcomed Bartram "to their country as a friend and brother, and then shaking hands heartily bid me farewell."

Though Bartram enjoyed astounding luck in his encounter with Atakullakulla, the experience must have left him unsettled, for he soon decided to turn back for the security of Cowee. The incident serves to indicate what a resourceful man this scholarly naturalist proved to be in the wilderness.

*Nantahala Lake*

The route now winds alongside the Nantahala River for 8.6 miles to the Aquone post office. Just past Aquone, Nantahala Lake is visible on the right. It is 1.9 miles from the post office to a marker indicating the trailhead for the Bartram Trail, which follows the same route William Bartram traveled. You can hike it from Nantahala Lake across Wayah Bald and into Franklin.

It is another 8.2 miles to F.R. 69. The crest of the ridge is Wayah Gap. The Wayah Crest Picnic

*Wilson Lick Ranger Station*

Wayah Bald
_____

Ground is on the right. Turn left onto F.R. 69, which travels to the top of Wayah Bald, elevation 5,335 feet. The drive is on a gravel road and will take approximately fifteen minutes.

It is 1.4 miles on F.R. 69 to the Wilson Lick Ranger Station, on the left. Built in 1913, it was the first ranger station in the Nantahala National Forest. You will also pass Wine Spring Bald and another sign for the Bartram Trail. It is approximately 2 more miles to the parking area at Wayah Bald, then a five-minute walk to the fire lookout station.

There is evidence that Indians used this bald as a hunting ground as early as 300 B.C. The Cherokees gave it the name Wayah, meaning wolf, because of the large number of wolves in the vicinity. During the 1850s and 1860s, there was a bounty on wolves in Macon County, which soon eradicated them from the area.

Another name the Cherokees had for the Wayah Gap was Atahita, or the Shouting Place, because of its role in the destruction of Ulagu, or the Great Yellow Jacket. The giant insect was said to be as large as a house. It would swoop down from its secret hiding place and carry off children from a village on the Nantahala River. In order to track the insect to its hiding place, the Cherokees killed a deer and tied a long white string to it. When Ulagu carried off his bounty, he found the load so heavy that he had to fly slowly, thus enabling the Indians to follow the string. It was at Wayah Gap that they saw Ulagu's nest in a large cave in the rocks on the other side of the valley. They gave a shout of excitement, and the site came to be known as the Shouting Place from that day. The Indians built fires around the entrance to the cave and smothered the insect with smoke. Some of the smaller yellow jackets escaped from the cave, and it is their descendants who may still be found in the area's forests.

After the Treaty of Washington established a boundary between whites and Indians along the crest of the Nantahala Mountains in 1819, it became apparent that it was only a matter of time before the Indians would be pushed completely out of the territory. In 1820, the town of Franklin was surveyed. In 1856, a toll turnpike was built from Asheville to the Tennessee state line, and mail and passengers traveled through the Wayah Gap on a daily basis. The bald, used primarily as pasture, then became a popular place for summer picnics as well.

The United States Forest Service took over the management of the bald in 1913. In 1933–34, the Civilian Conservation Corps improved the Wayah Road, and in 1935, they began the construction of Wayah Bald's rock fire tower. Completed in 1937 and dedicated to John B. Byrne, a well-loved national-forest supervisor, the tower was sixty feet tall. The second of its three floors was an observation level with twelve windows and an outside deck. The top floor housed two fire lookout men.

Unfortunately, there was a flaw in the mortar work. Water seeped in. In 1947, a contractor was hired to tear down the tower because it was unsafe. He removed the top two floors and built a new rock staircase on the outside of the south wall. In 1983, a new roof of hemlock beams and cedar shakes was constructed. The forest service removed many of the scrub trees that had grown up around the bald and pruned some of the azaleas there. The bald has since become a notable observation point during May and June, when the azaleas, rhododendrons, and wildflowers are in full bloom.

After enjoying the view atop Wayah Bald, retrace F.R. 69 to S.R. 1310 and turn left. It is 6.2 miles—most of it downhill—to the LBJ Civilian Conservation Center, on the right, and the Arrowhead Glade Picnic Area, on the left. There is an intersection after another 3.2 miles; a store is on the right. Turn right. It is a short distance to an intersection with U.S. 64. Turn left and it's about 4 miles into Franklin. Now that you have explored the Cowee Valley, you might want to stop off at the Gem and Mineral Museum, housed in a 150-year-old former jail in downtown Franklin. The free museum features a forty-nine-pound corundum crystal found at the Corundum Hill

*Fire tower on Wayah Bald*

*Gem and Mineral Museum*

Mine in Macon County in 1886. There are fossils, gems, and minerals from all over the world on display. There is also a display of Indian artifacts from the Little Tennessee River area and around the country. Follow Main Street to the courthouse and turn left onto Phillips Street. The museum is next to the statue on the right. This completes the tour.

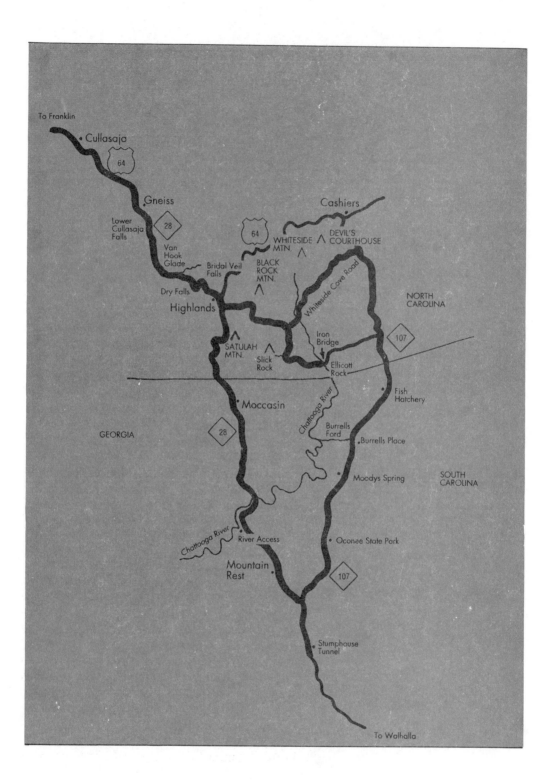

This tour begins in Franklin and travels through the Cullasaja Gorge to the town of Highlands. From there, it heads south along the Chattooga River to Stumphouse Tunnel Park and Issaqueena Falls. It then travels north to Whiteside and Horse coves before returning to Highlands. Total mileage: approximately 83 miles.

# ▲▲▲▲▲▲▲▲▲▲▲▲▲▲▲▲▲▲▲▲▲▲▲▲▲*The Highlands Tour*

*Cullasaja River*

To begin the tour, follow U.S. 64/N.C. 28 heading east from Franklin toward Highlands. It is 4.4 miles through a farming valley intersected by the Cullasaja River to the community named Cullasaja. The water from the Cullasaja River flows 1,500 miles via the Little Tennessee, Tennessee, Ohio, and Mississippi rivers to empty into the Gulf of Mexico. On the North Carolina portion of its journey, it flows through some of the most picturesque areas of the state.

Several sources from the early 1800s claimed that Cullasaja was the anglicized version of the Cherokee word for sugar water. James Mooney corrected that misconception in his 1898 report to the Bureau of American Ethnology after learning that it came from the Cherokee word *Kulsetsiyi*, meaning honey locust place. The honey locust tree was a religious symbol equated with the gods of thunder and lightning. According to Cherokee mythology, there was a throne made of honey locust in the home of the Thunder Man. The Indians believed there was a connection between the pinnated leaves of the tree and the lightning. The confusion started when white traders arrived with their sugar. The Cherokees had no name for this new sugar—the closest they could come was their word for honey. The traders further confused matters when they started to call any location featuring the Cherokees' revered honey locust Sugartown. One such settlement was near present-day Cullasaja. The place where the Little Tennessee River flows into the Cullasaja River was once known as Sugar Fork. Topographical maps still show a Sugar Fork along Ellijay Creek, which feeds into the Cullasaja.

*De Soto's Expedition*

In 1934, the Smithsonian Institution undertook the challenge of tracing the 1540 expedition of Hernando De Soto, the Spanish explorer who ventured into the mountains in search of gold. With the help of descriptions from the journals of several men who accompanied the expedition, the Smithsonian used landmarks to verify the route. Arriving from South Carolina, De Soto and his men left present-day Highlands and followed the Cullasaja River to the Cherokee village of Nikwasi, located where Franklin stands today. The area apparently didn't manage to hold De Soto's interest, because by 1541 he had reached the Mississippi River. Numerous historical markers all over the vicinity commemorate his visit.

*Cullasaja Gorge*

It is 3.7 miles from Cullasaja to another small community, Gneiss. Just past Gneiss, there is a sign designating the entrance to the Cullasaja Gorge. The next 7.5 miles constitute not only one of the most scenic routes in western North Carolina, but an amazing engineering feat as well.

In their 1883 book, *The Heart of the Alleghanies*, Wilbur Zeigler and Ben Grosscup described an older version of the route as "one possessing panoramic grandeur to an extent equalled by but few highways in the Alleghanies. . . . A series of picturesque rapids and cascades enlivens the way; and, in a deep gorge, where, on one precipitous side the turnpike clings, and the other rises abruptly across the void, tumbles the lower Sugar Fork falls [Lower Cullasaja Falls]."

In 1929, local people started lobbying for a good road through the gorge between Franklin and Highlands. North Carolina officials were reluctant to begin the project, knowing how difficult it would prove to be. The federal government further complicated matters by denying aid, since the proposed course was not the most direct or the least expensive route between the two towns.

When construction finally began, the first task

was to blast away parts of the solid granite mountains to allow space to build the road. Workers were lowered from the tops of the cliffs in rope slings tied to trees; gazing at the cliffs today, it doesn't take much of an imagination to envision what a popular job that must have been. Once the workers were lowered, they drilled holes in the granite and placed dynamite in the holes. They were then hauled back to the top, and the charges were set. The steel rods used to drill the holes were 10 feet long—meaning that only a 10-foot width of rock could be cleared at a time—so several trips down the face of the cliffs were required at each blasting site. The first load of gravel was laid in May 1931. The road was partially paved by 1932. Built on a granite shelf 250 feet above the river, it literally hangs on the rock wall.

The river drops 2,000 feet in the 7.5-mile gorge. Cascades and waterfalls are abundant. The first is Lower Cullasaja Falls, which is actually a dramatic series of cascades dropping more that 250 feet in 0.25 mile. The falls deserve a look, though stopping is tricky. Since the roadbed between the rock wall and the gorge barely allows space for two lanes, there is little room for a turn-out for tourists to stop and gawk or take photos. Stone parapets only a few feet high have been built on the edge of the gorge, and there is a small area where a few cars can pull over; it is not marked, so keep a sharp lookout. Many visitors find it easier to drive past the falls, park, and walk back, though the absence of a designated pedestrian path means that they have to walk close to the rock wall or out in the highway. If you decide to try to park at the pull-off, you will find the view well worth the effort.

The road continues to parallel the Cullasaja River, though the drop-off becomes a little less dramatic and unsettling. It is 4.6 miles to the entrance to Cliffside Lake Recreation Area, on the left. If you want to take a brief side trip, it is a 1.5-mile drive to picturesque Cliffside Lake and its swimming and fishing facilities—visitors should be aware that cold mountain lakes will make the adrenalin flow. The campground, the lake, the

*Lower Cullasaja Falls*

*Dry Falls*

*The Kalakaleskies
and Sequoyah Dam*

picnic area, and the several trails in the area are all part of the Nantahala National Forest. From the entrance to Cliffside Lake Recreation Area, it is 0.1 mile on U.S. 64/N.C. 28 to the Van Hook Glade Campground.

It is 0.8 mile farther to a parking area on the right for the popular Dry Falls. A short, paved path leads behind the 75-foot falls; the name for the waterfall comes from the fact that visitors can walk behind it without getting wet. Looking out through the falls toward the river is a unique perspective. An excellent photo opportunity, Dry Falls is well worth the stop.

It is another 0.8 mile to Bridal Veil Falls, where you can actually drive your car behind a 120-foot waterfall. Before the road was rerouted, motorists had no choice but to drive behind the falls, a startling experience for first-timers and those traveling at night. You now have the option of staying on the main road or making the slight detour. Either way, photos are usually in order. Legend says Indian maidens believed that if they passed behind the falls in the spring, they would wed before the first snowfall.

For the next 0.5 mile, the highway parallels a series of eighteen small falls known as the Kalakaleskies. At the head of the falls is Sequoyah Dam, built in 1927. Only 28 feet high and 175 feet wide, the dam nonetheless produces a scenic overflow of water from the seventy-six-acre lake behind it. Both the lake and the dam were named for Sequoyah, who invented the Cherokee alphabet around 1821, ultimately enabling thousands of Cherokees to read and write in their own language. Thus, much of their culture has been preserved.

Approaching Sequoyah Dam, you will see a sign announcing the town of Highlands. At 4,118 feet, Highlands was recognized as the highest town east of the Mississippi until 1981, when the community of Beech Mountain, at 5,005 feet, was incorporated.

In March 1874, an article appeared in *Scribner's Monthly* magazine describing the area around present-day Highlands. "For some time we had felt the exhilarating effects of the keen, rarified air, and had noticed the exquisite atmospheric effects peculiar to these regions," the article stated. "The land is of surprising fertility . . . and there are numerous quartz veins running through the hills, indicating the presence of gold in large quantities."

*Kelsey and Hutchinson develop Highlands*

It was inevitable that someone would develop the region, and soon. Two land developers, Samuel T. Kelsey and C. C. Hutchinson, were intrigued. Tradition has it that they studied a map of the United States and drew a line between the major population centers of Chicago and Savannah, then another one between New Orleans and Baltimore; their theory was that the intersection of the lines would one day mark the center of population of eastern America. When they saw that the lines met near present-day Highlands, they were on their way.

Kelsey and Hutchinson purchased 839 acres and began promoting their new town, Kelsey's Plateau. They soon changed the name to Highlands. In 1876, they produced their first promotional brochure, which proclaimed that there was "no better climate in the world for health, comfort and enjoyment" than that at Highlands. The advertisement went on to boast that "there are a dozen mountain peaks within a radius of as many miles. Almost to the very tops of these highest mountain peaks are beautiful coves and dells where gigantic forest trees stand guard over perennial springs of purest, softest waters, which send their cooling rills down the mountain's side."

Kelsey sent the brochures all over the country. It wasn't long before he began attracting permanent residents. By 1883, Highlands boasted a population of three hundred people from eighteen states. The town's first inn, still standing today,

*Highlands Inn*

was the Smith Hotel—now the Highlands Inn—built in 1879. The hotel's 1884 advertisement in the *Blue Ridge Enterprise* read, "Highlands is unsurpassed for equable climate, pure, invigorating air, pure, cold spring water and grand mountain scenery. All who try our very long, cool and delightful summers . . . pronounce this the best place east of the Rockies for those who seek health and natural scenery." The advertisement also pointed out that there were no mosquitoes and few flies in the area.

By 1887, Kelsey had produced a second set of brochures, focusing on the town's growing reputation as a health resort. Highlands was proclaimed a curative for consumption, ague, and yellow fever, to name only a few. Kelsey's brochures even supplied twenty-four testimonials to support his claims. Many who traveled to Highlands for their health ended up staying. Today, the town's wintertime population of approximately nine hundred explodes to between twelve and twenty thousand during the summer months.

While Highlands was still young, it was the site of a Western-style shootout. Just across the Georgia line in Rabun County, four brothers named Billingsley lived in the township of Moccasin. The brothers were well-known in the area for their moonshining activities. When two of their associates were arrested by federal agents for selling moonshine, the Billingsleys set out to free them. Since there was no jail, the prisoners were confined in a room in the Smith Hotel in nearby Highlands while they awaited trial. When the Billingsley forces arrived, they laid siege to the hotel. What followed was a classic showdown.

The federal agents, apparently assisted by some townspeople, armed and barricaded themselves within and behind the Smith Hotel. The eighteen members of the Billingsley gang took up a position across the street, and the two sides proceeded to exchange gunfire over the course of three days. The mayor of Highlands was even forced to temporarily declare martial law. When a man named Tom Ford finally climbed to the top of the hotel and killed one of the Moccasin troops, the Georgians withdrew from Highlands.

Several days passed before the Billingsley gang sent a messenger with the news that they intended to blockade the main road from Highlands to Walhalla, South Carolina, and kill any man from

*The Billingsleys*
*from Moccasin*

Highlands who attempted to pass. Since that route was one of the main arteries to the South Carolina low country, the blockade proved to be a great inconvenience to Highlands residents.

The Moccasin War, as it is called in some local histories, ended rather uneventfully. A local teamster named Joel Lovin finally decided to test the blockade. The story goes that he rode right past the Billingsley brothers, who made no attempt to stop him. The "war" was over.

When you reach the center of the Highlands business district, you will see the Highlands Inn on the left. Follow N.C. 28 as it turns right and heads south toward Walhalla, tracing the old route blockaded by the so-called Army of Moccasin. As you start the descent from the plateau, you will notice a large rock formation on the left 2 miles outside Highlands. Known as Satulah Mountain, it has an elevation of 4,560 feet. On the left at the foot of the mountain is a cascade called Satulah Falls, with a private home beside it. There is an overlook on the right after a short distance; in addition to a beautiful view of the Piedmont region, you can see the high, narrow waterfall known as Lower Satulah Falls or Clear Creek Falls below.

*Satulah Mountain*

The section of the route you are now following is known as the Walhalla Road. Constructed in 1920, it was preceded by four other roads between Highlands and Walhalla. There were regular runs of passengers, mail, and supplies on the Walhalla Road as early as 1895, but the road was so often muddy that the round trip of 64 miles took at least three days. One passenger on the ride north from Walhalla wrote, "Up in the clouds we certainly were. As we approached Satulah exclamations of delight were heard at the grandeur of the scenery, mingled with screams and clutches at whatever was within reach to cling to." Though the trip will take you considerably less than three days, the sublime views and the hair-raising curves have changed little since the turn of the century.

*Walhalla Road*

The next 20 miles of serpentine road pass through three states. It is approximately 6 miles

*Russell Farmstead*

*Floating Section of
Chattooga River*

from Highlands to Sassafras Gap and the Georgia border. It is another 1.4 miles to the boundary of the Chattahoochee National Forest and the beginning of the Moccasin precinct, home of the Billingsleys and their army. Another 7.8 miles bring you to the South Carolina border at Oconee County.

After an additional 0.8 mile, you will see a pair of chimneys that remain from the Russell Farmstead, listed on the National Register of Historic Places. It is said that William Ganaway Russell drove a herd of cattle west to California during the gold rush. He sold meat to miners near Sacramento and sewed the coins he took in exchange into his vest for his return home. He purchased land near the Chattooga River and built a small house in 1867, a structure that was enlarged three times over the next forty years and that served as an overnight inn for travelers making the stagecoach trip from Walhalla to Highlands. Russell's inn reportedly housed as many as eighty visitors. Still others camped in tents on the grounds when the Chattooga River was too deep to cross. There were sometimes enough guests at the inn to consume twenty turkeys at one meal. Russell's wife, Jane Nicholson Russell, bore fifteen children, in addition to serving as midwife, postmistress, and cook-hostess for the inn. Some of the ten outbuildings can still be seen, but fire destroyed the inn in 1988. Russell and his wife are buried nearby.

It is another 0.6 mile to a river access area for what is called Floating Section II of the Chattooga River. In 1974, the Chattooga was designated a Wild and Scenic River by Congress. That designation is reserved for rivers possessing not only outstanding scenery, but recreational, wildlife, geological, and cultural value as well. The Chattooga begins in the mountains of North Carolina and forms the boundary between the Sumter National Forest, in South Carolina, and the Chattahoochee National Forest, in Georgia, for almost 40 miles. The lower 31 miles are open for boating and constitute some of the best whitewater in the Southeast. Visitors who enter the river at the access

*Stumphouse Tunnel*

area can enjoy a 6-mile float to Earls Ford. This section of the Chattooga will prove a challenge for beginning whitewater boaters, and it is open for tubers—those riding inner tubes—as well. The largest of the twenty rapids in the area is Big Shoals, a Class-3 rapid, which can be portaged on an island in the middle of the river. Depending on the water level, it takes two to four hours to negotiate this section by canoe, and an extra hour by raft or tube.

Another 9.4 miles on S.C. 28 bring you to the Stumphouse Ranger Station, on the left. The entrance to Stumphouse Tunnel Park is an additional 0.4 mile. Turn left at the park entrance and drive 0.5 mile to the parking lot and picnic area. The top of Issaqueena Falls is to the right of the picnic area, while a short path to the left of the parking lot leads to Stumphouse Tunnel.

Stumphouse Tunnel was the longest of three tunnels proposed to complete South Carolina's portion of the Blue Ridge Railroad, which was to run from Charleston, South Carolina, to Cincinnati, Ohio. Work was begun in the 1850s. Irish immigrants, housed in a town named Tunnel Hill atop Stumphouse Mountain, provided most of the labor. They worked twelve hours a day for six days a week, pounding their way through the granite with sledgehammers, hand drills, and blasting powder. Stumphouse Tunnel was to be 5,863 feet long. Due to the scope of the project, all work was dropped on the other two tunnels and concentrated on Stumphouse by 1857.

The tunnel was to run 236 feet below the highest point of the mountain. Four vertical shafts were sunk to tunnel level, then dug horizontally toward each other. That way, work could proceed from a total of ten different surfaces. At the peak of the work, the men were able to tunnel 200 feet a month.

The work on shafts #1 and #4 did manage to connect with the tunneling from the outside, but the two middle tunnels were never completed. The company overseeing the work ran out of money, and the Civil War broke out before new funds could be raised.

The north end of Stumphouse Tunnel is now underwater, but the sixteen-hundred-foot section at the south end is open to the public. The temperature in the tunnel is fifty degrees year-round, and the humidity is always 90 percent. Thanks to the humidity, it is always raining at the base of the vertical shaft that rises to the top of the mountain.

The iron gate near the entrance to the tunnel and the brick wall past the vertical shaft were additions made in the 1950s by Clemson University. Clemson used the tunnel for experimentation in the manufacture of blue cheese. Since the temperature and humidity matched that of caves in France where blue cheese was aged, the tunnel was converted and used successfully for several years. Studies on the aging process were finally moved to the Clemson campus after the construction of a suitable building in 1956.

The name Stumphouse was given to the mountain sometime in the 1850s. Various stories have emerged explaining the origin of the name. Most seem to involve a one-room cabin that was located near the present tunnel. One version is centered around four large chestnut trees. The story goes that three of the trees were ideally suited to provide walls for the cabin, so they were cut down to stumps. A section of the fourth tree was cut to form the remaining wall. Though the cabin disappeared long ago, its unusual architecture apparently impressed travelers enough to name the mountain in its honor.

There are also numerous versions of the legend surrounding nearby Issaqueena Falls (frequently spelled Isaqueena). According to one of the most frequently told accounts, Captain James Francis and his two sons, Allan and Henry, established a Cherokee trading post sometime between 1730 and 1750 near the present-day community of Ninety Six, in Greenwood County, South Carolina. Through his business dealings with the Cherokee Chief Karuga, Allan Francis met and fell in love with a young maiden named Issaqueena, a captive Choctaw or Creek Indian (depending upon the version) who was living as Karuga's slave in the

*Issaqueena Falls*

village of Keowee, near present-day Lake Keowee in Pickens County, South Carolina.

When Issaqueena learned that Karuga planned to attack the white traders, she set out to warn her lover. The legend attributes various South Carolina place names—including Six Mile; Twelve Miles River; Eighteen, Three, and Twenty creeks; and even Issaqueena's destination, Ninety Six—to mileage points along her route. (The names actually indicate distances along an old trading path that ran the 96 or so miles between Keowee and Fort Ninety-six, but it still makes a good story.) It was at the falls at Stumphouse Mountain that Issaqueena completed her escape from her Cherokee captors. She leaped from the falls, landed on a ledge, and hid behind the falling water until the Cherokees left. Some versions say she had a baby in her arms when she accomplished this amazing feat.

It is a short hike along either side of the falls to the ledge where Issaqueena supposedly landed. The falls are about two hundred feet high, but the flow of water is so skimpy that it is hard to believe anyone could hide behind them. Healthy skepticism aside, it must be admitted that the falls still provide a great spot for a picnic.

*Oconee State Park*

Leaving Stumphouse Tunnel Park, retrace your route to S.C. 28 and turn right, heading north. It is 2.2 miles to an intersection with S.C. 107. Turn right. It is 2.4 miles to the entrance to Oconee State Park. This 1,165-acre park is centered around a 20-acre mountain lake ideal for swimming and fishing. There are nineteen fully furnished rental cabins, 140 family campsites, and a restaurant. Recreation and nature programs are available.

*Moodys Spring Picnic Area*

Continuing on S.C. 107, it is 6.4 miles to the Moodys Spring Picnic Area, on the left. Visitors can still use the spring where Wade Hampton II, hero of the Battle of New Orleans and the Mexican War, often stopped while traveling to his summer home at High Hampton. There is more information about Wade Hampton in the Cashiers Tour.

After another 1.4 miles, turn left onto F.R. 708.

*Burrells Ford*

*Chattooga Picnic Area*

*Whiteside Mountain*

It is about 2 miles to Burrells Ford, on the Chattooga River. There is a 0.5-mile trail southeast of Burrells Ford leading to King Creek Falls. It is an easy twenty-minute walk to the seventy-foot falls. There is also an easy fifteen-minute walk north to the sixty-foot Spoonauger Falls.

Retrace the route to S.C. 107 and continue in your original direction. It is 0.5 mile to the Burrells Place Campground, just past the overlook on the right. It is another 1 mile to the road leading to the Chattooga Picnic Area. A 1.9-mile side trip on a paved road leads to the picnic area and the United States Fish Hatchery, where you can view large numbers of trout being raised in pools. Both Burrells Place Campground and the Chattooga Picnic Area are good sites for picnics.

It is 9.1 miles up the mountain on S.C. 107 to the Wade Hampton Golf Club. You will cross the North Carolina border en route. After another 0.8 mile, turn left onto Whiteside Cove Road (S.R. 1107). Almost immediately, you will begin catching glimpses of the impressive stone face of Whiteside Mountain and its neighbor, Devil's Courthouse. This area was settled in 1827, when Barak Norton arrived from Virginia and built a cabin at the foot of Whiteside Mountain. Zeigler and Grosscup wrote an excellent description of the scene:

> We came out before the massive front of a peculiar mountain. Whiteside, or in literal translation of the Cherokee title, Unakakanoos, White-mountain, is the largest exposure of perpendicular, bare rock east of the Rockies. It is connected, without deeply-marked intervening gaps, with its neighboring peaks of the Blue Ridge; but from some points of observation it appears isolated—a majestic, solitary, dome-shaped monument, differing from all other mountains of the Alleghanies in its aspect and form. The top line of its precipitous front is 1,600 feet above its point of conjunction with the crest of the green hill, which slopes to the Chatooga [*sic*], 800 feet lower. The face of the mountain is gray, not white; but is seared by long rifts, running horizontal across it, of white rock.

*Grimshawes post office*

*Granite City*

*Slick Rock Vista*

*Ellicott Rock*

More information about Whiteside Mountain and the Devil's Courthouse is in the Cashiers Tour.

The pavement ends after 2.8 miles. It is another 0.8 mile to one of the most stunning views in the area—at the base of Whiteside Mountain is a lake that reflects the sheer, eighteen-hundred-foot white precipice.

As you circle the lake, you will see the restored Grimshawes post office on the right. Billed as the smallest post office in the United States, it measures six feet by eight feet. Established in 1875, the post office did not bear the Grimshawes name until 1909.

It is another 0.8 mile to the Whiteside Cove Church and its cemetery, on the left. Approximately 1.7 miles past the church, there is a trail—not readily marked from the road—leading to the right. It travels a few hundred feet to Granite City, the resting place of a number of huge boulders and once a popular summer attraction. Visitors have left alleys and lanes among the boulders—hence the name—but erosion has taken its toll, and many think of Granite City as little more than a bunch of big rocks today.

Continue on Whiteside Cove Road. After another 1.3 miles, you may elect to turn left (or east) onto Bull Pen Road (S.R. 1603) for a popular side trip. After 1 mile on Bull Pen Road, you will reach Slick Rock Trail, on the right, which will bring you to the Slick Rock Vista, for a view of the entire area. Back on Bull Pen Road, it is 0.2 mile farther to the Ammons Branch Campground, on the right. There is a trailhead at the campground for the Ellicott Rock Trail, which leads into the 3,030-acre Ellicott Rock Wilderness Area, a rugged tract on the Chattooga River that encompasses parts of three states. The 7-mile round-trip hike to Ellicott Rock is moderately difficult. When you reach the Chattooga, ford the river and go downstream approximately 0.1 mile. Commissioner Rock, ten feet downstream from Ellicott Rock, is now recognized as the boundary shared by North Carolina, South Carolina, and Georgia, though Ellicott Rock once held that distinction. Commissioner Rock bears the inscription "LAT 35

*The Iron Bridge*

*Horse Cove*

*Black Rock Mountain*

AD 1813 NC + SC," while Ellicott Rock has a simple "NC" chiseled into it.

Back on Bull Pen Road, it is another 2 miles to an old iron bridge on the Chattooga. A well-kept forest trail along the river and a waterfall make this a popular place to hike or picnic. After reaching the Chattooga, retrace your route to the intersection with Whiteside Cove Road to complete the side trip. (If you would prefer to travel to Cashiers rather than return to Highlands, continue on Bull Pen Road for 5.3 miles to N.C. 107. Turn left and it is 6.9 miles to Cashiers.)

If you return to Whiteside Cove Road, you should now head west on Horse Cove Road. The area you are driving through is called Horse Cove. There are a number of explanations for the name. Some say Indians used the area as pasture for their horses, while others say General William T. Sherman hid his horses in the cove one winter during the Civil War. Still others say it was Revolutionary War hero General Andrew Pickens who pastured his horses here. Regardless of the origin of the name, the scenic cove remains much as Zeigler and Grosscup found it in 1883: "Black Rock, with bold, stony, treeless front, looms up on one border, and on another, Satoola [Satulah], with precipitous slope, wood-covered, forms a sheltering wall for the 600 acres of fertile, level land below."

Horse Cove was settled soon after the Cherokees agreed to move out of the area in 1819. Its chief claim to fame is that Woodrow Wilson spent several weeks here with his mother and other relatives during the summer of 1879, just after he graduated from college.

Traveling through Horse Cove, you will notice Black Rock Mountain looming on the right. It was once believed that black lichens were responsible for the mountain's distinctive character, much as white lichens were credited for the appearance of the nearby landmark, Whiteside Mountain.

A little over 3 miles from the intersection with Whiteside Cove Road, Horse Cove Road begins its climb up the mountain. Zeigler and Grosscup wrote that "the road . . . leads up the Blue Ridge,

in zigzag course, through the forested aisles. . . .
Three miles and a half is the distance from its base
to the hamlet of Highlands. The engineering of
the road is so perfect that, in spite of the pre-
cipitousness of the mountain, the ascent is gradual." The ascent does not seem quite so gradual
today, for the road winds through thirty-seven
curves over the next 2 miles. From the crest,
however, there is a rewarding view of Horse Cove
and the surrounding countryside.

Continue for an additional 1 mile to the intersection with U.S. 64/N.C. 28 in the center of
Highlands to complete the tour.

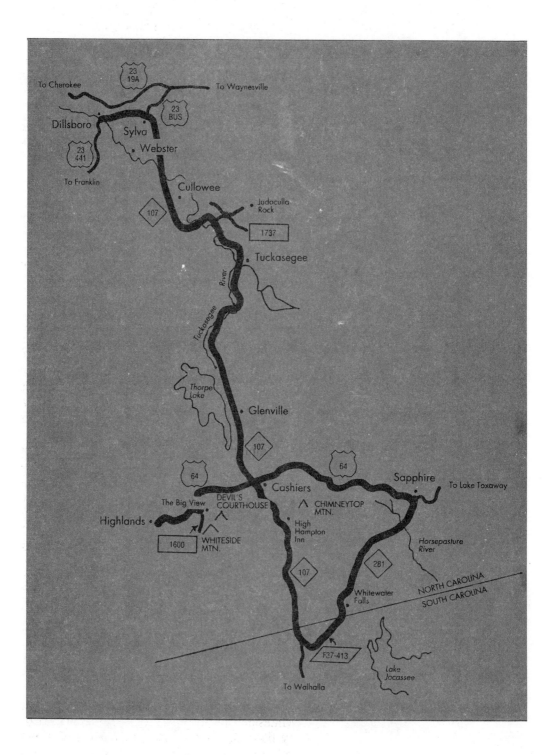

This tour begins in Highlands and travels to Whiteside Mountain. From there, it continues to the town of Cashiers, then heads south to Whitewater Falls. Next, it goes north to the Horsepasture River and Sapphire, then back to Cashiers before following the Tuckasegee River to Thorpe Lake and Judaculla Rock. The tour passes through Cullowhee and Sylva and ends in Dillsboro. Total mileage: approximately 83 miles.

▲▲▲▲▲▲▲▲▲▲▲▲▲▲▲▲▲▲▲▲▲▲▲▲▲▲*The Cashiers Tour*

*Whiteside Mountain*

From the main intersection in Highlands, follow U.S. 64 heading east toward Cashiers. It is 5.4 miles to the United States Forest Service's ranger station for the Highlands District of the Nantahala National Forest. The ranger station is on the right next to the entrance to the Cullasaja Club. It is a good place to pick up free pamphlets and ask questions about the area.

Continue for 1.5 miles to a sign on the right for Whiteside Mountain Road (S.R. 1600) and Wildcat Cliffs Country Club. (The sign is small, so start looking when you see the first indications of the country club on the right. If you reach the Jackson County line, you have gone one curve too far.) Turn onto Whiteside Mountain Road. It is approximately 1 mile to a parking area from which you can hike all or part of the 2-mile loop trail that goes to the top of Whiteside Mountain. The summit provides magnificent views of the Chattooga River Valley, Black Rock Mountain, and at least twenty-six other peaks in the area. The trail follows the edge of the 400- to 600-foot cliffs for 1.1 miles to another overlook, then descends to the parking lot.

Situated on the eastern continental divide, Whiteside Mountain rises 2,100 feet from the valley floor. Its summit has an elevation of 4,930 feet. Both the north and south faces feature stunning, sheer cliffs ranging from 400 to 750 feet in height. The cliffs consist of Whiteside granite, which contains a high content of feldspar, quartz, and mica. The south side of the mountain has little vegetation—its blue-gray color comes from the rock showing through. The white streaks on the south face are feldspar and quartz. The north side has a darker appearance because of the mosses and lichens that grow there.

Though you can reach the top of the mountain with relative ease today, that was not the case in 1880, when Rebecca H. Davis described her trip to Whiteside for *Harper's Magazine*. "When the top is reached, after a short stretch of nearly perpendicular climbing," she wrote, "the traveler finds himself on the edge of a sheer white wall of rock, over which, clinging for life to a protecting hand, he can look, if he chooses, two thousand feet down into the dim valley below."

Thrill seeking seems to have been the order of the day. In their 1883 book, *The Heart of the Alleghanies*, Wilbur Zeigler and Ben Grosscup described a similar experience: "As the observer to secure a fair view lies flat on the ground with part of his head projected over a space of dread nothingness . . . the pure, apparently tangible air of the void, and the soft moss-like bed of the deep-down forest bordered by a silver stream, have an irresistible fascination, especially over one troubled with ennui. Get the guide to hold your feet when you crawl to the verge."

According to James Mooney's 1898 report to the Bureau of American Ethnology, the Indians compared the cliffs to a sheet of ice. From Mooney's and other nineteenth-century accounts, it appears that the two separate peaks known as Whiteside Mountain and the Devil's Courthouse were once a single long ridge. The area adjoining Whiteside Mountain called Wildcat Cliffs is covered with lavish summer homes today. It was formerly known as the Sitting Down Place, since Indians using the trail that came up from present-day Whiteside Cove would often camp at the nearby spring.

Mooney recorded an interesting Indian legend

*Whiteside Mountain from the Big View*

about the area. The Cherokees believed Whiteside Mountain to be part of an enormous bridge that Utlunta, better known as Spearfinger, was building across the mountains. A terrible ogress who dwelt in the mountains, Spearfinger subsisted on livers plucked from the bodies of Indian children. Because Spearfinger could take on any appearance that suited her purposes, the Cherokees could never tell when she was around. She frequently disguised herself as an old woman. In her natural form, her body was covered with a skin as hard as a rock. Her most distinctive characteristic was a long, stony forefinger shaped like a spearhead, a device she used to stab children through their hearts or the backs of their necks preparatory to stealing their livers.

Legend has it that Spearfinger could lift huge boulders and cement them together by striking them against each other. Using that technique, she began building her bridge at Tree Rock—a rock that resembles a tree trunk—on the west side of the Hiwassee River about 4 miles from Hayesville, near the Georgia line. Spearfinger intended to extend the bridge all the way to Whiteside Mountain, but lightning destroyed it and scattered rock fragments along the entire ridge, where they can still be seen today.

The Cherokees eventually rid themselves of Spearfinger by digging a deep pit across a trail they knew she would use. Once she was trapped in the pit, they tried to shoot her, but their arrows were repulsed by her rock skin until a chickadee perched on her finger, alerting the Indians to her vulnerable spot. Once they shot her finger, they managed to reach her heart, and Spearfinger fell dead.

There were also myths placing the devil himself at Whiteside Mountain. Accounts from the 1800s use Whiteside Mountain and the Devil's Courthouse interchangeably. They often refer to a cave on Whiteside Mountain as the place where the devil kept his throne. There is another Devil's Courthouse in the Balsam Mountains just off the Blue Ridge Parkway (see the Cradle of Forestry Tour), but the one at Whiteside Mountain has been called the "supreme" courthouse to distinguish it from its lesser sibling. Zeigler and Grosscup noted that old Indian ladders—trees trimmed to stub branches—found in early days probably provided access to the cave.

It wasn't just Indians and mythological beings who left their imprint on the cliffs. Over 150 years ago, early settlers in the area discovered a Spanish inscription at the Devil's Courthouse. It was all but forgotten until developers explored the area in the 1950s. The letters on the inscription are two inches high and are carved a quarter-inch deep. The passage reads, "'T.T.' Un Luego Santa Ala Memoria." Many believe the inscription was left by one of Hernando De Soto's men in 1540. Researchers are fairly certain that De Soto's expedition followed the old Indian path that ascended Whiteside Mountain from Whiteside Cove, but the meaning of the words remains a mystery.

*Spanish Inscription*

Return to U.S. 64 and turn right. As you round the curve after crossing the Jackson County line, drive slowly so you can park on the left side of the road and enjoy what is aptly known as the Big View. This is probably one of the most photographed vistas in the vicinity, with its excellent view of Whiteside Mountain and the surrounding area.

*Cashiers*

Continue on U.S. 64 for 4.4 miles to the town of Cashiers (pronounced Cash-ers), elevation 3,486 feet. There are several explanations for the naming of the Cashiers Valley. The name may have come from a horse called Cash owned by Senator John C. Calhoun, who had a plantation near present-day Clemson, South Carolina; this version says that Cash wandered off to a valley pasture and that a search party yelled "Cash's here!" upon finding him. Or the name may have come from another horse called Cash, a horse whose considerable earnings from racing entitled him to spend his winters in the sheltered valley, as he preferred, rather than migrating to South Carolina with the rest of the stock. Or it may have originated with Cassius, one of the prize bulls owned by General Wade Hampton, who summered in the area. The least romantic explanation is perhaps the most likely one—Cashiers was named for an old hermit who lived in the Whiteside Cove area long before other white settlers arrived.

Zeigler and Grosscup described the Cashiers Valley as "a mountain plateau of the Blue Ridge, 3,400 feet in altitude, from four to five miles long and a mile and a half wide. Attracted by its climate, freedom from dampness, its utter isolation from the populated haunts of man, the rugged character of its scenery, and deer and bear infested wildwoods, years since, wealthy planters of South Carolina drifted in here with each recurring summer."

*Wade Hampton II*

One of the most famous of the South Carolinians was Wade Hampton II, who as a colonel in the Battle of New Orleans in 1814 was selected by General Andrew Jackson to deliver the report of victory to President James Madison. Hampton supposedly rode the 1,200 miles from New Orleans to Washington in ten days, using only one horse, to pronounce the message. He later set up a summer estate, Hampton Place, in the Cashiers Valley. The estate included a two-story, seven-bedroom cottage, a kitchen building, servants' quarters, and assorted outbuildings.

*Wade Hampton III*

His son, General Wade Hampton III, continued the tradition at Hampton Place. General Hampton was one of South Carolina's favorite sons and an important Civil War figure. After the death of J. E. B. Stuart, he was given command of the Confederate infantry and cavalry unit that came to be known as the Hampton Legion. It was Hampton who ordered the evacuation of Columbia, South Carolina, upon Sherman's approach. Sherman later accused him of burning his own city. Hampton went on to become governor of South Carolina; it was at Hampton Place that he learned of his election. He later served in the United States Senate. He continued to spend his summers in Cashiers until his death in 1902.

Turn right at the intersection with N.C. 107 and head south. It is 1.4 miles to the entrance to High Hampton Inn, on the left. The Hampton estate was purchased by the McKee family in 1924. A small inn was constructed on the property, but it was destroyed by fire in 1932. The present rustic inn, with its exposed beams and bark-covered exterior, was erected in 1933 and still operates as one of western North Carolina's most exclusive resorts. It is located at the foot of 4,625-foot Chimneytop Mountain, another sheer-faced peak. Chimneytop will remain in view on the left as you drive south.

It is 5.8 miles to the South Carolina line, where the highway becomes S.C. 107. It is another 0.9 mile to the Sloan Bridge Picnic Grounds, on the right. Immediately past the picnic area is a sign indicating that Whitewater Falls is 3 miles to the left. Turn left onto the road marked F37-413. It is 0.7 mile to an overlook on the right. The vista from the overlook includes Lake Jocassee and the South Carolina Piedmont. The Keowee River once had its origin here, where the Whitewater and Toxaway rivers merged just below the North Carolina–South Carolina line near the Cherokee village of Jocassee. The entire area is now covered by Lake Jocassee, one of two adjoining lakes created by Duke Power Company. The 7,500-acre Lake Jocassee boasts 75 miles of shoreline. It has established a reputation as one of the South's finest trout lakes.

According to legend, Jocassee was a Cherokee princess whose name signified "a full bosom" or "a fertile field," but she died before she fulfilled the promise of that name. In the mid-1800s, William Gilmore Simms wrote that Jocassee's lover was a man called Toxaway. When Toxaway died at the hands of Jocassee's brother, Chief Oconee, Jocassee disappeared from a canoe while crossing the river. The story goes that she leapt overboard when she saw the outstretched arms of her slain lover beckoning her to join him beneath the waters. Simms wrote, "She rose not once to the surface. The stream from that moment, lost the name of Sarratay, and both whites and Indians, to this day, know it only as the river of Jocassee." Toxaway, Oconee, and Jocassee survive in the names of various parks, waterfalls, lakes, and communities in the area.

*Lake Jocassee*

*Whitewater Falls*

*Horsepasture River*

*Drift Falls*

It is another 1.5 miles to an intersection with S.C. 130. Turn left and follow the signs to Whitewater Falls. It is 0.9 mile to the North Carolina line, where the highway becomes N.C. 281 as you enter the Nantahala National Forest. After 0.2 mile, follow the signs directing you to the Whitewater Falls Scenic Area, on the right. It is an easy five-minute walk from the parking lot to the Whitewater Falls overlook.

The falls measure 411 feet, the highest east of the Rockies. Simms described them in the journal he kept while traveling in the area: "The upper Fall is that of the White Water, which from the distance at which we behold it, is a galaxy, scintillating in the sunshine, with a perfect torrent of starlight. . . . [The river] darts over a cliff, and continues its headlong tumble for nearly three hundred yards, in a foamy and fearful conflict, with the great boulders and the fractured masses, through which it has torn itself a way."

There is a fairly easy 2-mile round-trip trail to the left. A steeper trail paralleling the Foothills Trail goes deep into the gorge. The latter is a 4-mile route. Its elevation change of 1,240 feet makes it a strenuous hike.

Return to N.C. 281 and turn right, heading north. It is 6.5 miles to the bridge over the Horsepasture River. In 1986, 4.5 miles of the river gorge—2 miles wide and 800 feet deep in places—were designated part of the National Wild and Scenic River System. The area was threatened when a private corporation revealed its plan to build a hydroelectric dam on the river, but local conservationists calling themselves FROTH (Friends of the Horsepasture) launched a grass-roots campaign that saved the falls.

A moderate to strenuous 2.8-mile round-trip hike along the Horsepasture River passes several waterfalls. Park along the guardrail on the narrow overlook above the river.

Downstream, you can see Drift Falls, a popular place for swimmers to slide on the rocks during the summer; it was once nicknamed Bohaynee Beach after a nearby community. Numerous steep, rocky spurs lead down to the river. It is

Rainbow Falls

Stairway Falls

Windy Falls

Shortia

fifteen minutes' walking time from Drift Falls to Umbrella Falls, or Turtleback Falls, then another ten minutes to Rainbow Falls, which thunders 150 feet into a deep pool, spraying a mist against the canyon walls that forms a rainbow when the sun is right. It is said that if the water level of the river is up during a full moon, rare moonbows can be seen at night arching over the falls. Rainbow Falls is also known as Horsepasture Falls or High Falls.

Another ten minutes brings you to Stairway Falls, which has seven steps averaging ten feet in height—hence the name. There is an unsettling story about the wife of a previous owner of Stairway Falls. In 1879, a woman named Eliza Dodgen died mysteriously; her body was discovered in the fireplace of her home along the Toxaway River. A coroner's inquest ruled that "the deceased Eliza Dodgen came to her death by falling into the fire from some unknown cause and burnt to death." A few months later, her husband, Adam Dodgen, purchased the land containing the stairway shoals, and for many years they were called Adam Shoals. Eliza Dodgen is buried on the ridge east of the falls.

An 0.8-mile descent over a treacherous route brings you to Windy Falls; extreme caution is urged if you choose to proceed. In *The Land of Waterfalls*, Jim Bob Tinsley wrote that "Windy Falls, creating almost constant breezes, is an ominous place of swirling spray, fog, and mist. In the main portion of the falls, a ceaseless resounding is heard, and a quaking of the earth is felt as the large river narrows down into a violent driving force of power, as if striking the very bowels of the earth, when it plunges into what is called the Ocean Hole." It is no wonder that the atmosphere seems ominous, since the Horsepasture descends nearly two thousand feet in the 6-mile gorge.

It is also in the Horsepasture River area that the rare and beautiful plant called shortia is found. Shortia is believed to occur naturally in the United States in only six counties, all in this immediate area. It blooms around the end of March or the beginning of April. Its leaves closely resemble galax, but shortia bears only a single large blossom—white or pink—on a slender stem. The plant was discovered by André Michaux when he was combing the Appalachians to collect specimens for the Royal Botanical Gardens in France. In 1787, Michaux placed a specimen in his collection and noted that it was found in "les hautes montagnes de Caroline" (the high mountains of Carolina). In 1842, Asa Gray, a well-known botanist from Harvard, stumbled upon the plant in Michaux's collection and named it *Shortia glacifolia*. Gray was particularly intrigued because the specimen was identical to a plant previously found only in Japan. He made trips to the mountains in 1838 and 1843 in search of shortia but did not manage to find it, though a few plants were collected by others in the following years. In 1886, Professor C. S. Sargeant located what was probably the site of Michaux's discovery, in South Carolina just across the border from Jackson County. After the exact location in the "high mountains" was ascertained, acres of the plant were found near an old Indian path along the Horsepasture River. Shortia has since been carried away by the wagonload, but it can still be sighted near the river on occasion.

It is 2 miles on N.C. 281 from the Horsepasture River to an intersection with U.S. 64 at the community of Sapphire. In 1892, the Sapphire Valley Mining Company began digging for corundum at the Burnt Rock Mine, 7 miles northeast of town. The company built a plant on the Horsepasture River that processed four hundred tons of corundum in 1892. It also constructed the fourteen-room Sapphire Inn as its headquarters. The mining town included a large store, several houses, shacks for the miners, and a twelve-foot-high dam that created a 1-mile-long lake. Though the Sapphire Valley Mining Company built a railroad spur to nearby Toxaway to shorten the haul to Hendersonville, it only worked the mines for a year. The Sapphire Inn was remodeled for the benefit of summer visitors in 1899, but it burned down in 1906.

*Sapphire*

Turn left (or west) onto U.S. 64 and drive the 10 miles to Cashiers. En route, you will notice that prosperity has returned to Sapphire Valley, with several exclusive residential developments complete with golf courses bordering the highway.

At the intersection with N.C. 107 in Cashiers, turn right and head north. After 3.5 miles, the road begins to parallel the shoreline of Thorpe Lake. In the late 1920s, the Aluminum Company of America (ALCOA) needed to expand its generating capacity to produce more aluminum. In 1929, it secured a charter that allowed the Nantahala Power and Light Company to develop power-production sites on the Little Tennessee, Nantahala, and Tuckasegee rivers. ALCOA's primary site was Fontana (see the Tour of the Lakes), a site desired by the Tennessee Valley Authority (TVA) as well. A compromise was worked out that allowed the TVA to build at Fontana and Nantahala Power to build on the Tuckasegee River. Nantahala Power constructed a dam at Glenville in 1941, a small dam for the Thorpe power plant in 1950, and other projects along the Tuckasegee in the 1950s. The lake formed by the dam at Glenville was first called Glenville Lake, but it was renamed in 1951 for J. E. S. Thorpe, Nantahala Power's first president. The lake is 4.5 miles long and covers almost fifteen hundred acres. The construction of dams along the Tuckasegee meant the loss of several well-known scenic landmarks, including High Falls, described in the book *Scenic Resources of the Tennessee Valley* as being "among [the] three or four most impressive and beautiful cataracts in the Tennessee Valley region."

It is 1.5 miles to the Glenville post office and another 1.4 miles to an intersection with Pine Creek Road (S.R. 1157), on the left. Signs indicate the way to Ralph J. Andrews Park, developed on Thorpe Lake in 1978 on land donated to Jackson County by Nantahala Power. The park is a seventy-eight-acre recreational area for camping, boating, and picnicking. A side trip of less than 2 miles takes you to the park entrance.

Returning to N.C. 107, a steep ascent begins after 0.3 mile and continues for the next 3 miles. Just before the road levels off, you will pass a dam and power plant. It is 7.2 miles alongside the river through a prosperous farming area from the Andrews Park turnoff to the community of Tuckasegee.

*Tuckasegee* _____

At the time that white men arrived in the area, Tuckasegee (Tsiksi'tsi) was one of the largest of the Cherokee Middle Towns. When the Cherokees backed the English during the Revolutionary War, North Carolina forces under General Griffith Rutherford marched to squelch them. Rutherford left Old Fort in September 1776 and headed through the Swannanoa Gap, following an old Indian trail that later became known as Rutherford Trace or the War Road. Rutherford initially bypassed the Tuckasegee settlements and headed for Macon County. Later, he sent Captain William Moore and a hundred horsemen back to the area. Captain Moore recorded, "We took a Blind path which led us Down to the Tuckyseige [Tuckasegee] river through a Very Mountainous bad way. Came upon a Very plain path, Very Much used by Indians Driving in from the Middle Settlement." Moore and his men destroyed a deserted village before departing.

The war was not over for the Cherokees. By March 1781, Colonel John Sevier—one of the leaders of the Tennessee forces that marched over the mountains to aid in the American victory at Kings Mountain—had returned home. After leading several raids that helped end the war on the frontier, Sevier and 150 select horsemen made a daring raid into Cherokee territory. James Mooney wrote that Sevier

> started to cross the Great Smoky mountains over trails never before attempted by white men, and so rough in places that it was hardly possible to lead horses. Falling unexpectedly upon Tuckasegee . . . he took the town completely by surprise, killing several warriors and capturing a number of women and children. Two other principal towns and three smaller settlements were taken in the same way . . . the Indians being entirely off their

guard and unprepared to make any effective resistance. Having spread destruction through the middle towns, with the loss to himself of only one man killed and another wounded, he was off again as suddenly as he had come.

The raid helped Sevier—nicknamed Nolichucky Jack—establish the reputation that eventually carried him to the governorship of Tennessee.

By 1802, Return J. Meigs and Thomas Freeman had surveyed a treaty line to separate Indian settlements from white farmsteads. The Meigs-Freeman line roughly paralleled the north bank of the Tuckasegee River. It served as a boundary for seventeen years.

Though there were a few early trading posts, most white settlement in the Tuckasegee Valley began around 1850. Cultivation of the valley proved prosperous, with a high percentage of farmers producing more grain than their families needed. They began to sell their excess grain to drovers en route with their herds to markets in South Carolina and Georgia. Soon, local families were raising and marketing their own herds.

It is 3.5 miles to an interesting monument by the side of the road overlooking the river. The bronze plaque on its massive slab of granite reads in part, "The boyhood home of Dr. John R. Brinkley and his Aunt Sally." Orphaned at the age of eleven, John Brinkley was taken in by his aunt, who lived on a nearby farm. A month after Sally's death, Brinkley struck out westward to make his fortune—and make it he did. It all started while he was practicing medicine in a small Kansas town. One day when a farmer complained of sexual problems, Brinkley remarked that the farmer ought to take his example from goats. When the farmer suggested that Brinkley actually transplant goat glands into his body, an entrepreneurial light clicked on in Brinkley's head.

It hasn't been preserved exactly which organs Brinkley used (though one can guess) and exactly where he put them in the farmer's body, but it's clear that the operation was a success. When people heard that Brinkley's goat-gland operation could create marvels of sexual potency, patients

*Tuckasegee River*

*Dr. John Brinkley*

*John Brinkley's monument
to his Aunt Sally*

flocked to his office. He built a hospital, then decided to build a radio station—one of the most powerful in the country—to advertise his services. Over the years, Brinkley performed his operation and used a subsequent nonsurgical treatment on more than sixteen thousand people, at a fee of $750 each. He also paid druggists a commission to act as agents for his products. It is believed that Brinkley netted $10,000 a week for thirteen years. He owned a fleet of Cadillacs, including a sixteen-cylinder model with his monogram on the doors. He owned three yachts, a palatial Texas estate where he raised his goats, and a big blue plane, the *Romancer*.

But Brinkley's lasting contributions to American culture came when he decided to run as a write-in candidate for the governorship of Kansas. He revolutionized political campaigning with the introduction of the use of radio, sound trucks, and airplanes. He also changed campaign strategies with the use of bands, bluegrass music, lollipops, bumper stickers, buttons, and banners—anything that would get his name before the public. Brinkley's billboard campaign was widespread. His radio station plugged his candidacy constantly. He promised free schoolbooks, free auto tags, and free medicine for the poor, as well as lower taxes, old-age assistance, and a lake in every county in the state. His radio slogan was "Let's pasture the goats on the statehouse lawn."

Though he sent out legions of cheerleaders to teach voters how to mark write-in ballots, he did not employ experienced poll watchers. Many think that Brinkley ballots were intentionally lost. The Democratic candidate won 217,171 votes and the Republican 216,914, while Brinkley amassed 183,278. He ran again in 1932 but lost to Alf Landon. He tried once more in 1934, but his heart didn't seem to be in it, as he hardly campaigned.

When the medical community and the government began harassing him, Brinkley moved his radio operation to Mexico and started a famous border station. He knew his world was crumbling. He died bankrupt before the government had a chance to bring him to trial for tax evasion. But

*Judaculla Rock*

*Webster and Sylva*

with the monument alongside N.C. 107, Jackson County at least has a memento of the man nicknamed the Goat-gland King or the Ponce de Leon of Kansas.

It is 0.7 mile on N.C. 107 to an intersection with Caney Fork Road (S.R. 1737). Turn right and drive 3 miles. A sign will direct you through a farm to Judaculla Rock, a large soapstone slab covered with rude carvings that have never been translated. The Cherokees believe that the carvings were made by the fearful giant Judaculla (or Tsulkalu, meaning "slanting eyes") when he leapt from his mountain farm—located on Tanasee Bald where Haywood, Jackson, and Transylvania counties meet—and landed at the creek near the rock. The markings predate recorded Cherokee history. There are theories that they represent a memorial to a peace treaty, a commemoration of a battle, or a boundary marker. Most people, however, like to think it's Judaculla's footprint on the rock.

Return to N.C. 107 and continue north. It is 3 miles to Cullowhee and the campus of Western Carolina University. Begun in 1889 as a small school for mountain children, it is now a comprehensive state university with over seven thousand students. An Indian mound on the campus was excavated in 1898; most of the artifacts recovered are housed in the Valentine Museum in Richmond, Virginia. The mound was leveled in an expansion project in 1956.

It is 9 miles from Cullowhee to a junction with N.C. 116, which leads to the town of Webster, the original county seat of Jackson County and the area's commercial center until the building of the Western North Carolina Railroad in the 1880s. Most local people wanted and expected the railroad to go through Webster, but a shorter route was plotted along Scotts Creek to Dillsboro. The traditional story goes that a county representative known to enjoy an occasional drink was taken aside at a crucial moment and given a sufficient quantity of alcohol to convince him to route the railroad to Dillsboro. Meanwhile, the town of Sylva, also on the railroad some 2 miles east of Dillsboro, was emerging as the county's new industrial and trade center. The rivalry between Sylva and Webster culminated in a 1913 vote that moved the county seat to Sylva, where it remains.

Stay on N.C. 107. You will reach Sylva after approximately 2 miles. The beautiful Jackson County Courthouse sits atop a hill in the center of town and is visible for miles. If you're looking for exercise, you can reach the courthouse by climbing a 108-step staircase.

*Dillsboro*

Turn left onto U.S. 23 Business and head past the courthouse. You will reach Dillsboro after approximately 2 miles. Dillsboro dates back to 1882, when William Allen Dills built what are known today as the Riverwood Shops. Dills's permanent home, adjacent to the Mount Beulah Hotel, was constructed in 1884. The hotel was renamed the Jarrett Springs Hotel in 1894, when R. H. Jarrett bought it and noted the sulphur spring at the rear of the property.

The railroad took the lead in promoting tourism. In 1886, the first summer vacationers arrived in Dillsboro—two women from Edenton, North Carolina, who shocked everyone by smoking in public. By 1888, Dillsboro had become an important town, with two sawmills, lumberyards, two clay mines, a corundum-crushing plant, two livery stables, six general stores, and a shoemaker's shop.

In 1975, Dillsboro residents began a successful effort to restore their town to its original appearance. The community has since become a marketing center for area craftsmen. The Jarrett Springs Hotel survives as the Jarrett House, a twenty-two-room inn noted for its family-style meals. Across the Tuckasegee River from the Jarrett House are the Riverwood Shops, a group of craft and gift shops featuring work by members of the Southern Highland Handicraft Guild, whose artisans are known for the quality of their craft. Dillsboro also offers a number of fine souvenir and food shops.

This completes the tour. You can take U.S. 23/441 south to Franklin, U.S. 23 north to Waynesville, or U.S. 19A to Cherokee.

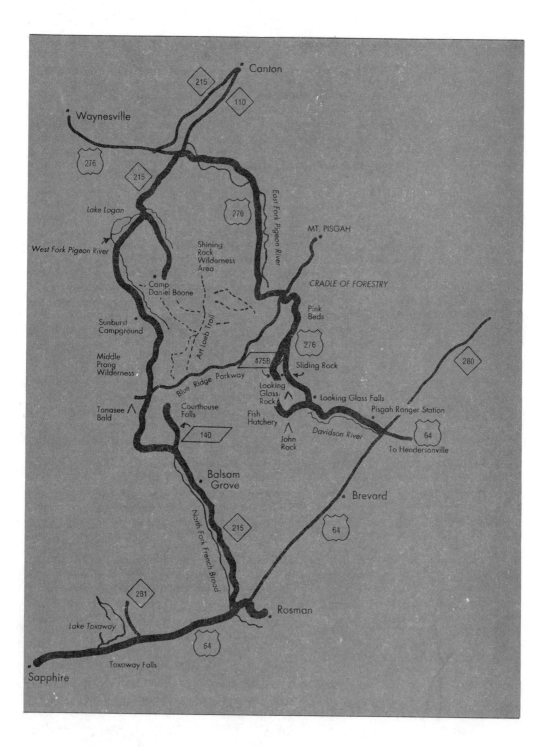

This tour begins near the community of Sapphire and passes Toxaway Falls before proceeding to Rosman. There, it follows the Forest Heritage National Scenic Byway, paralleling the North Fork of the French Broad River to Tanasee Bald. It then descends along the West Fork of the Pigeon River to Sunburst before turning to follow the Pigeon River's East Fork, which forms a boundary of the Shining Rock Wilderness Area. It then intersects with the Blue Ridge Parkway near Mount Pisgah and continues downhill to the Cradle of Forestry in America, Looking Glass Scenic Area, and the attractions of Looking Glass Falls and Sliding Rock. It ends at the entrance to the scenic byway and the boundary of Pisgah National Forest near Brevard. Total mileage: approximately 110 miles.

▲▲▲▲▲▲▲▲▲▲▲▲▲▲▲▲▲▲▲▲▲▲▲▲▲▲▲▲▲▲▲▲▲▲▲▲▲*The Cradle of Forestry Tour*

*Toxaway Falls*

From the intersection of N.C. 281 and U.S. 64 at Sapphire (a community described more fully in the Cashiers Tour), proceed east on U.S. 64 for 1.9 miles, where the highway crosses over the top of Toxaway Falls. You can park on either side of the dam and take a short walk to look down on the falls, a great, bare expanse of rock more than three hundred feet wide with a steady stream of water dropping three hundred feet to the bottom. The dam and the lake it created, Lake Toxaway, have an interesting history.

In the 1890s, a group calling itself the Lake Toxaway Company decided to build "a high class resort with the best of service in every particular," as one of their early brochures described it. After the construction of the dam and the formation of the 640-acre Lake Toxaway, with its 14 miles of shoreline, the mountainous setting lived up to its billing as "America's Switzerland."

The setting was not the only attraction that brought visitors to this isolated area. There was also a five-story wooden hotel with curving verandas overlooking the lake. It contained over five hundred rooms, each with a view of the lake and the mountains. The rooms had cut-and-grooved woodwork of walnut, cherry, chestnut, oak, pine, poplar, and beech. The hotel had electric lighting, refrigeration machinery, elevators, and steam heat—it even boasted that it was "equipped with baths" and had "Western Union and long distance telephones." Guests could dine on the finest of French cuisine, served in the chandeliered dining room with china, linen, crystal, and silver accompaniments. An orchestra played daily concerts. There was a ballroom for dancing. The hotel also offered tennis, boating, fishing, and hunting. A livery stable was available for drives and horseback rides, and a steam launch provided tours of the lake. There was also a mineral spring on the property for those who wished to take a mineral bath.

The railroad reached Lake Toxaway in 1903. Six passenger trains ran daily, some pulling private cars. Guests at the hotel included Henry Ford, the Wannamakers, the Dukes, and Thomas Edison. The good times began to come to an end in July 1916, when a great flood devastated much of the mountain region. The flood did not cause the dam to break but probably hastened its demise. When the dam gave way in August, water washed away livestock and property along the Toxaway River all the way into South Carolina. The railroad ran extra trains so sightseers could see the destruction and collect stranded fish in the drained lake. Facing numerous property settlements, the Lake Toxaway Company closed the hotel and abandoned the property. The hotel was torn down in 1948, but a new Lake Toxaway Company began to resurrect the property in 1960. Another dam was built. A five-story private home constructed between 1913 and 1916 was restored as a clubhouse for the new golf course. Today, the development thrives as a residential resort community.

It is 6.1 miles from the top of the Lake Toxaway Dam to an intersection with N.C. 215. Follow U.S. 64 for another 1.6 miles to an intersection with N.C. 178 and turn right, heading into Rosman.

From 1905 through the 1930s, Rosman was the most prosperous community in Transylvania County. It was built where four prongs of the French Broad River—the North Fork, the West Fork, the East Fork, and the Middle Fork—come together. The location had proven itself a good site for fording the river as far back as the days when the ancient Indian trading path called the Estatoe Trail ran nearby. A white settlement was formed in the early 1800s, but the community didn't begin to prosper until the coming of the Henderson-Brevard Railroad shortly after the turn of this century.

About the time the railroad made its appearance, Joseph Silversteen arrived from Pennsylvania and began his experimental tanning and tanning-extract operations. The settlement was called Jeptha at that time, but it was incorporated as the town of Toxaway in 1901. When the Lake Toxaway resort opened, its developers asked that the town's name be changed to avoid confusion. In 1903, the town became known as Estatoe, an unpopular choice that survived only two years. In 1905, it was called Rosman, a combination of the names of a couple of Joseph Silversteen's associates.

In 1910, Silversteen acquired thirty thousand acres of forestland from George Vanderbilt. He built a lumbermill and a company store for his three hundred workers. Silversteen's band mill sawed twenty-six thousand board feet of lumber daily. Two trains a day hauled logs out of what is now the Pisgah National Forest. Silversteen's tanning operations were suspended in 1956, and the lumbermill closed in 1966. The company store, now known as the Gloucester General Store, serves as a reminder of the prosperity Rosman once knew.

Retrace your route to the intersection with N.C. 215 and turn right, heading north. The railroad that delivered logs to the Rosman mill followed this course. The route has since become the first national forest scenic byway in North Carolina. In 1989, the Forest Heritage National Scenic Byway was dedicated to promote public enjoyment of outstanding scenic attractions in the Pisgah National Forest, thanks to the efforts of state and local agencies working in partnership with the United States Forest Service.

*Pisgah National Forest*

Most of the rest of this tour travels through the Pisgah National Forest. In 1889, George Vanderbilt, the grandson of railroad baron Cornelius Vanderbilt, began buying property at the confluence of the Swannanoa and French Broad rivers, near Asheville. Vanderbilt planned to build a reproduction of a sixteenth-century French château and surround it with a large game preserve. He purchased about sixty local farms and hired Frederick Law Olmstead, America's first landscape architect and the man behind New York City's Central Park, to plan his model farm. Part of Olmstead's master plan involved the restoration of exploited forestland. He hired Gifford Pinchot—the son of one of his friends—who developed the first example of managed forestry in the United States. American forestry was thus born.

*Gifford Pinchot*

Upon his arrival, Pinchot was struck by the abuse that the land had suffered. He recorded that destructive logging "had been done with an eye single to immediate returns and wholly without regard for the safety of the forests, and fires had been permitted to burn unchecked. There had been much injudicious clearing of upper slopes, which, after a few years of unprofitable cultivation, were generally abandoned to erosion."

Pinchot began a systematic mapping of the 7,280 acres on the Biltmore Estate. His plan was to harvest old trees so that young growth would have room to develop. He trained local men in the way to cut trees so that the least harm would be done to the forest. A sawmill was soon in operation.

Vanderbilt then sent Pinchot in search of land higher in the mountains to serve as a game preserve. This led to the purchase of the twenty-thousand-acre parcel called the Pink Beds. Vanderbilt later added eighty thousand adjoining acres on Pinchot's recommendation and named the entire tract Pisgah Forest, honoring the Biblical mountain from which Moses viewed the Promised Land.

*Carl Schenck*

Pinchot went on to found the United States Forest Service under President Theodore Roosevelt. He was replaced at the Biltmore Estate by a German forester, Dr. Carl A. Schenck. Since there were no accepted forestry standards in America at that time, Schenck was free to experiment. Forestry apprentices came to Biltmore to work under his guidance, many without remuneration.

After Vanderbilt's death in 1914, most of the Pisgah Forest was purchased by the federal government. In 1915, it became the first national game preserve east of the Mississippi River. Today, Pisgah National Forest covers 480,000 acres.

*French Broad River*

As you travel through the forest, you will be following the North Fork of the French Broad River. The river was named by eighteenth-century explorers and hunters who discovered that it differed from other rivers they knew in that it eventually turned west and flowed toward lands claimed by the French. They named it the French Broad to distinguish it from the rivers that flowed toward English settlements along the Atlantic Ocean. The Cherokees called it Long Man and its tributaries Chattering Children; they called some of the faster-moving parts Tahkeeostee, meaning "racing waters." Little has changed today.

*Alligator Rock*

After 1.7 miles on N.C. 215, you will see a rock ledge jutting over the highway on the right. Named Alligator Rock, it may give you the impression that you are entering the jaws of an alligator. It is another 4.3 miles to an intersection with S.R. 1326. A sign indicates that the Rosman Research Center is to the left. Because the mountainous environment is relatively free of electronic interference, the National Aeronautics and Space Administration built two dish-shaped antennas eighty-five feet in diameter at the Rosman Research Center. The facility was once used to track satellites. It is now operated by the Department of Defense.

It is 2.6 miles on N.C. 215 past the turnoff to the research center to the Balsam Grove post office, then another 2.1 miles to F.R. 140, which heads to the right up Courthouse Creek. The creek leads to the source of the French Broad River, located at the base of the west wall of the 5,462-foot summit known as the Devil's Courthouse. The Cherokees believed that the giant Tsulkalu (anglicized to Judaculla and translated as "slanting eyes") had a courtroom in a cave at the Devil's Courthouse. It was believed he held his judgment sessions there.

If you would like to take a side trip to do some hiking, head down F.R. 140. Veer left after 0.9 mile, then proceed another 2.2 miles (3.1 miles total) and park on the right for a moderately difficult 0.6-mile route to Courthouse Falls. The path is not marked, but you should hike downstream from the bridge on an old road. At 0.2 mile on the left is a narrow path with sections of steps that descends 0.1 mile to Courthouse Falls, where the creek plummets fifty feet into a round basin carved from solid granite. For a more strenuous hike to the Devil's Courthouse, drive another 0.8 mile to the parking area at the end of F.R. 140. (There is an easier approach from the Blue Ridge Parkway.) If you wish to make this hike, you would be well advised to get directions from a guidebook or a ranger station, since the trail is not marked. Retrace your route to N.C. 215 to complete the side trip.

N.C. 215 climbs for the next 6.6 miles to a crest at Beech Gap, where it meets the Blue Ridge Parkway. The bald on the left as you climb is Tanasee (or Tennessee) Bald. According to Cherokee legend, it was near here that Judaculla had his hundred-acre farm; it is said that because he cleared his fields, the area has remained bald to this day. It was also from this point—where

*Bald near Forest Heritage National Scenic Byway*

Jackson, Haywood, and Transylvania counties meet—that Judaculla made his famous jump. He landed near Caney Fork in the valley below, and the scratches left where his foot hit are still visible on Judaculla Rock (see the Cashiers Tour).

This area is also called the Devil's Old Fields. Cherokee legend tells of one occasion when some Indians intruded on Judaculla here. The slant-eyed devil-giant must not have cared for their visit, because he turned himself into a snake and swallowed all fifty of them in a single gulp.

*Middle Prong Wilderness Area*

Descending on N.C. 215, the area to the left is the Middle Prong Wilderness Area. Designated in 1984, the seventy-nine-hundred-acre tract is the newest addition to North Carolina's wilderness system. Much of the area was logged by the Champion Paper Company in the early 1900s, but the forest is growing back to the point where man's imprint is virtually unnoticeable, save for occasional evidence of abandoned logging roads and railroad grades.

The tour now follows the West Fork of the Pigeon River, which forms several cascades along the route. It is 8.6 miles from the intersection with the Blue Ridge Parkway to the Sunburst Campground. The logging town of Sunburst was

*Sunburst Campground*

once the center for ten of the Champion Paper Company's logging camps. The campground is actually located on the former site of the town of Spruce, which boasted a large band mill. The Sunburst Campground now provides an ideal base camp for hikes into the Middle Prong Wilderness Area. Because the trails into the wilderness area are not marked, visitors are advised to get directions from the forest-service ranger station near Brevard and to carry topographical maps and a compass.

Approximately 3 miles past the Sunburst Campground, you will begin to notice that the area has been reforested. Tall pine trees growing in symmetrical rows almost form a canopy over the road. It becomes obvious that you are riding through a resort area when a lake appears on the left. It is Lake Logan, a beautiful, private mountain lake built as a water supply for Champion's mills in 1932. Prior to the damming of the river, the community of Sunburst was located here.

Peter G. Thomson started the Champion Coated Paper Company in Ohio in 1896. His process of making paper and coating it on both sides in one operation was very profitable, but he owned no forests and was forced to buy wood from his competitors. He needed to make his own pulp, so he built a plant at Canton, North Carolina. Champion then began logging the fine hardwood forests of the area.

In 1906, Thomson sent his son-in-law, Reuben Robertson, on a fifty-day assignment to improve the company's operations. Robertson set out to make Sunburst a model logging town. He accomplished his task, and he and his wife ended up staying for over fifty years.

At the time of Champion's arrival, there were four hundred people living in Canton. By 1916, the population had grown to around six thousand, with another two thousand living in the surrounding area. Business boomed so much that Champion employed over a thousand men and shipped fifteen carloads of products from Canton daily. The large sawmill in Sunburst operated until the mid-1920s, when it was destroyed by fire. The railroad into the area was abandoned soon afterwards.

Champion is still a powerful economic force in the area, as evidenced by the recent political and legal battles between North Carolina and Tennessee over the company's emission of wastes into the Pigeon River, which flows northwest into Tennessee. Interestingly, Tennessee has been voicing its argument that Champion is polluting the river since 1927.

Circling Lake Logan on N.C. 215, it is less than 2 miles to a sign for Camp Daniel Boone, a Boy Scout camp. Turn right onto Little East Fork Road (S.R. 1129) and go 3.8 miles upstream to the camp. At the parking area at the south edge of the camp is a trailhead for the Art Loeb Trail System. Loeb was a hiking enthusiast and the leader of the Carolina Mountain Club. The trail system was dedicated to his memory and designated a nation-

*Art Loeb Trail System*

*Shining Rock Wilderness Area from Blue Ridge Parkway*

*Pigeon River*

*Mount Pisgah*

al recreation trail in 1979. Many experienced hikers feel that the system, which includes some of the longest and most challenging trails in the Pisgah National Forest, provides the most beautiful hiking in the area. There are several routes among the various interconnecting trails. One popular trailhead may be picked up off Milepost 420 on the Blue Ridge Parkway by turning onto N.C. 816 and riding 0.5 mile to a parking lot.

The trail beginning at Camp Daniel Boone ascends 2,926 feet. A strenuous hike leads to the heart of the Shining Rock Wilderness Area, where there are no comforts like water spigots, shelters, or picnic tables. The wilderness-area designation also means that no trail markings are allowed, though the trails are heavily used. Hikers are advised to take along trail guidebooks and topographical maps. The Shining Rock Wilderness Area was one of the first national wilderness areas in the East. It is accessible only by trail. The wilderness area was named for the white quartz that caps 6,000-foot Shining Rock Mountain. The highest peak in the area is Cold Mountain, with an elevation of 6,030 feet. Altogether, there are 30 rugged miles of trails in the Art Loeb Trail System. A properly outfitted, experienced hiker could occupy three and a half or four days in hiking them all. Look at a trail guidebook to help you decide which section of trail would suit you best. Whichever one you choose, the views are spectacular.

Retrace your route to N.C. 215. Turn right and travel 5 miles to an intersection with U.S. 276. Turn right. You are now following the East Fork of the Pigeon River. The route passes through a scenic farming valley that is becoming fairly developed. After you have traveled through the virtually deserted national-forest lands, the area may seem congested. For the next 14.5 miles, the road skirts the Shining Rock Wilderness Area, to the right. At the crest of the ascent, you will intersect the Blue Ridge Parkway.

If you exit U.S. 276 and drive north on the parkway, it is a side trip of 3 miles to Mount Pisgah. According to tradition, the 5,721-foot peak was named for the Biblical mountain by Reverend James Hall, an Indian-fighting chaplain who accompanied General Griffith Rutherford on his march through the area in 1776. Rutherford was on an expedition to subdue the Cherokees. George Vanderbilt later applied the name to his entire forest, as described earlier in the tour.

*The Pink Beds*

Continuing on U.S. 276, it is 4.5 miles downhill to the Pink Beds Picnic Area. The Pink Beds are an unusual forested upland bog with an average altitude of 3,250 feet. The name most likely came from the dense growth of pink rhododendron and mountain laurel that blooms in the late spring and early summer.

*Cradle of Forestry in America*

Almost next door, less than 0.1 mile farther on U.S. 276, is the Cradle of Forestry in America, a national historic site commemorating the birthplace of scientific forestry and forestry education in America. In 1898, Dr. Carl A. Schenck, the German who succeeded Gifford Pinchot in supervising George Vanderbilt's vast forest holdings, founded a school that he hoped would satisfy his questioning apprentices. The Biltmore Forest School was the first forestry school in America. Winter classes were held at the Biltmore Estate, while summer sessions were held in Pisgah Forest. Some of the students operated a trout hatchery and bred pheasants for the Vanderbilt game preserve. Students were told to find their own places to stay, and the campus soon encompassed several abandoned cabins and farmhouses with such descriptive names as Hell Hole, Little Bohemia, the Palace, and Rest for the Wicked. Schenck built several lodges, imitating architecture used in the Black Forest of Germany. He distributed lodges throughout Pisgah Forest to privately hired rangers, who watched for game violators and unauthorized timber cutters.

Schenck worked tirelessly to teach private owners of forests that they could insure future production of salable timber with proper management, including replanting and selective cutting. Pisgah Forest served as a demonstration site. In 1908, Schenck invited businessmen, lumbermen, educators, and politicians to a three-day Biltmore

Forest Fair. There, he showed them what practical forestry could do. Evidently, his demonstrations were successful, since many adopted his principles.

Schenck was discharged by Vanderbilt in 1909 in what was the beginning of an interesting feud between the two—Schenck described it in his book, *The Birth of Forestry in America*. His students remained loyal, and the Biltmore Forest School lived on, moving with Schenck to Germany; Cadillac, Michigan; and finally back to Sunburst. Schenck had a friend and admirer in Reuben Robertson of the Champion Fibre Company (Champion's official name at that time). Robertson offered Schenck the use of facilities at his newly built logging village, which was unoccupied because logging operations hadn't yet started in that area. The Biltmore Forest School was headquartered in Sunburst until it graduated its last class in 1913. In sixteen years, the school produced 367 graduates, who went on to become practicing professional foresters throughout the United States.

*Sliding Rock Recreation Area*

In 1968, Congress designated sixty-five hundred acres of the Pisgah National Forest as the Cradle of Forestry in America. Today, the site provides a gift shop, a snack bar, and a visitors' center with exhibits and a film. There are also two interpretive trails. One leads through restored and reconstructed buildings that depict the life of the first forestry students. The other duplicates the tour that Schenck gave visitors to the Biltmore Forest Fair in 1908. A small fee is charged at the gate for entrance to the area.

Continuing on U.S. 276, there is a sign for F.R. 475-B about 0.9 mile from the Cradle of Forestry. This is where you will reenter the highway if you opt to take the side trip mentioned later in the tour.

It is another 2.7 miles on U.S. 276 to the Sliding Rock Recreation Area, on the right. Sliding Rock is one of the hundreds of waterfalls in Transylvania County, nicknamed the Land of Waterfalls. Transylvania County has one of the greatest variations in elevation of any county in

*Sliding Rock*

*Looking Glass Falls*

the eastern United States, ranging from 6,025 feet atop Chestnut Bald to 2,220 feet where the Toxaway River crosses the South Carolina border. The county averages over eighty inches of rainfall annually, insuring that each of its acres is provided more than two million gallons of water per year. The rainfall also insures the continued existence of the waterfalls.

Sliding Rock is unusual as waterfalls go—visitors can slide down it. The granite incline provides a natural sixty-foot water slide. Eleven thousand gallons of water per minute glide over the granite into a six-foot-deep pool at the bottom. Bathers have been enjoying Sliding Rock since Schenck brought his students here in 1898. What has been called "the fastest sixty feet in the mountains" was rediscovered in the 1950s. The United States Forest Service constructed a bathhouse and a parking lot to accommodate summer visitors. A lifeguard is even provided from Memorial Day to Labor Day.

Continuing on U.S. 276, it is 1.3 miles to the Moore Cove Trail, on the left. Visitors can park near the stone bridge located between the highway and the creek, then hike across the bridge along an old railroad grade. The 0.7-mile trail leads to Moore Creek Falls. The creek drops fifty feet over a granite wall. Visitors can walk behind the falls.

It is another 1 mile on U.S. 276 to Looking Glass Falls, on the left. There is a parking area in front of the falls, which are thirty feet wide and drop unbroken more than sixty feet down a rock cliff. Because Looking Glass Falls is so accessible from the highway, there are usually lots of tourists taking photographs during the summer months.

Another 0.3 mile brings you to F.R. 475, where you will see signs for the Pisgah Forest Fish Hatchery. Turn right. It is 0.4 mile to a parking area for a trail to Looking Glass Rock. A 3.1-mile hike takes you to the 3,969-foot summit, which offers a beautiful view of the Pink Beds and the surrounding area. During wet springs or winters when the water freezes on Looking Glass Rock,

*Pisgah Forest*
*Fish Hatchery*

*John Rock Scenic Area*

*Looking Glass Rock*

the rock acts as a giant mirror, reflecting the sheer cliffs. The Cherokees called it the Devil's Looking Glass, since it is located so close to the Devil's Courthouse. Looking Glass Rock offers some of the best rock climbing in the South, so you may see climbers on its face.

It is another 0.5 mile to the fish hatchery. North Carolina has 4,000 miles of stocked trout streams, more than any other state in the Southeast. The Pisgah Forest Fish Hatchery, run by the North Carolina Wildlife Resources Commission, raises sixty thousand trout annually. Trout eggs are placed in large incubator trays, where water flows over them continuously, supplying oxygen until the eggs hatch in fifty days. When the trout grow to fingerling size (two to three inches), they are placed in circular tanks that simulate the action of a stream. They are kept in the tanks until they are taken to area streams.

At one time, this area was a logging community. During the 1930s, it served as a Civilian Conservation Corps camp. The hatchery, located at the foot of the John Rock Scenic Area, is now a popular place to bring children, who especially like to see the feeding frenzies. Fish food is available for those visitors who don't arrive at regular feeding times. There are several hiking trails around John Rock, which is part of a 435-acre area under consideration for the National Register of Landmarks.

Leaving the hatchery's parking area, you have two choices.

If you are not inclined to travel over gravel forest roads with washboard switchbacks, turn right and retrace your route to U.S. 276. Turn right.

If you're feeling adventurous, you can take a side trip that loops around Looking Glass Rock. Leaving the parking area, turn left and follow the gravel road marked F.R. 475-B, which heads up the hill to the right. As you ascend, you will see John Rock on your left. It is approximately 2 miles to a pull-off, with a trail on the right leading to Slick Rock Falls, so named because of the moss that covers the rocks on the brink. Several deer carcasses have been found below the falls. This should serve as a grim reminder to visitors of the tricky footing along the top.

As you continue on F.R. 475-B, Looking Glass Rock will be in view on the right. It is a little over 1 mile to another pull-off, where a trail following an old logging road leads to Looking Glass Rock. F.R. 475-B circles Looking Glass Rock for another 3.5 miles until it intersects U.S. 276 just below the Cradle of Forestry entrance. Turn right and travel approximately 5 miles back to the intersection with F.R. 475 to complete the side trip and rejoin the tour route.

Continue on U.S. 276. You will pass the Coontree Picnic Area on the right. Also on the right is the Davidson River. After the Revolutionary War, Benjamin Davidson moved into the area alongside what was then known as the Rolling River. Davidson's 640-acre land grant, given for his service during the war, was made official in 1797. He built a mill and dug ditches to drain the bottom lands so he could grow crops. It wasn't long before Rolling River became known as Davidson's Creek, and later Davidson's River. At the time that the Buncombe County Courthouse was built in Morristown (present-day Asheville), the main road from the communities in the southern part of the county still traveled along the river.

It is 3.5 miles on U.S. 276 to a visitors' center–ranger station. Information, exhibits, a gift shop, restrooms, and nature and exercise trails are provided.

It is another 0.2 mile to the Davidson River Campground, one of the largest family campgrounds in Pisgah National Forest. Its hot showers could explain the campground's popularity during the summer. Nearby is the Schenck Job Corps Center, a residential center operated by the United States Forest Service for underprivileged young men sixteen to twenty-two years old. There, they can complete their high-school education and learn vocational skills.

It is 2.1 miles to the Sycamore Flats Recreation Area, on the right, then another 0.4 mile to two stone columns erected to honor Transylvania

*Forest Heritage National Scenic Byway*

County residents who served their country during World War I. The columns also mark the entrance to Pisgah National Forest, the end of the Forest Heritage National Scenic Byway, and the conclusion of this tour. You are now at the junction with U.S. 64. If you turn right, you will have a short drive to Brevard. If you continue straight ahead, you will have a 22-mile drive to Hendersonville. If you turn left onto N.C. 280, you will be headed toward I-26 and Asheville.

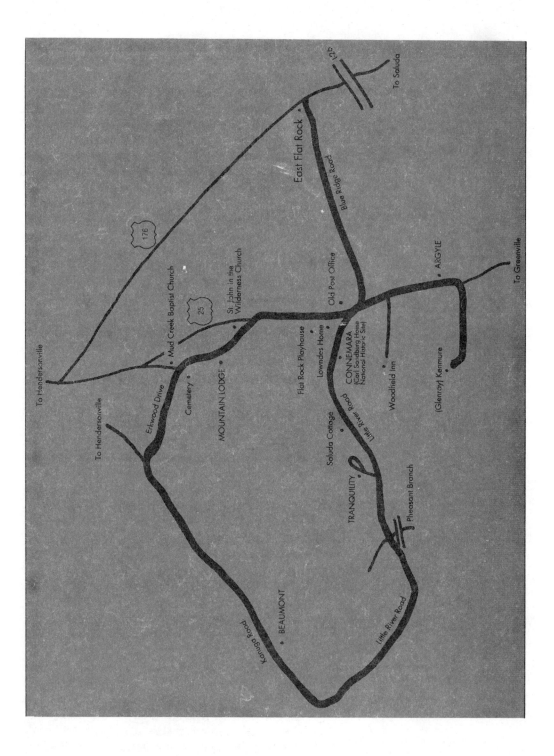

This tour makes a complete circle around the community of Flat Rock, once the summer social mecca for the aristocracy of Southern antebellum society. Although this tour covers a shorter distance than the others featured in the book, Flat Rock's wealth of history and legend certainly deserves a concentrated tour of its own. If a longer trip is desired, this tour may be combined with the Hunting Country Tour. Total mileage: approximately 22 miles.

▲▲▲▲▲▲▲▲▲▲▲▲▲▲▲▲▲▲▲▲▲▲▲▲▲▲▲▲▲▲▲▲*The Historic Flat Rock Tour*

*"If no passengers were alighting, the mail was simply thrown off the train."*

Flat Rock is located approximately 3 miles south of Hendersonville off I-26. Take Exit 23 (the exit for East Flat Rock) onto U.S. 176 and follow the signs for the Carl Sandburg Home National Historic Site.

Before reaching Flat Rock, you will pass through the community of East Flat Rock. When the area's first railroad was completed, it was routed through the middle of a forest 2 miles from Flat Rock, which was already a popular resort. Passengers wishing to visit Flat Rock were deposited in the woods at a location that eventually became known as East Flat Rock. They then had to walk or arrange transportation into town. If no passengers were alighting, the mail was simply thrown off the train. The small community of East Flat Rock grew up to accommodate rail passengers.

Turn left onto the Blue Ridge Road, following the route used by railroad passengers traveling to Flat Rock in the 1830s. Before white settlers moved into the area, the land between Knoxville, Tennessee, and the Watauga settlement in North Carolina, as well as that between the Watauga settlement and Greenville, South Carolina, was

## The Flat Rock

known on maps simply as the Wilderness. One Wilderness landmark—a large, flat rock—marked the location where Cherokee Indians held their annual hunting ceremonies. Some accounts also suggest that the rock marked the site of a camp from which Cherokee braves departed to attack the Block House in Tryon in 1776 (see the Hunting Country Tour). When frontiersmen retaliated by burning Indian settlements in the Smoky Mountains, the Cherokee families at the site of the flat rock turned their temporary settlement into a permanent camp that lasted until the early 1800s.

Once the Cherokees sided with the British during the Revolutionary War, it was only a matter of time before the victorious Americans pushed them farther west. With the opening of new roads, settlers from South Carolina were quick to move into this area. By 1827, the Buncombe Turnpike had opened the way for travel from Charleston, South Carolina, all the way to Tennessee and Kentucky.

## Charles and Susan Baring

Most settlements grew up for economic reasons, but Flat Rock was a summer haven for the rich almost from its inception. The story of Flat Rock starts with Charles Baring, a prominent Englishman associated with a banking firm in London. Baring was sent to Charleston on behalf of his cousin, Lord Ashburton, to arrange Ashburton's marriage to Susan Heyward, the widow of a wealthy rice planter. Fortunately for Flat Rock, Baring neglected his assignment and married Susan himself.

Although no one at the time understood what caused the dreaded summer outbreaks of yellow fever, Baring did know that he needed to protect his precious wife and her wealth in low-country plantations. Susan was already past middle age when she married Baring, who was actually her sixth husband, and she was in ill health during the first years of their union.

Bolstered by his personal theory that infertile soil at high altitudes made for healthy living, Baring set out to find the ideal place for a baronial estate for his wife. Though Baring's theory was

*Mountain Lodge* _____

*Judge Mitchell King* _____

right for the wrong reason, his judgment in selecting Flat Rock proved thoroughly sound—he lived to the age of ninety-two, and his wife to the age of eighty-three.

After purchasing several hundred acres, Baring built a replica of an English estate in 1827 and named it Mountain Lodge. The residence is still considered the patriarch of Flat Rock's many grand dwellings. The Baring estate also included a deer park, a billiard house, a gatekeeper's cottage, and a private chapel.

The Barings were soon joined by their friend Mitchell King, who was a lawyer, probate judge, and export merchant in Charleston. Judge King had become interested in the area upon touring it as a member of a survey team evaluating possible railroad routes. He purchased nine hundred acres in 1830 and began construction on Flat Rock's second great mansion. His first wife, Susan, and the wife he took after Susan's death, Margaret, were sisters. They were descended from Lord Campbell, Scotland's Duke of Argyle, so Judge King settled upon Argyle as the name for his new home. Since King had eighteen children, the arrival of his entourage each summer was a big event in Flat Rock.

King and Baring bought surrounding land until they owned over eleven thousand acres. It was Judge King who donated the tract that eventually became the county seat, Hendersonville. His slaves laid out the town's main street. It is ironic that Hendersonville now dwarfs Flat Rock, its older neighbor.

Flat Rock's founding families began spreading the word about their wonderful mountain summers to other members of the South Carolina aristocracy. The social season began with the two-week trek up from Charleston in May and lasted until October. It was one party after another. With plenty of slaves to care for their needs and maintain their estates, Flat Rock's wealthy enjoyed summers that epitomized gracious antebellum life.

The climax of the social season was Susan Baring's birthday party; Susan always came attired in royal purple and covered in diamond jewelry, with a headdress of flowing plumes. Her flair for the dramatic continued her entire life. Close to death, Susan declared that no one in nearby Greenville, South Carolina, knew how to conduct a proper funeral. She then ordered a hearse and carriages driven up to Flat Rock, decorated the horses' heads with plumes, and supervised the dress rehearsal for her upcoming funeral from her window.

*Little Charleston of the Mountains*

The Barings were instrumental in making Flat Rock a social mecca, but they were by no means the only important people to spend their summers there. So many low-country planters established mountain estates that Flat Rock became known as "the little Charleston of the mountains." The list of local landowners reads like a who's who of South Carolina society. It included the families of four signers of the Declaration of Independence, two members of George Washington's State Department, two secretaries of the treasury of the Confederacy, the French consul at Charleston, and the British consul at Savannah. The families that built the famous Magnolia and Middleton gardens in Charleston joined the fraternity, and in more recent years, poet Carl Sandburg selected Flat Rock as his home. With so many historical figures represented in such a small area, enjoying a tour of Flat Rock today is like taking a step back in time. Though a number of the large estates cannot be seen from the highway because of long entrance drives cut through forests, there are still several that can be viewed.

The intersection of Blue Ridge Road (formerly known as Depot Road) and U.S. 25 marks downtown Flat Rock. On the right, facing north, is the old post office, which now houses the Book Exchange. The town received its first post office in 1829; the preserved "old" post office dates from 1847. Follow the Little River Road (and the signs for the Carl Sandburg Home and the Flat Rock Playhouse) as it splits off to the left a few hundred feet from the post office. The grounds of the Flat Rock Playhouse are almost immediately on your right. The playhouse is the State Theatre of North

*Flat Rock Playhouse*

Carolina. Performances run throughout the summer. In front of the playhouse is the huge outcropping of gray granite that gave Flat Rock its name. The nearby house, built by the Lowndes family in 1885, serves as the playhouse's offices. It is said that while staying at Flat Rock, the Lowndes family raised the first Confederate flag in North Carolina.

Across Little River Road from the playhouse is the parking area for the Carl Sandburg Home National Historic Site. The white columns of the home, which is known as Connemara, can be seen atop a hill overlooking the parking lot. The original owner, Christopher Gustavus Memminger, christened the structure Rock Hill in 1838. An orphan born in Germany, Memminger was raised by Thomas Bennett, who later became governor of South Carolina. Memminger was such a success as a lawyer that he amassed the funds to build Rock Hill by the age of thirty-five. When the Civil War broke out, he chaired the committee that drafted the Confederacy's constitution. Jefferson Davis appointed him secretary of the treasury, a position from which Memminger organized the entire financial structure of the new country. But such responsibilities took their toll. After three years on the job, Memminger was forced to resign because of poor health. He retired to Rock Hill but kept in touch with his colleagues. When it appeared that Richmond was in danger, he wrote several leaders suggesting that they move the Confederate capital to Flat Rock, which could be defended more easily. Legend has it that Jefferson Davis sent the Provisional Seal of the Confederacy to Memminger in Flat Rock when it became evident that Richmond would fall. The seal has never been found. Some say Memminger buried it on Glassy Mountain, behind Rock Hill.

In 1945, Carl Sandburg moved here with his wife, Paula, the sister of famous photographer Edward Steichen. Paula ran the farm and raised prize-winning goats while Carl wrote. During his twenty-two years in Flat Rock, Sandburg produced only one novel—*Remembrance Rock*—

*Christopher Memminger*

*Connemara, the Carl Sandburg Home National Historic Site*

but he left one of the best-preserved writer's homes in America. It is now open to the public.

Leaving the national historic site, continue on Little River Road for 0.2 mile to the Saluda Cottage, on the right. This home was built in 1836 by Count Joseph Marie Gabriel St. Xavier de Choiseul. The count's family was active in court circles in France and Austria. It was his uncle who, as emissary of Louis XV to the court of Marie Theresa of Austria, arranged the marriage of Marie Antoinette to Louis XVI. The count himself was a former governor of Corsica and a cousin of Louis Phillip, the Duke of Orleans. He discovered Flat Rock while acting as French consul to Savannah and Charleston, and he was so taken with the social season that he settled his family here. The family members became so attached to Southern society that the count's son, Charles, joined the Confederate army. Charles was killed while fighting in Virginia in 1862 and is buried in Flat Rock.

*Saluda Cottage*

*Tranquility* _____

Little River Road winds through the valley as it passes the gates of a new residential development called Tranquility. The development is named for the Gay Nineties home that Christopher Memminger's son, Edward, built for his bride. The house still stands atop the hill, though it cannot be seen from the road. It was supposedly on this land that four Union prisoners hid after escaping from a Confederate prison. One of the soldiers, J. V. Hadley, wrote an account of his escapades entitled *Seven Months a Prisoner*. Hadley told how he and his cohorts were hidden by the daughters of tenants on the Memminger estate until they were able to make their escape to Knoxville. The fact that their feat was accomplished in such a Confederate stronghold is remarkable.

*Pheasant Branch* _____

After another 2.5 miles, you will pass a small creek called Pheasant Branch. In the days before the members of Charleston society built homes around Flat Rock, a man named Abraham Kuykendall—already advanced in age—moved to the area, purchased more than a thousand acres of land, and opened a tavern. A shrewd businessman, he made his patrons pay in gold or silver. The area was still untamed, and as the years rolled by Kuykendall began to worry about the safety of his money. Legend has it that one night he transferred his gold and silver to a large wash pot made of black iron, blindfolded two slaves, and instructed them to carry the pot. He led them into the forest, removed the blindfolds, ordered them to bury the treasure, and blindfolded them again for the return trip. He warned the slaves never to reveal what they had seen that night.

During Kuykendall's 104th year, the story goes, he found himself in need of money, so he set out to dig up his cache. That was the last time he was seen alive. His body was subsequently found facedown in Pheasant Branch. The only light the two slaves could shed on the mystery was that they had buried the treasure under a stooping white oak near a clear stream. Due to the location of the body, it was generally believed that the coins had to be somewhere near Pheasant Branch.

Soon after Kuykendall's death, night travelers on the Little River Road began to tell of seeing an old man digging frantically in the moonlight. Others told of seeing a wagon driven by an old man with a wash pot by his side; when the travelers came upon the wagon, it disappeared. Those who drive the road now may be moving too quickly to see ghosts. To this day the treasure has never been found.

A little over 1 mile later, Little River Road intersects Kanuga Road. Turn right. After 0.8 mile, you will pass the entrance to another new residential development—Beaumont Estates—that sprang up around one of the old Flat Rock mansions. In 1839, a wealthy rice planter named Andrew Johnstone brought a small army of slaves to the area, cut a large quantity of gray, mica-flecked granite from a quarry on Glassy Mountain, and constructed the home called Beaumont. When the low country was occupied by Union troops during the Civil War, Johnstone moved his family to Beaumont, thinking they would be safe.

Ironically, it was at Beaumont that Johnstone was shot in his own dining room after feeding some deserters who had demanded a meal. As his father lay dying, eleven-year-old Elliott Johnstone shot one of the unwelcome guests. That soldier was buried on the lawn at Beaumont, his grave marked by a stone bearing a devil's head.

After another 5.9 miles, turn right onto Erkwood Drive. It is 0.9 mile to Rutledge Drive. The Mud Creek Baptist Church, dating from 1805, is straight ahead. The old graveyard where Abraham Kuykendall is buried can be seen on the left. Turn right onto Rutledge Drive. Mountain Lodge—the Baring estate—sits atop a knoll behind huge pine trees about 0.4 mile down Rutledge Drive. Kuykendall's tavern was also located along this section of the road.

*Church of St. John in the Wilderness*

Another 0.4 mile later, you will see the Church of St. John in the Wilderness just before the intersection with U.S. 25. The Barings built the church as a private chapel and turned it over to the Episcopal Diocese of North Carolina in 1836. Nestled on a pine-clad knoll, it is considered one of the best examples of nineteenth-century Renaissance-style architecture in the nation.

A path ascends from the parking lot to a terraced walkway. The gray granite steps and the walls of the terraced burial plots surrounding the church blend with the old brick of the tower and the main structure. The bricks, imported from England, have aged to a soft yellow color. The sanctuary and the chancel were built in 1836. The nave was added in 1853. The interior copies traditional English country churches in its floor, its altar, and its posts supporting arches that converge in a pointed roof, all made of hand-hewn pine. The pews, also made of pine, each bear a family nameplate.

The driveway up the forested hill connects with a yellow brick walkway at the crest. This old carriage entrance is the subject of a story that gives an indication of the strong influence the Barings had over Flat Rock. On Sunday morning, Susan Baring, dressed all in white, would ride with her husband in their bright yellow carriage with its

*Susan Baring*

*Graveyard of St. John in the Wilderness Church in Flat Rock*

*James Brown*

*Woodfield Inn*

coat of arms, a carriage drawn by perfectly groomed horses harnessed with silver buckles and rings. The other members of their party would follow. Upon arriving at the carriage entrance, Susan's door would be opened by a footman, who waited for her to lay her prayer book and Bible on a velvet pillow he held ready. Another attendant would be sent to notify the rector that Susan was at the church door. Susan and her party would then enter, followed by a maid in a white turban bearing the velvet cushion with the prayer book and Bible. The maid would also be carrying a large turkey-tail fan, which she used to cool her mistress during the service. Only when the Barings were seated would the service begin.

The Barings are buried in a vault under the pews opposite the side door, beneath the spot where their large, square pew once sat. In the church cemetery are the graves of a number of Flat Rock's most illustrious citizens—Christopher Memminger, the wife and son of the Count de Choiseul, Reverend John Grimké Drayton (the man who created Charleston's Magnolia Gardens), and people with such historically important South Carolina names as Rutledge, Middleton, Laurens, and Haywood. Just outside the side entrance to the church is the grave of James Brown, a trumpeter in the Royal Scots Greys at the Battle of Waterloo and a charter member of the first congregation at the Church of St. John in the Wilderness. Some stories suggest that Brown was Susan Baring's coachman, while others maintain that he was the family's butler. It is said that on certain sultry nights when summer lightning flashes across the sky, you can hear a trumpet sounding a battle charge.

Leaving the church and graveyard, turn right (or south) onto U.S. 25. You will pass the old parsonage, built circa 1853, then the Flat Rock Playhouse and the Lowndes home again, this time from a different direction. The old post office is now on your left. Continue straight on U.S. 25 South.

It is 0.5 mile to the entrance to the Woodfield Inn. In 1847, several of the most prominent men

*Squire Henry Farmer*

*Woodfield Inn*

*Dr. Mitchell Campbell King*

in Flat Rock banded together to establish what they hoped would be "a good, commodious tavern on or near the Main Saluda Road." That tavern became known as the Flat Rock Hotel. The following year, Squire Henry T. Farmer bought them out, changed the name, and began the long tradition of the Farmer Hotel.

As relatives of Susan Baring's, Squire Farmer and his three brothers and three sisters had become wards of the Barings upon their father's death. Squire Farmer proved to be a shrewd businessman as an adult. Having worked as a building contractor before buying the hotel, he decided to make some of the furnishings to be used in his new establishment himself. The black walnut rockers made by Squire Farmer for the porch of his hotel became famous throughout the area. Known as Flat Rock Rockers, they were unique in the fact that they did not creep across the floor when they were rocked. They became so popular that Farmer opened a furniture factory to meet the demand. Unfortunately, the factory closed during the Civil War. Without Squire Farmer's mold, the chairs have never been duplicated. Though there are rockers on the huge porch of the inn and restaurant known today as the Woodfield Inn, they are only imitations.

Continue on U.S. 25 through an area lined with tall white pines. It is easy to imagine how grand the Buncombe Turnpike must have been when Flat Rock was in its prime. You may be able to glimpse some of the old homes behind the trees and shrubbery. On the right 1 mile from the Woodfield Inn is the entrance to a plush golf course that is surrounded by an exclusive residential development. The course and its environs were once part of the estate of Dr. Mitchell Campbell King, the son of Judge King. Dr. King was a beloved and highly respected physician not only in Flat Rock but in the entire area as well. Numerous stories about his life survive.

While pursuing postgraduate studies at the University of Göttingen in present-day Germany, Dr. King formed a friendship with a fellow student named Otto von Bismarck. It is said that one night during a discussion of politics, Dr. King bet Bismarck a case of champagne that Prussia would never become the most powerful nation on earth. Forty years later, finding himself one of the most powerful men in the world, Bismarck wrote Dr. King to remind him of their bet. Dr. King supposedly paid up, though that is not known for certain. It *is* known that the two men corresponded for many years. The letters Dr. King received from Bismarck are now housed in the Library of Congress in Washington.

It is also said that when one of the worst yellow-fever epidemics in memory struck Florida during the summer of 1888, Dr. King convinced the local commissioners to invite Florida residents to seek refuge in the Flat Rock–Hendersonville area. On his journeys throughout the world, Dr. King had observed some hard evidence that served to refine Charles Baring's simplistic early theory—yellow fever never occurred in high elevations, only in tropical climates. Dr. King had also noted that the fever did not spread once its victims fled to high altitudes.

Train after train brought an estimated total of ten thousand refugees. People in Georgia and South Carolina were so frightened by the epidemic that they sent armed groups to insure that the trains passed through their states without stopping. The summers that followed also brought refugees. No one in the area ever contracted the disease. Though Dr. King did not know the cause of yellow fever, his observations about its spread were correct. His efforts may be partly responsible for the large influx of Floridians who continued to come to the area long after the threat of disease disappeared.

When Dr. King decided to make Flat Rock his permanent home, he built an elaborate mansion named Glenroy across from his father's summer home. Now called Kenmure, Dr. King's home is the centerpiece of the golf course and residential development that bear the same name. The mansion sits atop a hill overlooking the course. It is open to the public as a restaurant.

Retrace U.S. 25 leaving Kenmure. On the right

*Dr. Mitchell Campbell King's home, Glenroy, now called Kenmure*

*Argyle*

after 0.2 mile is the entrance to Argyle, the home of Judge King. Built around 1830, the large, white Colonial home can still be seen from the highway.

It is less that 1 mile to the Flat Rock post office. There, you may either continue north on U.S. 25 to Hendersonville or turn right onto Blue Ridge Road, following the signs to I-26. At the junction of U.S. 176 and I-26, you have the option of extending your drive by embarking on the Hunting Country Tour.

*Flat Rock Post Office*

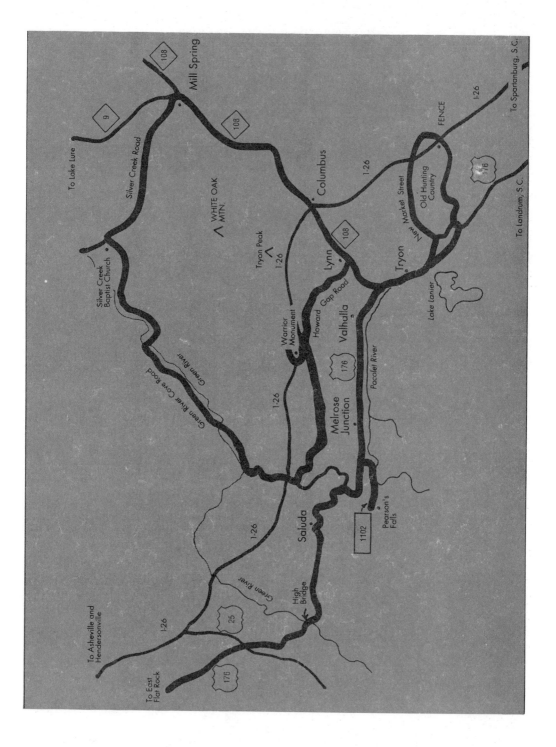

This tour travels from East Flat Rock to the community of Saluda. It follows the famous Saluda railroad grade, which parallels the Pacolet River, into Tryon. It then circles town, passing through the Old Hunting Country before traveling through Green River Cove and returning to Tryon. Total mileage: approximately 54 miles.

▲▲▲▲▲▲▲▲▲▲▲▲▲▲▲▲▲▲▲▲▲▲▲▲▲▲▲▲▲▲▲▲▲▲▲▲▲*The Hunting Country Tour*

The tour begins at the junction of I-26 and U.S. 176. Head east on U.S. 176 toward Saluda. Over the next 3 miles, the road descends through a series of sharp, steep curves until it comes to a bridge spanning the Green River.

The U.S. 176 bridge crosses 200 feet above the river. It is known locally as the High Bridge, though that is something of a misnomer. The original bridge across the river was built by Peter Guice around 1820; it was located out of sight from U.S. 176. When the U.S. 176 bridge was built across the Green River, it earned the title of High Bridge in comparison with Guice's span, which was much lower. That title was rendered a bit inaccurate in 1972 with the opening of a 220-foot-high bridge carrying I-26 across the river. Built near the site of Guice's original span, the new interstate bridge was appropriately named the Peter Guice Bridge. It remains one of the highest spans east of the Mississippi.

*The High Bridge*

You can park at either end of the High Bridge and walk to the center. Though the brush in the gorge is thick, you can still see the Green River flowing far below.

Just beyond the bridge, U.S. 176 passes under a

Saluda

trestle and begins to parallel the railroad for the 2-mile stretch into Saluda. The road curves sharply and crosses a railroad bridge before heading straight into downtown. The tracks pass through the center of Saluda. The quaint shops—highlighted by a restored depot on the left as you enter town—line the street across from the railroad tracks. The restored village serves as evidence that this once-thriving community is undergoing a renewal.

In the early 1800s, the area around present-day Saluda was known primarily as a crossroads. It was here that two well-traveled trading paths intersected—the Winding Stair Road led to Greenville, South Carolina, and Georgia; while the Howard Gap Road led to Spartanburg, South Carolina, and the low country. Local commerce had its beginnings when a family named Pace built an inn to serve the drovers who brought their livestock herds across the mountains to the South Carolina markets. The Pace family built a fence around the inn's yard so the drovers' stock could be penned up during their stay. The area soon became known as Pace's Gap.

Shortly after the Civil War, an engineer named Charles William Pearson was commissioned to locate a route for a railroad to be built from Spartanburg to Tryon and up the mountains to Hendersonville and Asheville. The obvious route followed the Howard Gap Road around Warrior Mountain, but it had a shifting roadbed caused by underground springs. Pearson settled upon a much steeper route following the gorge along the Pacolet River, and the famous Saluda grade was born.

The Saluda Grade

One of the first things to greet visitors in Saluda today is an historical marker across from the depot revealing that the steepest standard-gauge railroad grade in the United States crested here. With high fills, deep cuts, and a total of fifty curves, the 3-mile stretch from Saluda to Melrose Junction had a grade that varied from 4 to 7 percent, with an overall grade of 6 percent—considered very steep even today. Construction moved slowly in the early stages. Logs felled from

*Restored train depot in Saluda*

*The Helper at
Melrose Junction*

the virgin forests were sometimes greater in girth than the mules and oxen that had to drag them away. The construction crew had to blast through hills of granite, often using unstable blasting powder. The cuts they made tended to fill with water, while the fills they made tended to sink. Cold weather impeded progress, and the workers suffered from poor living conditions. The problems seemed insurmountable until the North Carolina legislature finally sent convicts to help build the grade. Three months later, on July 4, 1878, the first passenger train made the trip from Spartanburg to Saluda.

The completion of the railroad did not end its problems. By 1903, twenty-seven men had been killed by engines that went out of control on the downhill trip and jumped the tracks on the sharp curves. One ten-degree bend was so notorious that it earned the nickname Slaughterhouse Curve. The Southern Railroad Company was about to abandon the route when Pitt Bellew, an engineer who had been injured in a wreck on the Saluda grade, came up with a solution. He recommended a system of side tracks that would route runaway trains off the main route and onto dead-end lines running up the steep mountain. The system was built. If a train was under control, the engineer blew his whistle and the switchman gave him the main line. If a train was out of control, a different whistle was blown and the train was sent up a safety track, where gravity brought it to a halt.

The trains also experienced difficulty traveling uphill. The problem of supplying enough power to get them up the grade was solved by the introduction of a pusher engine known as the Helper. Built for traction, the Helper would be connected to the rear end of a train in Melrose Junction. It would push while the main engine in front pulled. Once the grade was attained, the Helper would be disconnected, to return on its own to Melrose Junction to await the next westbound train.

The arrival of the Carolina Special became the center of local activities. The westbound train arrived from the low country in the mornings, and the eastbound train returned in the afternoons. The trains were met by boys carrying trays of fried chicken, coleslaw, and lemonade to sell to the passengers. As the community's popularity as a resort increased, so did the number of inns and hotels. At the height of popularity, there were thirty-seven hostelries in town.

By 1881, Pace's Gap had grown so prosperous that it was chartered as the town of Saluda. The name came from the nearby Saluda Mountains and Saluda River. Saluda was supposedly the white man's phonetic spelling of a Cherokee chief's name that translated as "corn river."

The town was the height of fashion in the early 1900s, not to mention a haven for sufferers of tuberculosis. As highways were improved, train travel lost its allure, and Saluda lost much of its vitality, but signs of new life are evident in the town today.

Continue on U.S. 176, which parallels the Saluda grade and the valley of the Pacolet River. After about 1 mile, you will see the Orchard Inn on the right. Now a bed-and-breakfast inn, it was built as a vacation retreat for the Brotherhood of Railway Clerks. After another 2 miles, you will see a sign directing you to Pearson's Falls. Turn right onto S.R. 1102 and follow the signs for 1 mile.

*Pearson's Falls*

When Charles Pearson was surveying the area around the Pacolet River for a railroad route, he became so taken with the land that he purchased a large tract between Tryon and Saluda that included one of the area's most beautiful waterfalls. In June 1930, naturalist Donald C. Peattie wrote to the Tryon Garden Club asking that Pearson's prize spot be rescued from lumber operations. The club raised enough money to purchase the falls, which they named in honor of Pearson. The Tryon Garden Club still owns the tract, and it has set the land aside as a preserve for native flora and fauna. The preserve attracts naturalists from all over America, who come to study mountain plant life. Others can visit the park for a reasonable fee. There is an easy 0.25-mile trail leading to the ninety-foot Pearson's Falls. At the foot is a great tablelike rock. En route, the trail passes more than two hundred species of ferns, as well as various species of mosses, trilliums, and orchids.

Return to U.S. 176 and continue in your original direction for 0.1 mile to Melrose Junction, the community from which the Helper began pushing trains up the Saluda grade. Traveling down this scenic route, you may notice the prolific kudzu vine, so well known to native Southerners. Kudzu was introduced to this country from the Orient in 1876. It burst into prominence in the South through the soil-conservation programs of FDR's New Deal. Kudzu adapted so well to the Southern environment that it soon became a formidable pest. It grows so rapidly that it will completely cover trees, abandoned buildings, and anything else that stands still long enough.

*Kudzu*

If you travel through the Pacolet River Valley in early spring, you will also notice the prevalence of a distinctive tree bearing purple flowers. It is the paulownia, or princess tree. Locals know it as "the coffee tree." A Dutch botanist named it after Anna Pavlovna, daughter of Russia's Czar Paul and granddaughter of Catherine the Great. Native to Japan and China, the tree was once the exclusive property of the Japanese imperial family. The crest of the empress of Japan featured three leaves surmounted by an equal number of blossoms from the paulownia. The ruling family was so possessive of the paulownia that if a tree was found growing outside the imperial forest, it was removed and its owner beheaded. Since each of the paulownia's pods produces two thousand winged seeds, the executioner must have been a busy man.

*The Paulownia Tree*

Introduced in this area when it was planted in the gardens of George Vanderbilt's Biltmore Estate in Asheville, the paulownia found its way to the Pacolet River Valley as early as the 1890s. Blue and violet are rare colors for tree blossoms, so the dense clusters, sometimes a foot in length, are easy to spot. The paulownia is also conspicuous in winter, since its seed balls remain after most local trees have lost their foliage. The one sad note is that the paulownia is quickly disappearing. Light, soft, and easily worked, its highly prized wood takes on a satin finish. Those characteristics cause it to be in great demand among craftsmen who carve bowls and other wooden utensils.

Kudzu vines and paulownia trees are just two products of a phenomenon that has given the Pacolet River Valley an unusual climate. The mountain slopes of the region surround a thermal belt in which there are no frosts or freezes like those at slightly higher altitudes. Nineteenth-century visitors like R. H. Edmonds of Baltimore wrote glowing descriptions of Polk County's climate: "The peculiarity of this circling mountain range gives to this country a protection from cold, and adds to the wonderful charm of the climate throughout this far-famed mountain section a freedom from coldness and dampness that can only be appreciated by those who have felt its exhilarating influence."

*The Thermal Belt*

By the 1880s, new residents who had come because of the thermal-belt climate began to plant apple and peach orchards and vineyards. A little over 1.5 miles from Melrose Junction, the tour passes through the community of Valhalla. It was on the slopes of nearby Warrior Mountain, located on the left, that some of the area's earliest vineyards were established.

George Edward Morton arrived in 1886 after his physicians had given him less than a month to live. He recovered and prospered for another thirty years. In addition to founding the *Tryon Bee*, nearby Tryon's first newspaper, Morton was a pioneer in growing the famous Tryon grape at his Valhalla Fruit Farm. W. T. Lindsey started a nearby vineyard in 1893; Lindsey even sent his fruit to the New York State Fair, and the reputation of the superior quality of Tryon grapes spread. On the east side of nearby Piney Mountain was the Doubleday vineyard, started by the son of poet Sidney Lanier and the son of General Ulysses Doubleday of Civil War fame. Around 1890, Doubleday supposedly brought Alexis La Morte, a French-Swiss grape grower, to Tryon to

*Valhalla Fruit Farm*

*Doubleday Vineyard*

improve his vineyards. A story is told that all trains stopped in Tryon except the Carolina Special, the main train between Charleston and Chicago in those days. The citizens of Tryon flagged down the Carolina Special one day and served Tryon wine to all on board, and from that date, the train never failed to stop. In 1896, Polk County began its first commercial shipment of grapes. A hundred thousand pounds were marketed that year. But by the 1950s, the vineyards were abandoned and the clearings overgrown.

It is 2.8 miles from Valhalla to the Tryon city limits. In 1730, representatives of the English colonial government met with leading Cherokee chiefs and drew up what was supposed to be a perpetual treaty of peace. A lucrative trade developed between coastal settlements in South Carolina and the Indians of western North Carolina. Villages and trading posts appeared along the frontier until the French and Indian War broke the "perpetual peace." When Indians attacked upcountry settlements around 1756, forts were built to protect the frontier. They included Earle's Fort, near present-day Landrum, South Carolina; the Block House, near Tryon; and Young's Fort, near present-day Mill Spring.

*William Tryon*

After the war, conflicts between white settlers and Indians grew so numerous that William Tryon, the royal governor of the colony of North Carolina, came west in 1767 to negotiate a new boundary line. He met with John Stuart—an agent trusted by the Indians—and a group of Cherokees led by Ustenaka. On June 4, a survey was begun from Reedy River—near present-day Greenville, South Carolina—northward to "a Spanish oak standing on the top of a mountain called by us Tryon Mountain, on the headwaters of White Oak and Packolato Creeks," as described in the treaty. The landmark cited as Tryon Mountain was actually the highest peak on present-day White Oak Mountain. It is now known as Tryon

*Tryon Peak*

Peak, and it dominates the landscape for miles. (If you were approaching from the south on I-26, Tryon Peak would come prominently into view directly ahead at the boundary between North

*Skyuka and the Battle*
*of Round Mountain*

*Tryon's wooden horse*

and South Carolina. I-26 passes just to the left of the peak at Howard Gap.) By 1839, a frontier post office at the foot of the peak bore Governor Tryon's name as well. The community eventually grew into the town of Tryon.

The efforts of Governor Tryon and the boundary team were futile. White settlers continued to encroach upon Cherokee lands, and ill feelings frequently erupted into violent warfare. When the Revolutionary War began, the Cherokees sided with the English. In the spring of 1776, a group of Indian braves gathered on the side of what is now known as Warrior Mountain, near present-day Tryon. They planned to attack the Block House and then descend upon Earle's and Young's forts. Their plan might have succeeded save for a traitor in their midst. An Indian named Skyuka made his way to Captain Thomas Howard, who had assembled a small band of American patriots at the Block House. Legend says that Howard had once saved Skyuka's life after Skyuka was bitten by a rattlesnake. Whatever the case, Skyuka led Howard through a gap in the mountains to the rear of the Cherokee forces. Howard and his men overwhelmed the surprised Indians in the battle of Round Mountain, which ended Cherokee dominance in the area. The trail Skyuka showed Howard became known as the Howard Gap Road.

The coming of the railroad in the 1870s transformed Tryon into a popular tourist resort. With the tourists came a whole new class of settlers, who proceeded to leave their distinctive mark. Driving U.S. 176 (Trade Street) through downtown Tryon today, their influence is everywhere. Most of the old inns have disappeared, but the depot on the hill on the right has been restored. Around the corner from the depot, at the intersection of Melrose Avenue and Chestnut Street, is the Lanier Library, a tribute to the literary interests of Tryon's residents. The Lanier Club was organized in 1890; its weekly meetings were directed toward procuring a library for the town. What they achieved was not only a fine example of a small-town library, but a social center for the community as well.

At the main intersection in town—at Trade and Pacolet streets—stands a large wooden horse, a Tryon landmark since 1928. The horse was designed by Eleanor Vance, who moved into a cottage on the Biltmore Estate with Charlotte Yale in 1901. The classes they conducted in woodcarving, weaving, and various other crafts evolved into what is known today as the Biltmore Industries. In 1915, they moved to Tryon and opened the Tryon Toymakers and Woodcarvers Shop, which became famous across the country for its hand-carved toys.

Just before crossing the railroad tracks, turn left off Trade Street onto New Market Street, following the signs for the Pine Crest Inn. A sign on the left at the top of the hill indicates the entrance. In 1918, Carter P. Brown, owner of a hotel in Michigan, transformed a former tuberculosis sanatorium into the Pine Crest Inn, still known for its rustic charm.

In 1925, Brown played an instrumental role in forming the Tryon Riding and Hunt Club, a club that accounts for much of Tryon's present reputation. Most people who have heard of Tryon equate it with horses. It was Brown and the guests at the Pine Crest Inn who began mounting their horses and following hounds across an area between the Pacolet River and Landrum, South Carolina. That area is now known as the Old Hunting Country. Though the original hunts were informally organized, regular drag hunts were being scheduled by 1926. In a drag hunt, participants ride over a course after a fox scent has been dragged along the trails. There are frequent jumps, so a drag hunt resembles a steeplechase. In 1935, a club known as the Tryon Hounds was recognized by the Masters of Foxhounds Association of America. Hunts are still held today. The Tryon Hounds and the Tryon Riding and Hunt Club are responsible for the steeplechases held in April and October. Both events have turned into social occasions well attended by spectators from all over the Carolinas.

Continue past the entrance to the Pine Crest Inn. Bear left at the fork in the road, following

*Carter P. Brown*

*Tryon Riding and Hunt Club and the Tryon Hounds*

*View of White Oak Mountain from the Old Hunting Country*

New Market Street for 1.5 miles to a stop sign. Turn right and go to the next stop sign, at S.R. 1501 (Hunting Country Road). Turn left. Beyond the fields on the right, you will see the Block House and some of the fences set up for steeplechases and fox hunts.

After its days of service as a fort, the Block House became a popular stop for drovers, and later a hideout for deserters during the Civil War. In its original location, the building touched two states and three counties. Its unusual geographical site made it a natural choice for such illegal activities as cockfighting and whiskey manufacture. Depending upon whose laws were being violated, participants could walk a few feet to a neighboring county or state and avoid law officers appearing from any direction. The building was later moved to its present location.

Carter Brown saved the Block House when he bought and restored it for a family that wanted a home near Tryon. The new owners, the Plamondons, invited local riders to run a steeplechase over their property. The Block House Steeplechase, held in April, was run here until its steady growth in popularity led it to be moved to a larger facility a few years ago.

S.R. 1501 passes one large horse farm after another. It is 1.5 miles to Morgan Chapel Baptist Church, which is on the right immediately after I-26. Turn right just past the church. It is 0.6 mile to the Foothills Equestrian Nature Center (FENCE) properties, the site where horse shows, horse trials, and steeplechases are now held. In addition to riding trails and courses, FENCE has nature trails for hikers.

The road makes a sharp uphill curve approximately 0.2 mile past the stables on the FENCE property. Take the road to the right in the middle of the curve and go a few hundred yards to Columbus Avenue. Turn right and go 0.6 mile, then turn right onto Greenwood Road, which travels through an area that is clear-cut save for the single row of large pine trees bordering the road. Drive 2.2 miles, then turn right onto Block House Road, which is just before the junction with U.S.

*The Block House*

Foothills Equestrian
Nature Center (FENCE)

176. You are now traveling along the backside of the Block House property. In front of the house is a large stone that marked the 1772 dividing line between North and South Carolina. Follow Block House Road to another intersection with U.S. 176. Turn right and head back through downtown Tryon, following U.S. 108 East when the road splits. It is 1 mile to the Mill Farm Inn, on the left. Built in 1939 on the site of an old gristmill, the lovely stone house is now a bed-and-breakfast inn.

*Mill Farm Inn*

It is another 0.4 mile to the community of Lynn and the first of its two historic landmarks. On the right is the Mimosa Inn, which can lay claim to two hundred years of history. In the eighteenth century, King George of England granted ninety thousand acres of mountain land to a man named John Mills. The trading trail that later became the Howard Gap Road passed by Mills's inn. He and his son, Columbus, became widely known for their hospitality. After the Civil War, the inn was sold to Dr. Leland McAboy, a Presbyterian minister from Pennsylvania, and the McAboy House continued the fine tradition. The township of Lynn, established before either Tryon or Columbus, was named for McAboy's son. Aaron French and David Stearns bought the property in 1903 and changed the name to the Mimosa Inn. They installed new plumbing, heating, and lighting equipment—even an hydraulic elevator. They built a casino with billiard tables and a bowling alley in the rear. Each room at the inn had hot and cold running water, steam heat, gaslights, and call bells. Each floor had men's and women's bathrooms—progressive accommodations in those days. The Mimosa Inn quickly became one of the most popular resort hotels in the South. When it burned in 1916, Stearns rebuilt the former casino. He created twelve bedrooms with baths, a dining room with seating capacity for a hundred guests, and a nine-hole golf course. The current status of the inn is uncertain, but it is to be hoped that someone will return it to its former grandeur.

*Mimosa Inn*

Across the road is the former home of Lemuel

Wilcox. Built in 1869, the house became a landmark when Sidney Lanier, a Southern poet, died in an upstairs bedroom. Lanier suffered a long, severe illness after spending five months in a Union prison camp during the Civil War. He came to the area seeking relief from his tuberculosis. When he and his wife arrived in Lynn in 1881, the McAboy House was full, so Dr. McAboy sent them across the road to his son-in-law's home. Lanier was never to leave. Best known for his poems "The Symphony" and "The Marshes of Glynn," Lanier left an indelible stamp on the area. After his death, his family moved to Tryon and resided for years on Lanier Street. His son started a vineyard as described earlier in the tour. The Lanier Club, the Lanier Library, and Lake Lanier all serve as testimony to Tryon's devotion to his memory.

Though the Mimosa Inn contributed greatly to local prosperity, Lynn's fate was sealed when the new road from Tryon to Saluda bypassed the town. In 1965, the North Carolina legislature passed a bill repealing Lynn's articles of incorporation.

Follow U.S. 108 through Columbus (discussed in the Hickory Nut Gorge Tour). It is approximately 4 miles to the community of Mill Spring, where U.S. 108 intersects N.C. 9. In the 1740s, Young's Fort, located in Mill Spring, protected local settlers against Indian attacks. Ambrose Mills moved to the area in 1766 and established a trading post and a sawmill near two springs in a natural basin chiseled from granite rock. The vicinity soon became known as Mills Springs. In recent years, a postmaster with illegible handwriting caused the terminal *s* to be dropped from each word in the name.

Turn left onto N.C. 9, heading north toward Lake Lure. Take a quick left 0.2 mile later onto Silver Creek Road (S.R. 1138). Farmland still borders the road, but there are occasional signs of new industry related to the area's recreational attractions. After 3.7 miles, you will come to the Silver Creek Baptist Church, on a hill on the left. The Green River Cove Road (S.R. 1151) is on the left between the church and its cemetery. Turn

*Green River Cove*

*Warrior Monument*

left. The road soon becomes gravel. It is 0.8 mile to a Private Property sign. The next 10 miles pass through land owned by Duke Power Company. The public can travel the area and use the designated recreational and parking facilities, but they must observe posted regulations.

The route soon drops to the bottom of the gorge and follows the Green River through what was once one of the most productive agricultural areas in western North Carolina. The thermal-belt climate meant that the first vegetables of the season were sure to come from here. It was the first area to produce truck crops on a commercial scale. Cabbage growers from neighboring counties planted seedbeds here to produce early plants. A devastating flood in 1916 destroyed the best farmland, and the area has largely reverted to its natural state.

It is 1.3 miles to the Big Rock Access Area, a recreational area open to the public. The Green River Cove Store (the only store in the vicinity) is 4.2 miles farther. During this portion of the tour, you may see rafters, canoeists, and kayakers coming down the Green River, a popular whitewater river. The Fish Top Access Area is 2.8 miles from the store. After another 1.8 miles, the road begins its narrow, steeply winding way out of the gorge. It is 0.5 mile to an intersection from which you can see I-26 to the right. Turn right and go under I-26 for 0.5 mile. Turn left onto S.R. 1122 (Warrior Mountain Road). Warrior Baptist Church is on the left as the road turns to gravel.

It is another 2.6 miles to an intersection where you must turn left or right. Head left up the unpaved road for 0.3 mile to Warrior Monument. Erected in 1909 by the Daughters of the American Revolution, Warrior Monument commemorates the battle of Round Mountain, discussed earlier in the tour. When the old Howard Gap Road was incorporated into I-26, the state removed Warrior Monument, stored the stones, and relocated the monument upon the completion of I-26. It can be seen from the interstate today. The view from its present location down into South Carolina is stunning.

Retrace your route to S.R. 1122 and follow it down the mountain. You will travel through a scenic valley nestled at the foot of Tryon Peak, with White Oak Mountain on the left. Approximately 3 miles from Warrior Monument, you will intersect N.C. 108 at the Mill Farm Inn. You may either turn right to go back into downtown Tryon or turn left to reach I-26 at the Columbus exit.

*Tryon Peak*

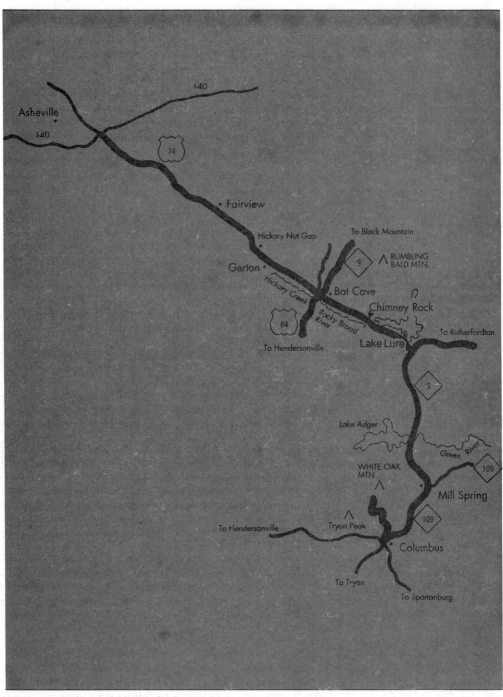

This tour begins near Asheville, travels through the Hickory Nut Gap to Bat Cave, and follows the Rocky Broad River to Chimney Rock and Lake Lure. It then travels to Columbus and White Oak Mountain before ending at I-26. Total mileage: approximately 50 miles.

▲▲▲▲▲▲▲▲▲▲▲▲▲▲▲▲▲▲▲▲▲▲▲▲▲▲▲▲▲▲▲*The Hickory Nut Gorge Tour*

To begin the tour, take U.S. 74 East off I-40 just east of Asheville. After approximately 3 miles, you will pass through the community of Fairview. Another 5.2 miles will bring you into a scenic valley that extends to the foot of a chain of mountains that opens at the Hickory Nut Gap.

As the road ascends through a series of corkscrew curves, you will begin to see signs for the Hickory Nut Gap Farm. In the fall, the signs also advertise the farm's apple orchard. This is the first of many such orchards you will see, since a great deal of this tour travels through Henderson County, which claims to rank seventh among American counties in the production of apples. Henderson County produces 70 percent of North Carolina's apple crop.

*Sherrill's Inn*

In front of the Hickory Nut Gap Farm is an historical marker about Sherrill's Inn. Bedford Sherrill held the contract to haul the mail from Salisbury via Lincolnton and Rutherfordton to Asheville. In 1834, he purchased property at Hickory Nut Gap and expanded the existing house there into a tavern, which served as a well-known stopping place until 1909. One Civil War–era story about Sherrill's Inn concerns a Union cavalry unit that stayed the night when they were crossing through Hickory Nut Gap. It is said that

Mrs. Sherrill, a Southern sympathizer, emptied the dirt from her shoes onto the eggs she was forced to fry for the Union soldiers' breakfast the next morning. That was certainly not the type of hospitality for which Sherrill's Inn was famous.

Gerton

It is 2.6 miles to the Gerton post office, originally called the Pump post office in 1883. According to volume 3 of Frank FitzSimons's *From the Banks of the Oklawaha*, the name came from a spot near a local water pump. If a person left a quarter or a half dollar on the spot, he would find a jar of liquid the color of water in its place upon his return. The liquid was unlike water in that "it had a bead and was much more potent." Such was the way the moonshine business operated in the mountains.

FitzSimons also related the story of how the post office's original name came into disfavor. It seems that a cancellation stamp issued by the government to be used by the local postmaster was discovered to read "Rump, N.C." It was then that the people of Pump decided that a name change was in order. They chose to honor Gertrude Freeman, a local teacher. Though justifiably flattered, Mrs. Freeman thought that a post office named Gertrude would be unbecoming for a lady. When the name Gerton was offered as a compromise, everyone was happy.

After 4.8 miles, U.S. 74 East merges with N.C. 9 and U.S. 64 at the place where the Broad River comes into Hickory Creek from the left. The Broad River—also known as the Rocky Broad River to avoid confusing it with the French Broad River—now becomes the primary waterway through the gorge. Next, the tour enters the community of Bat Cave. On the right is Bat Cave Mountain. The name comes from a huge, dark cave near the top of the mountain that runs hundreds of feet back under the hillside. The cave has been a refuge for a huge colony of bats for generations.

Bat Cave

It is 4.3 miles to the Bat Cave Apple House, on the right. A suspension bridge behind the apple house crosses the Rocky Broad River to a trail that ascends to Bat Cave. The path is treacherous enough to require a guide. A woman named Sarah runs the apple house; she is also the caretaker of the privately owned property on which Bat Cave is located. The owner has designated the area a nature preserve and insists that there be no commercialization of the property. There is a free guided tour once a week. Wednesday was tour day in 1989, but Sarah said that she "may change the day next year," so check at the apple house. Visitors should be forewarned that some tourists are deterred from making the trek up the mountain when they learn of the strong possibility of encountering the rattlesnakes that congregate around the cave during summer. Some are also put off by the fact that entering the inner chamber of the cave with a flashlight disturbs the natives—visitors may find themselves surrounded by flying bats.

Across the road from the apple house, you can see the remnants of the turnpike that once ran through the gorge. The tollgate was located near the boundary between Henderson and Rutherford counties in an area known as Parris Gap. It was run by a man named Joe Williams, who charged twenty-five cents for a wagon pulled by two horses or a yoke of oxen and five cents a head for the herds of cattle, horses, mules, sheep, and hogs that traveled the route. People on foot or horseback were allowed to go around the tollgate without charge.

## Parris Gap

There is a ghost story about the area near the old tollgate. In 1830, Christopher Bechtler and his son August came to Rutherford County from the grand duchy of Baden, in present-day Germany. They established a private mint in Rutherfordton for the coinage of gold, the only private mint in the Southeast recognized by the United States government. They operated their mint for nine years, turning out approximately $2,250,000 in $1, $2, and $5 gold pieces. Legend has it that in 1840, Christopher Bechtler was returning from business in Asheville by way of the turnpike late one afternoon. He passed through Joe Williams's tollgate, but that was the last time he was seen alive. Bechtler's smashed buggy was later found on the river rocks below the turnpike. It was said that he had been carrying a large sum of gold with him at the time. Neither the gold nor Bechtler's body was ever discovered. For years after the disappearance, people reported hearing a buggy riding along the Rocky Broad River on moonlit nights. No one ever claimed to have seen a vision

## Christopher Bechtler

of the buggy itself.

It is less than 1 mile to the Esmeralda Inn, which sits atop a hillside on the left. The original inn, built by Colonel Tom Turner, opened in the spring of 1892. After a fire destroyed the main building in 1917, the inn was rebuilt on the original foundation. Colonel Turner named the Esmeralda for the book of the same name by Frances Hodgson Burnett, who also wrote *Little Lord Fauntleroy* and *The Secret Garden*. Burnett penned *Esmeralda* while staying in the area.

In 1915, the motion-picture industry discovered Hickory Nut Gorge. Several silent movies were made in the vicinity of the Esmeralda Inn. Stars like Mary Pickford, Gloria Swanson, Douglas Fairbanks, William S. Hart, and Clark Gable stayed at the inn while filming. Author Lew Wallace finished the script for the Broadway production of his *Ben Hur* while staying in room nine.

It was a custom at the Esmeralda for visitors to write their comments in the register. Colonel Bob Ingersoll took the opportunity to wax eloquent on the subject of Colonel Turner's "Mountain Dew":

> Col. Turner's moonshine is the most wonderful whiskey which ever drove a skeleton from the feast or painted landscapes in the brain of man. It is the mingled soul of corn and rye. In it you will find the sunshine and the shadows that chase each other over the billowy fields; the breath of June; the carol of the lark; the dews of night; the wealth of summer and autumn's content—all golden with imprisoned life. Drink it and you will hear the voices of men and maidens singing the harvest home; mingled with it is the laughter of children; drink and you will feel within your blood the scarlet dawns; the dreamy, tawny memory of many perfect days. For many years this liquid has been within the happy staves of oak, longing to touch the lips of man and maiden.

While it makes no pretense of being able to duplicate such an extraordinary beverage, the Esmeralda Inn continues to offer hospitality and fine food today.

While traveling this route, it is impossible not to take notice of the high cliffs and the cascading Rocky Broad River. Travelers have remarked upon the scenery for generations. It seems that little has changed. In 1859, Henry E. Colton wrote in his book *Mountain Scenery* that "the road . . . winds upon the banks of the Broad River, the contortions of whose troubled waters are beyond description. They curvet and lash around each rock, as if caressing it, then scornfully, seemingly with coquettish glee, dash on, singing a wild song, as if murmuring at the barriers which nature has put in its course."

Of course, any natural phenomenon that could inspire such lofty thoughts would also figure to have inspired legends about its origin. The Hickory Nut Gorge is no exception.

In his 1849 book, *Letters from the Alleghany Mountains*, Charles Lanman preserved the Cherokees' explanation for the appearance of the gorge, as told to him by Chief Flying Squirrel, also known as All Bones. Flying Squirrel spoke of a time when the Cherokees had found themselves without their beloved Tso-lungh, or tobacco weed. Many became sick and died. The Cherokees knew that tobacco grew in the east, but the gateway to that country was closely guarded by a group of malicious spirits known as the Little People. (These should not be confused with the Yunwi Tsunsdi, a kindly band of Little People who lived in another region of Cherokee territory, as discussed in the Standing Indian Tour.) Anyone who tried to travel along the river in the vicinity of the gateway found the Little People raining rocks upon him from the high cliffs.

*The Rocky Broad River*

A young warrior was sent to bring back tobacco from the east. When he failed to return, a magician arose and offered his services. On his first attempt, the magician turned himself into a mole and tried to burrow past the Little People, but they spotted him, and he was forced to return. The magician found more success when he turned himself into a hummingbird, though he was only able to bring back a small amount of tobacco. Finally, he turned himself into a whirlwind and "stripped the mountains of their vegetation, and scattered huge rocks in every part of the narrow valley." The Little People scurried away in fear. The magician was able to return with a load of the fragrant weed to save his people. Tobacco still grows abundantly in the area, though the cliffs remain barren of growth thanks to the magician's heroics.

It is 2 miles from the Esmeralda Inn to Chimney Rock, the most striking landmark in the area. Chimney Rock, too, has inspired abundant praise from travelers over the decades. Charles Lanman wrote,

> The highest bluff is on the south side . . . and midway up its front stands an isolated rock, looming against the sky, which is of a circular form, and resembles the principal turret of a stupendous castle. The entire mountain is composed of granite, and a large proportion of the bluff in question positively hangs over the abyss beneath, and is as smooth as it could possibly be made by the rains of uncounted centuries. Over one portion of this superb cliff, falling far down into some undiscovered, and apparently unattainable pool, is a stream of water, which seems to be the offspring of the clouds.

During the late 1800s, the entire area between the Rocky Broad River and the top of the mountain was owned by Jerome B. "Rome" Freeman. The mountain was covered by giant virgin black walnut trees at that time. A London firm contracted with Freeman to cut and deliver the logs to the railroad in Hendersonville. After the timber was cleared, Freeman recognized the possibility of developing the chimneylike rock standing apart from the mountain into a tourist attraction. He opened a trail from the village at the base and began charging a fee for guided tours to the top. The reputation of the view spread, and Chimney Rock was soon known all over the Southeast.

Lucius Morse was a physician from St. Louis who, like so many others, came to the area seeking a favorable climate. In 1902, he purchased sixty-four acres of the mountain from Freeman. Dr. Morse replaced the trail with a well-graded, hard-surfaced road that allowed automobiles to drive to the top. Norman Gregg operated the attraction for the Morse family. Gregg had a 196-foot tunnel cut along the bottom of Chimney Rock and a 258-foot shaft chiseled to the top, for a total of 454 feet through solid granite and quartz. The tunnel and the elevator shaft were finished in 1949. It took eighteen months, fifty thousand man-hours, and more than eight tons of dynamite to complete the project. The Morse family

*Chimney Rock*

owns more than a thousand acres in the area today. They continue to operate the park. Visitors can pay a fee at the ticket office at the foot of Chimney Rock and drive almost to the top, where a twenty-six-story elevator ride whisks them the rest of the way up.

You can also see the dramatic, 404-foot Hickory Nut Falls at the foot of the mountain. If you decide to pay the park entrance fee, you will have access to trails that lead to the top or bottom of the falls.

Chimney Rock was in the newspapers long before Rome Freeman arrived in the area, built a trail to the top, and began attracting tourists. On July 31, 1806, a widow named Patsey Reaves reported that she and her two children had seen a "very numerous crowd of beings" atop Chimney Rock. She went on to say that the beings were clad in brilliant white raiments and that they seemed to rise in unison. Though the Cherokees would have dismissed it as a gathering of the Little People, the sighting managed to create quite a stir in western North Carolina.

Other witnesses came forward to report similar hilltop gatherings, but things were relatively quiet until September 1811, when a husband and wife who lived below Chimney Rock spotted two opposing armies of horsemen high up in the air. The riders were mounted on winged horses. It was obvious that they were readying for combat atop Chimney Rock. The couple reported that when the preparations were over, the two armies dashed into each other, cutting, thrusting, and hacking. The wife distinctly "heard the ring of their swords and saw the glitter of their blades flashing in the sun's rays." Newspaper accounts of the sighting created so much excitement that a public meeting was held and a delegation with a magistrate and a clerk was appointed to visit the couple and take their affidavits. The delegation also reviewed the testimony of three more locals who witnessed similar cavalry gatherings on subsequent evenings.

In 1878, Silas McDowell, a well-known farmer, scientific observer, and man of letters in the area, came forward with the explanation he found most plausible. "In autumn," McDowell proclaimed,

*View of Lake Lure from Chimney Rock*

"when the atmosphere is clear, before a change in weather, the lower atmosphere in the ravine is surcharged with vapor, and to all objects in the upper atmosphere, seen through this medium, this vapor acts with telescopic effect and swells in size a bunch of gnats when at play in the sun's rays to the appearance of a squadron of winged-horse." Regardless of how much credence one gives McDowell's theory of the gnats, it is fun to look up at Chimney Rock around twilight during the fall and imagine a ghostly cavalry fight.

*Buried gold on Round Top*

There is also a legend about Round Top, the mountain opposite and just to the north of Chimney Rock that forms one wall of the valley. In the 1700s, a group of Englishmen who owned a mine farther north were on their way to the coast with a load of gold when they were attacked by Indians. The Englishmen retreated to a nearby cave and tried to fight. All but one of them died. The lone survivor managed to reach the coast and sail back to England. He intended to return to America for his gold, but a loss of eyesight forced him to dictate a map showing the location of the cave as he remembered it. A search party was dispatched to look for the treasure. Subsequent parties were organized over the years, but no gold was ever found. Rumors circulated that there was a copy of the Englishman's map on file in the Library of Congress. So many requests were made for the map that an official explanation was finally issued: "From time to time the Division of Maps has received requests for a manuscript showing the location of a cave near Chimney Rock, N.C., where gold is said to have been hidden by a party of Englishmen in the 18th century, but we have never located such a map. The statement that the map is in the Library of Congress is said to have been printed in the 1890s and has been copied repeatedly since, but without basis so far as we have been able to ascertain." So don't write them and ask.

It is 0.5 mile to the heart of the Lake Lure community. In 1927, the Morse family—the developers of Chimney Rock—drastically changed what was a cross-shaped agricultural valley by building a dam 115 feet high and 600 feet wide across the Rocky Broad River. The resulting

*Lake Lure*

*Rumbling Bald Mountain*

lake—Lake Lure—covers 1,500 acres, with 27 miles of shoreline and depths of up to 100 feet. Lake Lure has been described as one of the most beautiful man-made lakes in the world. The resort community that grew up around the lake covers an estimated 88 square miles, making it one of the largest towns in North Carolina in area.

If you stop in front of the Lake Lure Inn, you can look across the lake to Bald Mountain. From January 3, 1874, to the early summer of that year, the mountain shook with such force that it "rattled plates on pantry shelves in the cabins in the valley [and] shook windows to pieces in their sashes," in the words of one local resident. The series of shocks dislodged huge boulders and opened a fissure in the mountainside. Another resident noted that "dust, smoke, and weird noises" issued from the fissure. One writer claimed that the rumbling steadily increased in intensity to the point that the inhabitants began fleeing the area, thinking they were one step ahead of a lava flow. Another source put his finger on what was perhaps the only positive result of all the geological activity—those residents who remained in the area had to send "ten miles for an itinerant preacher who conducted so successful a revival that twenty-five new members connected themselves with the Baptist Church."

The rumblings continued, though they were not as severe as those from the six-month period in 1874. In July 1940, the National Speleological Society sent a team of scientists from Washington, D.C., to try to discover the cause of the noise. The scientists found that the rumblings were caused by boulders breaking loose from the tops of subterranean crevices and thundering down to the bottoms of caves inside the mountain. The shape of several caves was such that they served to amplify the sound.

Of course, there are less scientific explanations as well. According to one legend, a family that lived on Bald Mountain was known for the size and strength of the father and his several sons. The family was an argumentative bunch. They had constant quarrels among themselves that often ended in physical fights.

After attending a logrolling one day, the father

and one of his sons did not return. A search was conducted, but no trace was found of them. Years passed. An urgent request finally arrived from the long-lost son, who was on his deathbed out west. His brothers hurried to his side in time to hear his confession. The long-lost brother confessed that he and his father had quarreled violently on the day of the logrolling. The ensuing fight had left the father dead. The son had piled logs on the body and attempted to destroy the evidence of his crime, but the smoke had risen to the top of Bald Mountain and transformed the rock into the profile of his late father.

Though the brothers had never noticed before, they clearly saw their father's face on Bald Mountain upon their return to North Carolina. When the rumbling started in 1874, local people familiar with the tale said that the brothers were still fighting inside the mountain.

Just across from the Lake Lure Inn are signs for the Bottomless Pools, another of the area's main attractions. You can enter the park for a fee. Water has carved three pools into one of the oldest rocks on earth, the Henderson granite gneiss. The Bottomless Pools form a most unusual "pothole." They were featured in a "Ripley's Believe It or Not" cartoon on June 29, 1939. The Lower Pool has circular walls and a strong whirlpool. Sticks and other floating objects revolve for hours under the force of the current. They rarely escape. The pools are estimated to be between twenty-five thousand and a hundred thousand years old.

Continue east for 3.5 miles, then turn right onto N.C. 9, heading toward Tryon. After approximately 6 miles, you will see the Green River on your left. On the right are the Lake Adger power plant and dam. It is a little over 4 miles to Mill Spring, described more fully in the Hunting Country Tour. Turn right onto N.C. 108, heading south. It is another 3.5 miles to the Columbus city limits.

Columbus is the county seat of Polk County, which had a rather difficult beginning as a governmental unit. The North Carolina legislature approved the formation of Polk County in 1847, but there was so much squabbling over the location where a county seat should be built that the mat-

## Columbus Mills

*Polk County Courthouse in Columbus*

ter was not settled until 1855. Even then, it took a specially appointed commission of three men from outside the new county to make the final site selection. Instructed to choose a site as near the center of the county as possible, the committee purchased a hundred acres of wilderness land in an area known as Foster's Racepath.

One man who worked especially hard to see Polk County become a reality was Dr. Columbus Mills, the great-great-grandson of Ambrose Mills, one of the area's first settlers. Ambrose Mills showed bad judgment in siding with the English in the Revolutionary War, and he was hanged as a Tory traitor shortly after the American victory at Kings Mountain. Columbus Mills's father exercised better judgment, serving on the American side as a colonel in the War of 1812. Upon his death, he left his land along the Pacolet River to Columbus. As a North Carolina legislator, Columbus Mills fought for the settlement of the dispute over the Polk County seat. His efforts were rewarded when the legislature stipulated that the new town be named for him, not for Schuywicker—the Indian hero of the battle of Round Mountain—as had originally been proposed. (See the story of Skyuka in the Hunting Country Tour.)

Mills served the Confederate cause during the Civil War. It is ironic that when he returned to Polk County at the end of the war hoping to find peace, he instead found himself a prime target for raiding by renegades, since he was one of the area's most affluent landowners. After the repeated plundering of his plantation—which stood on the site now occupied by the Mimosa Inn—Mills was forced to flee in the middle of the night. He escaped to Cabarrus County, sold his plantation, and never returned to Polk County, even though he had fought so hard for its creation.

Mills at least stayed long enough to see the town of Columbus become a reality. The Greek Revival courthouse was completed in 1859. It was built by slaves using bricks made of native clay baked near the site. The bell housed by the graceful white belfry has rung every day Polk County Court has been in session. It was once feared that the wood in the belfry was rotting and that the bell might fall, but it turned out that there was little cause for alarm. Upon investigation, it was discovered that over a hundred years' worth of bird droppings had encased and completely preserved the wood.

A second man who greatly influenced the development of Columbus arrived in 1888. Frank Stearns had made a fortune with his grindstone quarry in the village of Berea, Ohio, just outside Cleveland. He first learned of Columbus because of its thermal-belt climate. So convinced was Stearns of the area's potential for commercial development that he purchased three thousand acres—including much of present-day Columbus, as well as land on Tryon Peak and the multiple peaks of White Oak Mountain—by 1912.

Stearns went to work immediately after his arrival, focusing on a development on White Oak Mountain that he called Spring Mountain Park. He advertised it as "the coming sanitorium and Switzerland of America." To make Spring Mountain Park easily accessible, Stearns built what he called a "serpentine drive" all the way to the 3,102-foot summit. He bragged that the grade was "so easy that a horse could trot all the way up." On the summit, he constructed the Log Cabin Inn, which soon established itself as an elite mountain resort. In 1894, Stearns's brother David and a man named Aaron French added a large, four-story frame structure they named the Skyuka Hotel. David Stearns and Aaron French later remodeled what was formerly the McAboy House to create the Mimosa Inn (see the Hunting Country Tour).

Driving into Columbus, you will see the Polk County Courthouse on the left. The Stearns School—lasting evidence of Frank Stearns's commitment to education—is on the right. Turn right onto Houston Road at the second stoplight. The road forks just after passing under the I-26 bridge. Bear right, following Houston Road and the signs for White Oak Mountain. Turn left into the entrance for the White Oak Development, which was once a part of Spring Mountain Park.

In following the paved road to the top of White Oak Mountain, you will be tracing the route of the "serpentine drive" that Frank Stearns constructed

## Frank Stearns

*Shunkawauken Falls*

Old Bill Williams

to the Log Cabin Inn. En route, you will pass an impressive waterfall on your right. The waterfall was known as Horse Creek Falls until 1891, when Stearns changed the name to Shunkawauken Falls in honor of an Indian chief. The current name is one of the few remaining imprints of Stearns, a man who once controlled the entire area.

It is 0.7 mile from the falls to an overlook in front of the White Oak Condominiums. You can see I-26 curving up from the Piedmont through Howard Gap. After enjoying the view, retrace your route to N.C. 108 and turn right.

Just before reaching I-26, you will see an historical marker on the left at the foot of Skyuka Mountain commemorating the birthplace of Old Bill Williams, christened William Sherley Williams in 1787. Old Bill lived near where Horse Creek flows into the Pacolet River until the age of eight, when his family moved to St. Louis. He went on to become, in the words of Albert Pike of Pikes Peak fame, "the bravest and most fearless mountaineer of them all." Thanks largely to the literary exaggerations of Frederick Ruxton, Old Bill established a legendary reputation as a drinker, a trapper, and a guide in the West from the early 1800s through the middle of the century. There are many tales of Old Bill's exploits. One of the best concerns an encounter with three Blackfoot braves who ambushed him while he was trapping alone. Bill took an arrow in the leg but managed to escape. After cutting the arrow out, he tracked the Indians for four days without the aid of rifle, horse, or pack, surviving mainly on berries. Bill slit the throats of two of the Indians while they slept, then kicked the third awake and sent him fleeing. Asked later why he spared one brave, Bill retorted that if he'd dispatched them all, the Blackfeet would never have known who killed them. Old Bill Williams died in an Indian attack in 1849. In Arizona, a nine-thousand-foot mountain and a nearby stream still bear his name.

The tour ends at the junction with I-26. You can continue on N.C. 108 to Tryon, or you can follow I-26 north to Hendersonville and Asheville or south to Spartanburg, South Carolina.

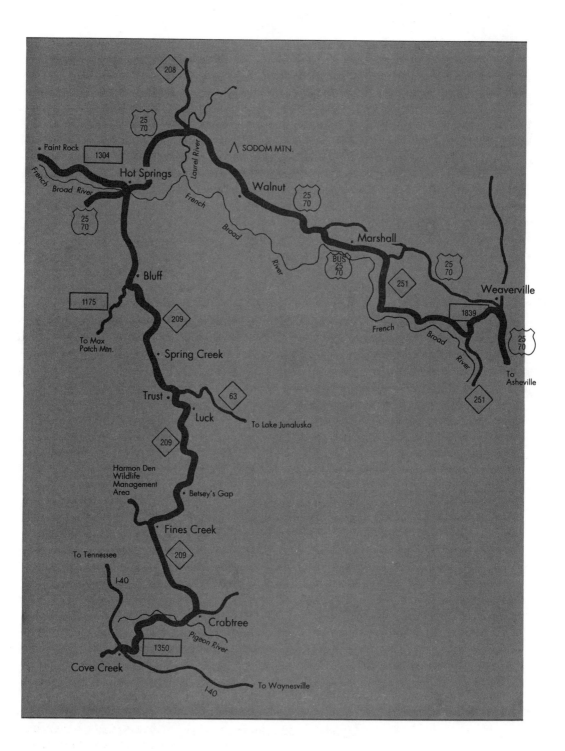

This tour begins at Cove Creek in Haywood County, near the old Cataloochee Trail. It follows the Pigeon River, then travels northeast to Madison County. There, it heads to Hot Springs and Marshall, then follows the French Broad River before ending near Weaverville. Total mileage: approximately 78 miles.

▲▲▲▲▲▲▲▲▲▲▲▲▲▲▲▲▲▲▲▲▲▲▲▲▲▲▲▲▲ *The Haywood to Madison Tour*

*The Cataloochee Trail*

Take Exit 20 off I-40 west of Lake Junaluska and Clyde—the exit for U.S. 276 and Maggie Valley. When you reach the stop sign at the end of the offramp, head straight across onto Rabbit Skin Road (S.R. 1350). If you were to follow the signs for U.S. 276, you would see an historical marker on the other side of I-40 for the famous Cataloochee Trail. Across from the sign is Little Cove Road, which follows a path similar to that of the old trail. You are in the vicinity of the Cove Creek community.

Cataloochee is the anglicized version of the Cherokee Ga-da-lu-sti, which meant "standing up in a row," according to James Mooney in his 1898 report to the Bureau of American Ethnology. It apparently referred to the high mountain ranges in the area, now within the boundaries of Great Smoky Mountains National Park, a few miles north of Exit 20. The Cataloochee Trail was first used by the Indians as a route across the mountains into present-day Tennessee. It was later used by white settlers driving their cattle to the good rangeland atop the peaks. Cattle would be brought to the peaks in the spring and allowed to graze until late fall, when their owners returned for the roundup.

One early traveler along the trail was Francis

## Bishop Francis Asbury

Asbury, who arrived in America in 1771 and became the first bishop of the Methodist church in this country in 1784. In the forty-five years after his arrival, Asbury traveled an estimated 275,000 miles in an effort to save the new settlers' souls from wickedness and whiskey. Though he had covered other areas in the mountains, it wasn't until 1810, and the age of sixty-five, that he followed the Cataloochee Trail from eastern Tennessee. Asbury's description of the journey is preserved in his journal, which reads in part, "Friday, our troubles began at the foaming, roaring stream which hid the rocks. At Catahouche [Cataloochee] I walked over a log. But O, the mountain—height after height, and five miles over! After crossing other streams, and losing ourselves in the woods, we came in, about nine o'clock at night, to Vater Shuck's. [Located near present-day Clyde, Shook's Campground was a well-known site for camp meetings.] What an awful day."

Asbury passed near Exit 20 on that "awful day." If you have a desire to follow in his footsteps, you can hike the 7-mile Francis Asbury Trail, located inside Great Smoky Mountains National Park. If you are not up to the hike, you can at least take comfort in the fact that you will cross paths with Bishop Asbury again on this tour.

## Iron Duff and Rabbit Skin

Continue on Rabbit Skin Road, which travels through the Iron Duff township. The name has an interesting history. One of the early white settlers in the area was a Scot named Aaron McDuff. He must have been a popular man—the territory was known as Aaron Duff's Bend until 1873, when the first local post office was established. The name Aaron Duff was suggested in the petition sent to Washington, but the word *Iron* was somehow substituted for *Aaron*. The new township accepted it as a matter of fate.

At least Iron Duff doesn't carry a negative connotation like Rabbit Skin, the locals' name for an area within the township. The latter name supposedly arose one day when a village wag remarked, "Looky here, fellers, at this pore, rotten thin soil—hit's as rotten an' thin as a rabbit's skin." The analogy must have been a good one, because the name stuck.

*Pigeon River*

After 3.4 miles on Rabbit Skin Road, you will round a curve to see the Pigeon River flowing beside you. The Pigeon River's name had a much less imaginative source—the large flocks of pigeons that once lived along its banks. They are no longer in evidence. Approximately 0.3 mile after your first look at the Pigeon River, you will see a bridge on the left. Turn onto the bridge. After crossing the river, turn right onto S.R. 1355 and follow the scenic route known locally as Riverside Drive.

It is another 2.4 miles along the Pigeon River to an intersection with N.C. 209 at the community of Crabtree. Turn left and begin the drive through scenic farmland. It is 5.3 miles to the place where N.C. 209 takes a sharp right turn at the Ferguson Supply Store. This is the Fines Creek Township,

*Fines Creek*

which received its name in the early 1790s, when white settlers along the Holston River in present-day Tennessee found it necessary to send raiding parties eastward to retaliate against the attacking Cherokees. The story goes that one such party, led by Captain Peter Fine, came through this area searching for a more direct route into Tennessee. Fine had followed some fleeing Cherokees into North Carolina, and his brother had been killed in a resulting skirmish. The ground was too frozen to dig a grave, so the party decided to break the ice in the nearby creek and submerge the body at a still place. They reasoned that the broken ice would refreeze and that the body would be preserved until their return. The body was never found, but Fine's name stuck.

*Boudinot Boundary*

The Fines Creek area was once part of a sixty-thousand-acre tract called the Boudinot Boundary. A man named Daniel Huger obtained the original grant in 1795, but it was Elias Boudinot who left his name on the area. A native of Philadelphia, Boudinot is remembered as much for the way he signed his name—"Ph.D. and Curator of the Mint"—as for anything else. The tract went through several owners until it was finally divided in 1876. The Harmon Den Wildlife Management Area, located several miles north of Fines Creek, is managed by the federal government. It covers a large segment of the original Boudinot Boundary.

*View from Betsey's Gap*

*Max Patch Mountain*

*Reynolds and Morgan
discover hot springs*

N.C. 209 now climbs to Betsey's Gap, elevation 5,895. It is approximately 4 miles from the turn at the Ferguson Supply Store to the Madison County line, at the crest of the range. There is an incredible view of the surrounding peaks from the top. It is another 4.7 miles to the small community of Luck. You might not even notice Luck, since it consists principally of a store and a bridge. It is 1.4 miles farther to the community of Trust, which has a substantial general store and a cafe. N.C. 209 intersects N.C. 63, which leads to Lake Junaluska 22 miles to the south. Turn left and continue on N.C. 209 toward Hot Springs.

Your route is following Spring Creek. The landscape opens into a scenic valley. It is 4.7 miles—past a volunteer fire department, a school, and a Methodist church, all named Spring Creek—before you reach the sign for the actual community of Spring Creek.

It is another 3.1 miles to a sign indicating that Max Patch Mountain is to the left on S.R. 1175. Standing 4,629 feet, Max Patch Mountain is located near the boundary of the Harmon Den Wildlife Management Area. The Appalachian Trail crosses the top of the mountain's grassy bald. Some have called Max Patch Mountain "the crown jewel of the Appalachian Trail" because of the panoramic view from its summit. It is 0.7 mile past the turn-off to the mountain to the community of Bluff, whose name is easily understood—your route immediately begins climbing the bluffs overlooking Spring Creek. It is 3.1 miles to the Rocky Bluff Recreation Area, which offers camping, picnicking, and two trailheads for hiking.

It is another 3.3 miles to the outskirts of Hot Springs. In 1778, two men named Henry Reynolds and Thomas Morgan were acting as advance scouts, watching for Indian movements. Spotting some stolen horses on the other side of the French Broad River, they left their own horses on the bank and waded across. While doing so, they noticed that the water was unusually warm. It turned out that the site was fed by an underground natural hot spring. Reynolds and Morgan spread the word when they returned to their settlement. Soon thereafter, invalids began journeying to the area to take the waters in the hope that they would be healed.

But it was a completely different phenomenon that put the town originally called Warm Springs (the name was changed to Hot Springs in 1886) on the map. At the turn of the nineteenth century, drovers from Kentucky and Tennessee began taking their herds of cattle, hogs, and horses to markets in South Carolina and Georgia. The most popular route ran from Greeneville, Tennessee, through Warm Springs, along the French Broad River, past present-day Asheville, and on to Greenville, South Carolina. In the fall months, a steady stream of livestock moved south along the French Broad. It has been estimated that between 150,000 and 200,000 hogs were driven along the route every year.

*Drovers' route*

In the early days, the drovers simply slept on the ground at night, but as the number of herds increased, stock stands sprang up—places where drovers could contain and feed their animals for the night and enjoy some rest and relaxation of their own. It was not uncommon for ten to twelve herds numbering from three hundred to one or two thousand animals apiece to stop overnight and feed at the stands. Each drove had an individual lot to itself. Wagons were driven through the lots with ten or twelve men scattering enough corn to literally cover the ground. The facilities that accommodated the men at the stock stands were little better than sleeping on the ground. There was usually a large room with an immense fireplace. The men were given a blanket or two each. They formed a semicircle, their feet to the fire, and slept on the bare floor. Several communities that grew up around the stock stands will be pointed out on this tour.

*Stock stands*

The year 1828 saw the opening of the Buncombe Turnpike, a toll road that ran from the Saluda Gap at the South Carolina line through Asheville and Warm Springs to the Tennessee line. It was a considerable improvement over the previous route. One description of conditions on the earlier road came from Bishop Asbury, who journeyed into this area in the autumn of 1800. "My roan horse . . . reeled and fell over, taking the chaise with him," he wrote. "I was called back, when I beheld the poor beast and the carriage,

*Buncombe Turnpike*

bottom up, lodged and wedged against a sapling, which alone prevented them both being precipitated into the river." Neither did the bishop write favorably of the people of Warm Springs: "My company was not agreeable here—there were too many subjects of the two great potentates of this Western World, whisky, brandy. My mind was greatly distressed."

*The Pattons' hotel*

The Buncombe Turnpike brought regular stagecoach traffic, as well as private carriages. In 1831, James Patton and his son John bought the drovers' stand (hardly what we would call a hotel today) in Warm Springs and began to upgrade its accommodations. The place burned in 1838, but the Pattons rebuilt. This time, they constructed a masterpiece. The principal structure was a 250-foot-long brick building. Two stories high, it had a piazza fronting the river studded with thirteen 20-foot columns representing the original states. The hotel could accommodate 500 guests, and the dining room could seat 240. A bar, a ballroom, a large stable, and the therapeutic baths were a few of the attractions.

Charles Lanman discussed the springs in his 1849 *Letters from the Alleghany Mountains*. "The water is clear as crystal, and so heavy that even a child may be thrown into it with little danger of being drowned," he wrote. "As a beverage, the water is quite palatable, and it is said that some people can drink a number of quarts per day, and yet experience none but beneficial effects. The diseases which it is thought to cure are palsy, rheumatism, and cutaneous affections. . . . The Warm Springs are annually visited by a large number of fashionable and sickly people from all the Southern States. . . . As a resort, especially for the latter part of summer, it has no superior in any State."

The hotel's brochure claimed that the waters could "bring bloom back to the cheek, the lustre to the eye, tone to the languid pulse, strength to the jaded nerves, and vigor to the wasted frame."

When the Civil War broke out in 1861, tourism in Warm Springs dropped considerably. In 1862, the hotel was purchased by James Rumbough, the operator of a stagecoach company that ran between Greeneville, Tennessee, and Greenville,

South Carolina. Rumbough and his wife, Carrie, were Confederate sympathizers, and their move to Warm Springs was inspired by the uncomfortable conditions in Unionist Greeneville, Tennessee. The story is told that Rumbough was captured while in active service with the Confederates in 1865 and that Carrie, pregnant at the time, rode to Morristown, Tennessee, to beg for his release. She succeeded, and Rumbough returned to Warm Springs to operate the hotel. It was under his ownership that the hotel saw its golden years.

In 1875, the Rumboughs' oldest daughter, Bessie, married Andrew Johnson, Jr., the son of the Unionist who became president of the United States after Abraham Lincoln's assassination. Though Bessie's father had been a Confederate colonel and her mother had burned the bridge in Warm Springs upon hearing of the approach of Union troops, there is no record of any objections to the marriage.

The following year, Rumbough's hotel received an unexpected and highly profitable endorsement from a popular novel. *"The Land of the Sky"; Or, Adventures in Mountain By-Ways* was a travel tale based on an actual excursion taken around 1874. Its author was Frances Christine Fisher Tiernan, writing under the nom de plume Christian Reid. Manly Wade Wellman described Reid's novel in *The Kingdom of Madison*: "In it, a socially elegant party visits the North Carolina mountains, exclaiming over the scenery and carrying on flirtatious exchanges in terms that . . . seem cumbersomely self-conscious." Though it might be difficult to understand the popularity of *The Land of the Sky* today, Reid's descriptions of Warm Springs and Rumbough's hotel brought guests flocking.

Rumbough used most of his profits to improve the hotel. He added a pair of three-story wings and hundreds of feet of porches. As many as a thousand guests were frequently accommodated. By that time, sixteen springs had been discovered, varying in temperature from 98 to 117 degrees. Guests could bathe in a shower of warm water, or they could choose an enclosed tile tub whose water was piped in from the springs. They could also use the large outdoor pool, where the water ran directly out of the springs. Hunting, horseback riding, fishing, hiking, billiards, bowling, tennis, carriage rides, and balls were other popular activities.

By January 1882, the Western North Carolina Railroad was completed all the way to Paint Rock, outside Warm Springs. From there, the new line connected with the East Tennessee Railroad, which brought passengers from the Midwest. With the new means of transportation, business increased even more.

The hotel burned in 1884. Rumbough lacked the funds to rebuild, so he sold the property to a group of New York investors who changed the name of the town to Hot Springs and built a new

*Mountain Park Hotel*

inn called the Mountain Park Hotel. Their resort had steam heat, electricity, and approximately 0.25 mile of broad porches enclosed by glass. It also boasted a modern bathhouse with sixteen marble pools measuring nine feet by six feet each, with depths of up to six feet. The investors overextended themselves, and they were forced to sell to pay their bills. Rumbough bought the property back and took over the operation as before. In 1875, the first golf course in the Southeast was built on the grounds.

With the outbreak of World War I, things slowed down for the Mountain Park Hotel. Rumbough negotiated with the federal government to house twenty-seven hundred officers and crew

*German prisoners-of-war*

members of German merchant vessels captured in New York Harbor at the declaration of war. Barbed wire was strung up around the hotel grounds, but since the prisoners were noncombatants, security was relatively relaxed. Only one prisoner escaped—he reportedly wrote from New Mexico saying that things were better in Hot Springs. Tents were pitched for the enlisted men, while officers were housed in the hotel itself. The prisoners requested and were granted materials to build a more substantial community of shelters resembling the inn's chalet style. On Sunday afternoons, the band from the ship *Vadderland* gave concerts for the townspeople. When the armistice was announced, the band played all night. Most prisoners and townspeople had only

*View of the French Broad River from Hot Springs*

*Dorland-Bell Institute*

fond memories of each other.

After the war, renovations were started on the hotel, only to be halted by another disastrous fire in 1920. The property passed through several owners but never regained its former grandeur. The last remaining part of the hotel burned in 1976. There was some hope of reviving the area as a resort when a new interstate through the mountains was being discussed, but the plans died when I-40 passed west of Hot Springs, leaving it off the beaten path. The vacant lot where the hotel stood is once again for sale.

Entering Hot Springs, N.C. 209 merges with U.S. 25/70 to become Bridge Street. A quick tour of the town is recommended. At the corner of Bridge and Walnut streets, you will notice an historical marker on the right commemorating the work of musical scholar Cecil Sharp, who visited the area in 1916 to collect mountain folk songs. Across from the marker, turn left and follow U.S. 25/70 as it heads up the hill. At the top, you will pass a large stone monument whose inscription tells you that it was built "in loving memory of Robert E. Lee." Behind the monument is a stately home constructed around 1902. It now serves as the Jesuit Residence. Also on the property is a Hikers' Hostel, used frequently by hikers on the Appalachian Trail. Follow U.S. 25/70 until you see a private home atop the high bluff overlooking the French Broad River Valley. The owners of the home were considerate enough to construct an overlook for those who wish to view the scenery. All they request, as indicated by the signs on the overlook, is that visitors sign the guest book.

Retrace your route to Bridge Street and turn left. In the first block on the left, you will see the Dorland Memorial Presbyterian Church, built in 1900. Dr. Luke Dorland came to Hot Springs in 1887 and opened a school under the auspices of the Presbyterian church. Many guests at the hotel contributed to the school, and its campus spread around the town. In 1918, the Dorland Institute merged with the Bell Institute, founded in nearby Jewel Hill. The Dorland-Bell Institute subsequently merged with the Asheville Farm School in 1942 to become Warren Wilson College, which is located in Swannanoa. Many of the buildings still standing in Hot Springs served as dormitories or classrooms for the original Dorland Institute. Across the road from the Dorland Memorial Presbyterian Church is the office of the French Broad Ranger District, where visitors may obtain information about Pisgah National Forest.

Continue on Bridge Street across the railroad tracks. The vacant lot on the left between the railroad tracks and the French Broad River is the former site of the Mountain Park Hotel. Continue across the bridge over the river. You will see an historical marker for Paint Rock on the left. Turn left just past the marker onto River Road, or Paint Rock Road (S.R. 1304). Circle back under the bridge. You will soon see Carolina Wilderness Adventures, an outfitters' headquarters. Just past an area where rafters prepare to depart on the French Broad, you will see an imposing rock bluff called Lover's Leap.

Retrace River Road under the bridge and continue straight, following the signs to Paint Rock. It is a scenic 4.7-mile drive alongside the French Broad River to one of the area's best-known landmarks. In 1799, a commission was appointed to establish the boundary between North Carolina and Tennessee once and for all. David Vance, Joseph McDowell, and Mussendine Matthews assembled at the Virginia border that May with surveyors James Strother and Robert Henry. The men worked their way south. Strother kept a daily journal that provides some of the best material available about early frontier life. On June 28, the men dropped a plumb line from the top of Paint Rock and established its height as 107 feet, 3 inches. Strother reported that Paint Rock "rather projects out," and that "the face of the rock bears but few traces of its having formerly been painted, owing to its being smoked by pine knots and other wood from a place at its base where travellers have frequently camped. In the year 1790 it was not much smoked, the picture of some humans, wild beasts, fish and fowls were to be seen plainly made with red paint, some of them 20 and 30 feet from its base." Strother also put to rest the argument voiced by some Tennesseans that the "painted rock" referred to in the Act of Cession—the act by which North Carolina

*Paint Rock*

ceded its western land for the creation of a new state, as detailed in the Burnsville to Mars Hill Tour—was farther downstream. Strother wrote that Paint Rock "has, ever since the River F. Broad was explored by white men, been a place of Publick Notoriety."

After viewing Paint Rock, retrace your route to U.S. 25/70 and turn left. It is approximately 5 miles to the Laurel River and an intersection with N.C. 208. Turn right, continuing on U.S. 25/70 toward Marshall and Asheville. It is 2.2 miles to S.R. 1319 (Stackhouse Road). The community of *Stackhouse*, to the right, was a stop on the Western North Carolina Railroad. It was named for Amos Stackhouse, who built a house, a store, and a bridge near the river in 1876 and induced the owners of the railroad to construct a station at the east end of his bridge. On the other side of U.S. 25/70, S.R. 1319 winds around Sodom Mountain and up to the area that won Madison County the Civil War nickname *Bloody Madison*. The communities near Laurel River and Laurel Creek are called Rich Laurel, Big Laurel, Little Laurel, Sodom Laurel, Wolf Laurel, and Shelton Laurel. They served as a center for Unionist activities.

Madison County was one of the most hotly divided areas in the South during the Civil War, but it took a shortage of salt in the winter of 1863 to bring matters to a head. Shopkeepers in the town of Marshall tended to be Southern sympathizers. They frequently denied salt to Union supporters. That January, some fifty armed men from Shelton Laurel traveled to Marshall and plundered the town's salt depot and stores. A company under Confederate Lieutenant Colonel James Keith was dispatched to round up the culprits.

Fifteen men and boys were captured on the first sweep. They were quartered in a cabin and denied food while the search continued. Another thirteen suspected culprits were then captured. Thirteen of the twenty-eight prisoners were subsequently marched to a field near Shelton Laurel Creek. They were ordered to their knees and told to pray, and then they were shot. Their bodies were thrown into a nearby sinkhole. Four women who had followed to see what would happen to their loved ones protested. One of them was stripped

*Stackhouse*

*Bloody Madison*

bare and flogged. The other three were tied to trees with ropes around their necks.

The local militia leader wrote Zebulon Vance, the governor of North Carolina, that twelve "Tories"—an apparent miscalculation—had been killed, with another twenty, including the four women, captured. Vance ordered his friend Augustus Merrimon, the solicitor for the Eighth Judicial District, to visit the scene and send him a report. Merrimon submitted a horrified account that read in part, "Such savage and barbarous cruelty is without a parallel in the State and I hope in every other." He charged that Keith's men had killed the captives without any semblance of a trial, and that it was Keith who ordered the captives to kneel and then shot them without warning. Merrimon also estimated that "probably eight of the thirteen" who were executed were not in the band of looters. Ultimately, only four prisoners—not twenty—were brought in alive. Governor Vance pronounced the incident "a horror disgraceful to civilization" and demanded that court-martial proceedings be brought against Keith. Others found it difficult to blame Keith for his reaction to the hot resistance he had encountered from snipers in Shelton Laurel. He was finally allowed to resign without facing a court-martial, and the relatives of the slain swore revenge. The incident earned the county the sobriquet Bloody Madison.

It is another 3.1 miles on U.S. 25/70 to S.R. 1155, the turnoff for the community of Walnut. During the days of the stock stands, this area was known as Jewel Hill. When a bill was introduced to establish Madison County in 1850, there was disagreement about whether the county seat should be located at Jewel Hill or Lapland, another stock-stand community. While the dispute was being ironed out, court sessions were held in Jewel Hill. Augustus Merrimon, the man later sent by Governor Vance to investigate the killing of the thirteen Union supporters, was in those days a young attorney. He attended a court session in Jewel Hill in 1853 and recorded his observations in his diary. The son of a Methodist minister, Merrimon was a bit shocked by what he saw. He recorded that Judge David T. Caldwell "opened

*Vance sends Merrimon to investigate*

*Walnut or Jewel Hill*

court in a verry [*sic*] bad house—open without seats fit to sit in and without any place to do business. . . . Some twenty or thirty women were present and most of them drunk, or partially so, and the majority of the men were drunk.—I do not know any rival of this place in regard to drunkenness, ignorance, superstition and the most brutal debauchery." The next day, he noted, "Such a drunken crowd I have seldom seen. . . . As I passed along to my lodgins [*sic*] I saw several persons so drunk they could not walk, and their friends were dragging them along to their homes."

Merrimon returned in 1854 and found that things had not improved. "Women sell themselves to prostitution of the basest character not infrequently for whisky," he lamented. "O wretched state of morals." Jewel Hill was obviously not one of Merrimon's favorite stops on the judicial circuit.

*The murdering innkeeper*

Two popular stock stands near Jewel Hill have frequently been cited as the location of a notorious robbery-murder conspiracy. Some tales say that Sam Chunn's tavern was the site, while others lay the burden on William Barnett's stand. The story goes that a drover staying at a stock stand overheard screams during the night, screams that the owners of the establishment denied having heard the next morning. Shortly after continuing on his journey, the drover was ambushed by a man with a blackened face. The drover killed his attacker and ran to the tavern to report what had happened. When he announced the news to the wife of the owner, she screamed that he had killed her husband. She then fled, never to be seen again. An investigation discovered that the couple had been killing boarders and ambushing travelers along the road, then robbing them and disposing of their bodies down a long chute that ran from an upstairs room in the inn to the French Broad.

The version centered around Barnett's stock stand says that the drover began to suspect something was up when the tavern owner showed him to his room and locked the door behind him. The drover saw blood on the floor and discovered a body under his bed. He placed the body in the bed and hid behind the door when the murderers came in later that night. He escaped while they were committing the crime intended for him on the hapless corpse. By the time the drover returned with help, the tavern owners had fled. It was then that searchers discovered the chute to the river.

The story of the murderous innkeeper is an archetypal gothic tale that appears around the world. But if the truth be known about Sam Chunn and William Barnett, both men died of natural causes, and their establishments were reputable places during their lifetimes. Chunn served in the North Carolina General Assembly in 1846. His tavern operated profitably until 1904. Barnett sold his stand in 1857 and lived in Madison County until his death in 1863. Neither man fit the description of the murderous innkeeper. Still, the legend persists.

Approximately 4 miles past the turnoff to Walnut, turn onto U.S. 25/70 Business and head into Marshall. Formerly known as Lapland, the town was Jewel Hill's rival for the distinction of becoming the county seat of Madison County. Marshall won the dispute after an election in 1855. Wilbur Zeigler and Ben Grosscup described the town in *The Heart of the Alleghanies*:

*Madison County Courthouse in Marshall*

> Its situation is decidedly Alpine in character. Its growth is stunted in a most emphatic manner by these apparently soulless conspirators—the river, mountain and railroad. The three seem to have joined hands in a determination regarding the village which might read well this way: "So large shalt thou grow, and no larger!" It is sung by the river, roared by the train and echoed by the mountain. . . . Such a location is unfavorable for a man whose gait is unsteady; for a chance mis-step might precipitate him out of his front yard, with a broken neck.

In the Work Projects Administration's *North Carolina: A Guide to the Old North State*, Marshall was depicted as "one mile long, one street wide, and sky high." It hasn't changed much since that description was written in 1939.

There is so little space in Marshall between the mountains and the French Broad that the local high school was built on Blannderhasset Island, in the middle of the river—the structure can still be seen there today. Local folklorist John Parris reported that the town was so geographically confined that cobblers found it impossible to stretch their thread to arm's length, so they were forced to use wooden pegs in their shoes instead of sewn soles.

David Vance was the son of the former congressman killed in the famous duel described in the Overmountain Victory Trail Tour. During the days of the stock drives, Vance kept a tavern at the upper end of Marshall that was reportedly 150 feet long. It is said that Vance fed 90,000 hogs during one month in 1826. Hezekiah Barnard, another proprietor, claimed to have fed 110,000 hogs over the same period.

At the Ivy River Bridge on the southern end of town, follow N.C. 251 instead of continuing on U.S. 25/70. The route parallels the French Broad River. In his 1859 book, *Mountain Scenery*, Henry Colton quoted from a *Southern Quarterly Review* article that described a trip along a similar course: "In the vague and misty twilight the first flashings of the foaming torrent rose in sight; and, as the opposite shores could not be distinguished at that early hour, and in consequence of the heavy mist which overhung them, the illusion was perfect which persuaded us that we were once more on the borders of the great Atlantic Sea." Several roadside picnic areas maintained by Buncombe County offer similar views.

It is 9.8 miles from the Ivy River Bridge to Ledges River Park, where the water breaking over the rock ledges resembles whitecaps on an ocean. This is a choice spot for a picnic, and it also serves as an access area for boaters on the French Broad River. After another 1.5 miles, N.C. 251 intersects S.R. 1839 and curves to the right, heading toward a prison. Turn left onto S.R. 1839. It is 1.4 miles to a junction with U.S. 19 Business on the outskirts of Weaverville. This marks the end of the tour. You may turn left and follow the signs to U.S. 25/70. If you turn left at the first stoplight, U.S. 25/70 will take you south into Asheville.

*View of French Broad River from Ledges River Park*

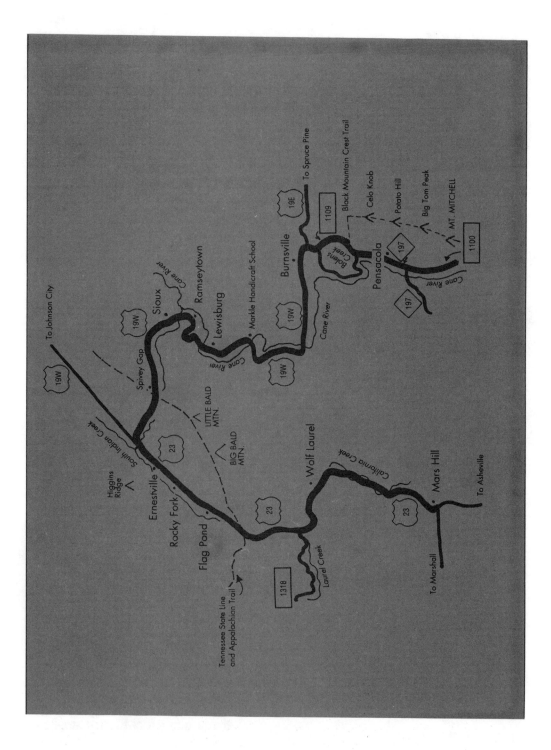

This tour begins in Burnsville, the county seat of Yancey County. It travels to the old Big Tom Wilson Motor Road near Mount Mitchell, follows the Cane River to Spivey Gap, and continues into Tennessee. It then turns back into Madison County, North Carolina, and ends in Mars Hill. Total mileage: approximately 76 miles.

# ▲▲▲▲▲▲▲▲▲▲▲▲▲▲▲▲▲▲▲▲▲▲▲▲▲▲▲▲▲▲▲*The Burnsville to Mars Hill Tour*

*Burnsville*

*Nu-Wray Inn*

The tour begins at the town square in the center of Burnsville, a scene that has changed little since Charles Dudley Warner described it in his 1888 book, *On Horseback*: "Burnsville is not only mildly picturesque, but very pleasing. . . . [It] is more like a New England village than any hitherto seen. Most of the houses stand about a square, which contains a shabby court-house; around it are two small churches, a jail, an inviting tavern, with a long veranda, and a couple of stores. . . . The elevation of Burnsville gives it a delightful summer climate, the gentle undulations of the country are agreeable, the views noble, the air is good and it is altogether a 'liveable' and attractive place."

The shabby courthouse was replaced by a 1908 building that now houses the police department. An attractive neo-Colonial structure built in 1965 serves as the courthouse today. The inviting tavern is now the well-known Nu-Wray Inn. Constructed in 1833, the same year Yancey County was formed, the inn is one of the oldest in the region. It is noted for its family-style dinners, at which guests sit at long tables set with heaping platters of food. After the meal, most diners choose to make use of the rocking chairs that line the front porch.

An addition to the town square since Warner's visit is a statue of Otway Burns, the man for whom the town is named. Burns won fame in the War of 1812 by building one of the fastest sailing vessels of the time, the *Snap Dragon*. With his ship's speed and his extensive knowledge of the North Carolina coast, Burns set out to capture and destroy English vessels. Atop his home in Beaufort, he built an observatory that commanded an extensive view of the ocean. Lookouts notified the crew of the *Snap Dragon* whenever English ships were in sight of the coast.

Burns caused so much damage that the British offered fifty thousand dollars for his capture, dead or alive. They even went so far as to construct a special vessel to capture him. The *Snap Dragon* was finally taken in 1814, but Burns, shorebound that particular voyage due to a bout of rheumatism, escaped.

His life after the War of 1812 proved unexciting by comparison. He managed to spend most of the fortune he had amassed during the war. His friend Andrew Jackson appointed him keeper of the Brant Island Shoal Light, where Burns "sank into his anecdotage, fond of his bright naval uniform, his cocked hat, good whiskey, and a good fight," according to the Work Projects Administration's *North Carolina: A Guide to the Old North State*.

*Statue of Otway Burns with Nu-Wray Inn in the background*

The cocked hat is a notable feature of the statue standing in the Burnsville town square. It gives the statue an unusual look. A story is told that a visitor at the unveiling remarked, "I didn't know he was an Indian."

According to court reports, Yancey County's early days were wild and woolly. Many blamed the easy availability of mountain moonshine for the full docket of cases involving drinking, fighting, and murder. Today, the area is attractive to tourists because of its eighteen peaks above 6,300 feet. The most famous is Mount Mitchell, at 6,684 feet the highest peak east of the Black Hills of South Dakota.

Leaving the Burnsville town square, head north on U.S. 19E for approximately 1 mile. Turn right onto N.C. 197, heading south toward Pensacola. After about 0.7 mile, turn left onto Bolens Creek Road (S.R.1109). After 2.5 miles, you will pass the Bolens Creek Church, where the road begins its steady climb to the crest of the ridge. You will see a cemetery on the right. On the left just past the cemetery is the trailhead for the Black Mountain Crest Trail, a strenuous 12-mile route to the top of Mount Mitchell. The trail follows an old logging road and is not well marked. There may be a chain across the road to prevent cars from driving on it. The twelve-hour hike passes several old mines worked in the early 1900s before it crosses Celo Knob, ascends to Deep Gap, and crosses Cattail Peak and Potato Hill. It continues through Big Tom Gap and crosses Big Tom Peak and Mount Craig before reaching the parking lot at Mount Mitchell. There are several other trails in the extensive system in Mount Mitchell State Park. Maps are available at the Pisgah National Forest's ranger station in Burnsville.

Follow Bolens Creek Road until it rejoins N.C. 197 after 1.3 miles. Turn left, following the Cane River for 1.8 miles to the community of Pensacola. Another 1.5 miles, following the river through a valley rimmed with steep peaks, bring you to a place where N.C. 197 makes a right-angle turn. Instead of turning right, continue straight on S.R. 1100 (the Ewart Wilson Road), which follows the same course along the river that the Big Tom Wilson Motor Road did in the 1920s and 1930s.

It is believed that in 1789, French botanist André Michaux became the first white man to set foot in these mountains, called the Black Mountains. But it was not until Dr. Elisha Mitchell arrived in 1827 that anyone had much of an idea how tall the Black Mountains really were.

Dr. Mitchell became a professor at the University of North Carolina in 1818. In those days, there were only three faculty members and ninety-two students at the university. Mitchell's initial appointment was in mathematics and natural philosophy, a discipline that included botany, zoology, and some of the physical sciences. He later took the university's other science professorship in chemistry, geology, and mineralogy. Mitchell also acted as bursar for the university and superintendent of its buildings and grounds. An ordained Presbyterian minister, he even

*Elisha Mitchell*

*Archway beside highway
leading to Pensacola*

*Thomas Clingman*

preached regularly. Mitchell was a well-rounded individual, to say the least.

In 1825, he took charge of the North Carolina Geological Survey, the first statewide survey anywhere in the nation. In the course of fulfilling his duties, he made his first visits to the western part of the state. In an 1829 geological report, Mitchell stated that he felt the Black Mountains contained the highest land between the Gulf of Mexico and the White Mountains of New Hampshire. He returned to the Blacks in 1835 to take measurements. The first peak he climbed was Celo Knob, elevation 5,946. There, he noted "peaks considerably more elevated farther South." Mitchell took measurements of barometric pressure and temperature and compared them to measurements taken at his base in Morganton. He then used a formula to determine that the peak that later became known as Mount Mitchell stood 6,476 feet above sea level. He proclaimed it "the Highest Peak of the Black."

Mitchell returned to Chapel Hill and made his revelations public in a lengthy article that appeared in the *Raleigh Register* on November 3, 1835. "The Black Mountain [range]," he noted, "has some Peaks of greater elevation than any point that has hitherto been measured in North-America, East of the Rocky Mountains, and is believed to be the highest Mountain in the United States." Mount Mitchell turned out to be 208 feet higher than Mitchell's figure. Had he correctly measured Morganton's elevation, he would have missed by only 6 feet.

He returned in 1844 to try to erase the doubts in his mind as to whether he had actually found the highest peak in the chain. General Thomas L. Clingman, a member of Congress and a man of scientific tastes, was taking measurements in the area at that same time. Clingman published a statement claiming that he had found a peak higher than the one measured by Mitchell. It was agreed that the peak Clingman measured was the highest, but controversy lingered as to whether that peak might be the same one measured previously by Mitchell.

Dr. Mitchell returned again in 1857 to settle the matter. He set out alone. He was scheduled to meet with his son during the course of his travels, and when he failed to do so, a search party was organized. Ten days later, the frustrated group enlisted the aid of Big Tom Wilson, a legendary hunter and tracker who lived in the Cane River area, at the foot of the Blacks. Charles Dudley Warner described Big Tom Wilson as "six feet and two inches tall, very spare and muscular, with sandy hair, long gray beard, and honest blue eyes. He has a reputation for great strength and endurance; a man of native simplicity and mild manners."

*Big Tom Wilson*

The searchers eventually agreed to let Wilson take the lead. Following seemingly invisible clues—broken limbs and faint impressions in the earth—Big Tom brought the group to a fifty-foot waterfall. There, in a pool at the foot, was the perfectly preserved body of Dr. Mitchell. It was surmised that he must have become lost in the fog and fallen over the falls while following the stream. His body was buried in Asheville and later moved to the top of the peak that now bears his name.

*Mitchell's death*

Big Tom Wilson's tracking ability was soon known far and wide. By the time he retired from bear hunting several years later, Big Tom supposedly had 113 black bears to his credit. Upon visiting Big Tom, Warner wrote, "His backwoods figure loomed larger and larger in our imagination, and he seemed strangely familiar. At length it came over us where we had met him before. It was in Cooper's novels. He was the Leather-Stocking exactly. And yet he was an original; for he assured us that he had never read the Leather-Stocking Tales."

Warner was so impressed with Wilson that he couldn't resist investigating what tales Big Tom might tell from his Civil War days. "What a figure, I was thinking, he must have made in the late war! Such a shot, such a splendid physique, such iron endurance! . . . Yes, he was in the war, he was sixteen months in the Confederate army, this Homeric man. In what rank? 'Oh, I was a fifer'!"

Another story is told of Big Tom's eloquence at a banquet in Asheville given in his honor after his retirement. When asked to say a few words, Big Tom remarked, "I'm glad I seed you, because if I hadn't seed you I wouldn't have knowed you."

Wilson was hired by a Mr. Murchison to watch

for game poachers and keep foraging cattle off the thirteen thousand acres he owned, a tract that included most of Mount Mitchell. Wilson raised ten children on the land and became so revered throughout the area that the government began designating his home territory on the Cane River as "Big Tom Wilson's" on topographical maps. In 1946, a nearby peak only seventy-seven feet shorter than Mount Mitchell was officially named Big Tom.

Tourists began discovering Mount Mitchell in the early 1850s. Accommodations were built on and near the mountain. Most visitors approached the peak from the southern slope. In 1915, the Perley and Crockett Logging Company adapted their logging railroad to provide passenger service to the top of Mount Mitchell. Despite the popularity of the service, they halted its operation in 1919 to devote the railroad exclusively to removing timber. In 1922, Perley and Crockett terminated their logging. The tracks were taken up and the grade was realigned to create the toll road known as the Mount Mitchell Motor Road.

Not to be outdone, Ewart Wilson, Big Tom's grandson, constructed another toll road along one of the logging-railroad grades on the Cane River side of the Blacks. Completed in 1925, it was named the Big Tom Wilson Motor Road. Since it hooked into the Mount Mitchell Motor Road, motorists could take both roads and make a complete loop through Burnsville and Mars Hill back to Asheville.

When the local section of the Blue Ridge Parkway opened in 1939, the state of North Carolina carried out its promise to keep roads free of tolls by taking over the Mount Mitchell Motor Road. As a consequence, the continued operation of the Big Tom Wilson Motor Road was not economically feasible. The road no longer exists, though you can drive the old route for 1.5 miles along the river on S.R. 1100. At that point, state maintenance ends and the road becomes private property. Big Tom's family continued to operate Camp Wilson, at the entrance to Mount Mitchell State Park, until 1960. Park officials considered the camp an eyesore and finally acquired its land in 1962. But Tom Wilson's legacy lives on in area landmarks.

*Mount Mitchell Motor Road*

*Big Tom Wilson Motor Road*

Historically, logging has been an important industry in the Black Mountains. The Murchison Lumber Company (also known as the Brown Brothers Lumber Company) was headquartered in nearby Eskota, while the Carolina Spruce Company had a fifty-two-hundred-acre tract with headquarters in Pensacola. Logging operations boomed during World War I. When the labor shortage grew critical, about four hundred Italian and Austrian workers were brought into the Cane River Valley. Pensacola grew into a thriving community, complete with a department store, a grocery store, a hardware store, a drugstore, a feed and seed store, and a barbershop. There was even a makeshift theater where movies were shown every Friday and Saturday night. Business decreased after the war, and the railroad tracks between Eskota and Burnsville were finally removed in 1933.

After touring Big Tom Wilson's former domain, retrace your route to U.S. 19E outside Burnsville. Turn left, heading west. It is approximately 5 miles to U.S. 19W. Turn right onto U.S. 19W, heading north. You will again be paralleling the Cane River. In her 1913 book, *The Carolina Mountains*, Margaret Morley wrote, "There is no more romantically beautiful valley in the mountains than that of Cane River, which, in its upper part, is over three thousand feet high, and nowhere falls below twenty-five hundred feet. . . . From it one sees round-pointed mountains delightfully grouped in the landscape, and quaint houses placed in a superb setting of mountains and streams." The river was supposedly named for the heavy canebrakes in places along its banks. The canes were used for fishing poles, pipestems, and reeds for looms. One interesting feature of the valley is the large number of footbridges that span the river, connecting the houses with the highway.

*Former location of the
Markle Handicraft School*

It is 5.5 miles on U.S. 19W to an interesting group of stone buildings along the Cane. They were once the site of the Markle Handicraft School, which was established to preserve traditional native crafts. The school was overseen by the Presbyterian church, but the project has since been abandoned.

It is 2.7 miles to the Egypt-Ramseytown Volunteer Fire Department at the community of Lewisburg. Bear to the right with U.S. 19W. It is another 4.6 miles to a sign announcing the community of Ramseytown, then 1.7 miles to the place where the Cane River flows off to the right, with U.S. 19W following Big Creek to the left. Another 0.7 mile on U.S. 19W brings you to the community of Sioux, where the road winds its way past several white clapboard storefronts built close to the highway.

## Spivey Gap and the Appalachian Trail

After crossing a valley, the road ascends to Spivey Gap (elevation 3,252 feet) and an intersection with the Appalachian Trail, the longest continuous marked trail in the world. The Appalachian Trail extends from Mount Katahdin in northern Maine to Springer Mountain in Georgia, the southern terminus of the Blue Ridge Mountains. For 2,000 miles, it winds through the most scenic areas in the eastern United States, crossing privately and publicly owned land that includes eight national forests, two national parks, and numerous state parks. Several books and trail guides are available if hiking any or all of the Appalachian Trail intrigues you.

## Big Bald Mountain

It is a 6.2-mile hike on the Appalachian Trail from Spivey Gap to Big Bald Mountain, also known as Greer's Bald because it was once home to an interesting character named David Greer. Greer came to the mountains in 1798 and worked for David Vance, who had a farm near present-day Weaverville. Vance was the grandfather of Zebulon Vance, governor of North Carolina during the Civil War. David Greer fell in love with Vance's daughter, but his affections were not returned. Some believe that being spurned left Greer crazed. In any event, he fled to the wilderness and the summit of Big Bald Mountain in 1802. He converted a cave into living quarters, and he remained undisturbed until the appearance of settlers.

## David Greer

An educated man, Greer declared himself the sovereign of *his* mountain. He wrote his own articles of government, along with a code of laws that postulated that every man had the right to take executive power into his own hands. He also wrote a tract on his religious views that revealed him to be a deist. Unfortunately, his notebooks were lost several years ago in a house fire.

One story about Greer centers around the time the sheriff of Burke County climbed Big Bald Mountain to collect an unpaid tax. When Greer refused to pay, he was summoned to court. He appeared with a loaded gun and ordered the judge, the sheriff, and others outside while he proceeded to break all the windows in the courthouse. The case was eventually dropped because it was decided Greer lived in Tennessee, not North Carolina.

He frequently shot at people who ventured into his domain, and he mutilated cattle that grazed on his land. In a quarrel with a neighbor named Holland Higgins over the ownership of a cherry orchard, Greer ambushed and killed Higgins while the latter was on his way to Jonesborough, Tennessee, to check his claim. Brought to trial, Greer was acquitted on the grounds that he was insane. He was so incensed at being judged insane that he published a pamphlet defending his action and sold it to anyone he could interest in his side of the story.

*Footbridge across the Cane River*

In 1834, he took some farming tools to George Tompkins's blacksmith shop for repairs. The tools were not ready upon Greer's return to the shop, and he grew furious. When Greer left, Tompkins's other customers warned the blacksmith that he had just signed his death warrant—Greer was seen building a blind in the bushes outside the shop. The customers took a gun, put Tompkins's hat on it, and stuck it out the door. When the hat flew across the shop with a bullet hole in it, Tompkins was convinced. Assuming he had killed Tompkins, Greer left his blind and headed up the road. Tompkins seized the opportunity and shot him in the back. No one ever complained that Tompkins wasn't brought to trial. Greer's thirty-two-year reign of terror had come to an end.

Dotting the landscape on top of Big Bald are hundreds of small mounds of earth. Inside the mounds are rocks—anywhere from a single large one to several small, round ones. Scientific studies have attempted to explain the phenomenon, but the best story involves Greer, sometimes called Hog Greer—behind his back, undoubtedly—because he raised hogs. He gave the impression that he lived like one as well. At any rate, terrified neighbors spread the story that after planting several potato hills, Hog Greer discovered stones, not potatoes, inside them at digging time. Regardless of whether a deity seeking justice or neighbors seeking revenge were behind the stones, local people took to calling the mounds Greer's Potato Hills.

From Spivey Gap, U.S. 19W passes the Spivey Gap Campground. It is 3.1 miles from the intersection with the Appalachian Trail to the Tennessee state line. The road follows a plateau, then ascends again. The numerous cascades along the ascent include a particularly impressive series of falls 2.3 miles from the state line. A primitive overlook on the left, marked by large boulders, allows you to look at the falls below.

It is another 4.2 miles to an intersection at South Indian Creek. U.S. 19W goes right, while U.S. 23 goes left. Turn left and follow U.S. 23 for 0.3 mile to the community of Ernestville. You are paralleling South Indian Creek. The tall peaks on the right comprise Higgins Ridge. This area was once a part of the short-lived State of Franklin.

In 1784, North Carolina ceded its western lands (which now constitute the state of Tennessee) to the federal government, an action that was repealed later that same year. Many settlers in the ceded area were dissatisfied with the shoddy military protection they received and with the inconvenience of traveling long distances over the mountains to resolve judicial matters. They met in what is now Jonesborough, Tennessee, and organized their own state—Franklin—electing John Sevier their first governor. Political infighting led to the state's collapse in 1787. By 1790, North Carolina was prepared to cede its western lands again. The region was finally admitted to the union as Tennessee in 1796.

During that chaotic time, area settlers were having trouble with the Cherokee and the Chickamauga Indians. In January 1789, Sevier learned that a large body of warriors was gathered at Flint Ridge and that they planned to venture forth in small groups to raid isolated cabins and settlements. Sevier gathered a force and marched up South Indian Creek, while another force entered the opposite side of the gorge from Devil's Fork Creek. After the ensuing battle, Sevier buried 145 Indians. Only 5 of his own men were killed. The battle proved to be one of the last engagements with Indians in the area. At the community of Rocky Fork, approximately 4.5 miles from Ernestville, U.S. 23 travels to the left. It was near this area that the Flint Creek Indian battle took place.

It is 2.2 miles over a route designated a scenic highway by the state of Tennessee to the community of Flag Pond. It is 5.5 miles farther to the North Carolina line and another intersection with the Appalachian Trail at Sam's Gap.

The tour now travels through Madison County. You will soon see signs of the Upper Laurel community. It is 2.9 miles from the state line to Little Creek Road (S.R. 1318), which goes to the right. The communities along Laurel Creek assumed names like Rich Laurel, Big Laurel, Little Laurel, Sodom Laurel, Wolf Laurel, and Shelton Laurel. If you were to travel on Little Creek Road, you would pass through most of them. Along with Upper Laurel, they constituted the center for Union sympathizers in Madison County during the Civil War (see the Haywood to Madison Tour).

It is 1 mile on U.S. 23 to the road that leads to the Wolf Laurel Ski Resort, on the left. Continuing through Upper Laurel, it is 4.1 miles to the valley created by California Creek. The distinctive church on the left was built in 1917. Recently used as a restaurant, it now stands empty.

It is approximately 6 miles to the outskirts of Mars Hill. The life of this community has always centered around Mars Hill College, a Baptist liberal-arts college founded in 1856. There is a story that upon the completion of the first building on campus, local fund-raisers found themselves eleven hundred dollars short of the needed sum. The sheriff supposedly seized a man called Old Joe, the slave of one of the donors, and held him as security until the debt was paid. It is on the campus of Mars Hill College that the tour ends. You can either follow U.S. 19/23 south to Asheville or take N.C. 213 to Marshall.

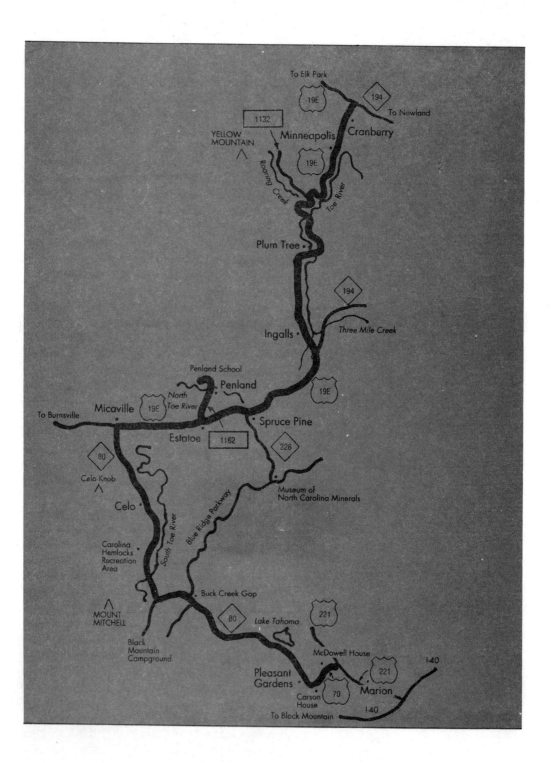

This tour begins at Pleasant Gardens, near Marion, the county seat of McDowell County. It follows Buck Creek to the Blue Ridge Parkway near Mount Mitchell, then follows the Toe River to Micaville. It visits the Penland School of Crafts, travels to Spruce Pine, and picks up the Overmountain Victory National Historic Trail through Plum Tree, Minneapolis, and Cranberry in Avery County. Total mileage: approximately 82 miles.

# The Overmountain Victory Trail Tour

Follow U.S. 221 North through downtown Marion to the junction with U.S. 70 West just outside town. Turn left onto U.S. 70 West. On your immediate right is an historical marker commemorating Pleasant Gardens, the estate of Joseph McDowell.

One of the earliest white settlers in present-day McDowell County was Hunting John McDowell. It is believed that McDowell came to the area in the 1760s and earned his nickname because of his considerable prowess as a hunter. In *Reminiscences and Memoirs of North Carolina and Eminent North Carolinians*, John H. Wheeler described Hunting John McDowell: "To a late period of his life, he could be seen on his way to the mountains, with four large bear traps tied behind him on his horse, with his trusty rifle on his shoulder. On these excursions he would go alone, and be absent for a month or more."

McDowell purchased land near the Catawba River and named it Pleasant Gardens. He also found time to marry and raise four children. One of his sons, Joseph, became a Revolutionary War hero for his leadership during a skirmish at

*Hunting John McDowell*

*Pleasant Gardens*

Cowan's Ford, on Cane Creek in present-day McDowell County, and for his role at the battles of Kings Mountain and Cowpens. When McDowell County was formed in 1843, the citizens chose to honor their hero by naming the new county after him.

It was Colonel Joseph McDowell who constructed the stately, white frame McDowell House, which stands behind the historical marker near U.S. 70. Built in the 1780s of hand-hewn beams and lumber and of bricks that were probably made by slaves in the kiln near the home, the McDowell House now contains several stores. It has seen better days, but its former grandeur is still apparent.

In 1780, American forces were not doing well in their battle to gain independence from Britain. Major Patrick Ferguson, commander of the British forces in the South, was convinced that the rebellion in his territory could be quickly squelched. That's where he made his big mistake. Ferguson sent word to Colonel Isaac Shelby, one of the American commanders in the area, that if Shelby and his fellow leaders "did not desist from their opposition to the British Arms," he would march his army over the mountains, "hang their leaders, and lay waste to the country with fire and sword."

Shelby relayed Ferguson's sentiments to John Sevier in present-day Tennessee, William Campbell in Virginia, and Benjamin Cleveland in the Watauga settlements. In September, those leaders rendezvoused for a battle against Ferguson. Since the majority of the two thousand men who marched to the battle site at Kings Mountain came across the mountains, they became known as the Overmountain Men. Their victory at Kings Mountain proved to be a turning point in the war. Ironically, Major Ferguson, who had promised to hang the leaders of the rebellious forces, was killed in the battle.

In September and October 1975, the route across the mountains was retraced by several hundred participants as part of the nation's bicentennial celebration. It was christened the Overmountain Victory National Historic Trail. Although our tour travels in the direction opposite that taken by the Overmountain Men, its second half follows much of the route of Sevier's men, who marched from Sycamore Shoals, Tennessee. Since Colonel Joseph McDowell led troops from Burke and Rutherford counties into the decisive battle, it seems appropriate to begin at Pleasant Gardens.

_Carson House_

Approximately 0.8 mile across the Catawba River on U.S. 70 is an historical marker for the Carson House, built in 1780 by Colonel John Carson. The Carson House was constructed of twelve-inch walnut logs covered with white clapboards. John Carson had an interesting marital history. His first wife, Rachel, was a daughter of Hunting John McDowell. She bore him seven children. Carson later married the widow of Joseph McDowell, Mary Moffitt McDowell, who also happened to be his sister-in-law. She bore him five children.

Unlike its sister home—the McDowell House—the Carson House is still beautifully landscaped. It now serves as a museum and research library. In former days, it was a stagecoach stop and an inn for travelers venturing between Asheville and Salisbury. The Carson House served as the seat of local government from the time of McDowell County's organization until a courthouse was built two years later. During the Civil War, the Carsons conducted a private school for young women in their home. The women and girls were terrified when Major General George Stoneman's Union raiders swept through the area and confiscated supplies, but the house itself was left unscathed.

_Carson-Vance duel_

Samuel Price Carson, one of John Carson's sons by his second marriage, was a United States senator who became involved in a scandalous duel. In 1827, Carson was running for reelection against a former friend, Dr. Robert B. Vance, who was a member of a well-known western North Carolina political family; Robert Vance was the uncle of a future governor, Zebulon Vance. Accusations were exchanged between the two opponents. Soon, family reputations were dragged into the matter. In the climate of the times, the only honorable way to settle the dispute was a duel. Since North Carolina law forbade dueling, Vance and Carson met at Saluda Gap, just across the South Carolina border, on November 5. Carson shot Vance, and the wound proved fatal. Davy Crockett, a friend of the Carsons' who was present at the duel, rode to the Carson House to deliver the news of the outcome. Carson was not prosecuted for his actions, a fact that sheds some light on the prevailing attitude toward dueling. He later moved to Texas, where he served as the first secretary of state during the time when Texas was an independent republic.

The Carson House and the entire valley still possess much of the beauty that Wilbur Zeigler and Ben Grosscup described in 1883 in *The Heart of the Alleghanies*:

*Old casino at Lake Tahoma*

> Bursting from a twilight wood, I beheld lying before me a valley scene of striking beauty. A broad and level tract of farming land, covered with meadows, corn and pea-fields, stretched away from the forested skirts of hill-sides. . . . On the right lay low hills. On the left [were] the summits of a lofty line of peaks, behind which the sun was sinking. . . . That night I stopped in Pleasant Gardens, one of the richest and most beautiful valleys to be found in any land. . . . The large, frame house [Carson House] and surroundings . . . showed evidence of thrift and neatness, and withall a certain ancestral air, one that only appears with age.

It is 1 mile on U.S. 70 to an intersection with N.C. 80 (Lake Tahoma Road), which follows Buck Creek through the valley. Turn right. It is 1.8 miles to the dam that forms Lake Tahoma. The dam's spillway creates a scenic waterfall that can be seen on the right. The lake was created in 1924 for the purpose of promoting the sale of real estate along its lakefront. When developers began the enterprise, they sponsored a contest to name the new lake. Tahoma supposedly translates as "mountain lake of God" or "God's mountain lake" in some unknown Indian dialect. A large casino constructed of rock was built over the water. It was there that big-name bands such as those of Kay Kyser, Hal Kemp, and Jan Garber played for weekend dances. The development proceeded nicely until the stock market crash of 1929. Work on a forty-room hotel was abandoned; only the foundation is left. The property has passed through several owners and is now controlled by a small number of stockholders. It still provides a scenic interlude as the road begins its climb to Hazelnut, or Buck Creek Gap.

It is almost 10 miles to the Yancey County line, at the crest of the mountain. The road winds through more than thirty hairpin curves before reaching the overlook at Buck Creek Gap, just below the Blue Ridge Parkway. The view from the overlook is worth the drive through the treacherous curves.

If you care to take a side trip, head south on the Blue Ridge Parkway for 11.3 miles to N.C. 128, which serves as the main entrance to Mount Mitchell State Park. It is 5 miles from the parkway to the parking lot near the summit of Mount Mitchell.

Good trails are available for those who prefer to avoid the crowds and approach Mount Mitchell on foot. Continue on N.C. 80 past the Blue Ridge Parkway. It is 2.3 miles to F.R. 472 (South Toe River Road). Turn left and drive the 3 miles to the Black Mountain Campground, located at the foot of Mount Mitchell. A 5.2-mile trail to the top of Mount Mitchell and a trailhead for the Black Mountain Crest Trail, which reaches almost to Burnsville, are available in addition to the camping facilities.

Mount Mitchell State Park was established in 1916 as the first state park in North Carolina and one of the first in the South. But the mountain actually began attracting tourists as early as the 1850s, when relative prosperity and improved transportation led to an interest in the scenic attractions of western North Carolina. Word filtered out through newspaper and magazine articles.

A Charlestonian named William Patton got things started by purchasing land in the area. In 1851, he erected a two-story cabin at an altitude of fifty-two hundred feet and called it Mountain House. To reach Mountain House from his lower cabins, Patton constructed a 2-mile horse trail,

*Buck Creek Gap*

*Black Mountain Campground*

*Mount Mitchell State Park*

*Mountain House*

## Camp Alice

which made access to the high peaks relatively easy. Others followed suit in building tourist accommodations. Talk began circulating about constructing a turnpike.

The Civil War brought a temporary halt to such ideas, but the creation of the Mount Mitchell Railroad from a logging railroad in 1915 changed the mountain forever. As many as seven passenger cars carried a maximum 250 people a day the 21 miles from Mount Mitchell Station, near the present-day town of Black Mountain, to the upper terminus at Camp Alice. The trip up took three hours and the return trip three and a half. In 1916, some 10,000 visitors disembarked at Camp Alice between mid-May and mid-October. In one week alone, almost 1,600 tourists made the trip.

Camp Alice consisted of a large, rustic dining hall and several platform tents for those who desired to spend the night. The dining hall served family-style food to overnight visitors, as well as preparing lunches for others who ascended the mountain. It was a moderately difficult 1-mile hike from Camp Alice to Mount Mitchell's summit.

## Mount Mitchell Motor Road

In 1919, Perley and Crockett, the owners of the logging railroad whose tracks were used for the excursion train, halted passenger service. When their logging operations were completed, the tracks were removed and the grade was realigned for the Mount Mitchell Motor Road, which opened in 1922. The following year, nearly thirteen thousand people drove the 19-mile toll road to Camp Alice. Because the road was not wide enough for two-way traffic, an interesting set of rules developed. Automobiles were required to start their ascent between the hours of 8:00 A.M. and 1:00 P.M. They had to head down the mountain between 3:30 P.M. and 5:30 P.M. Visitors who stayed overnight were required to arrive at the lower terminus before 7:30 A.M. or wait for the 3:30 P.M. departure.

When the section of the Blue Ridge Parkway from N.C. 80 to Black Mountain Gap was completed in 1939, the state of North Carolina took over the Mount Mitchell Motor Road and removed the toll. When the present N.C. 128 was completed after World War II, Camp Alice was bypassed. The stone foundations are all that remain today. If you hike the trail to Mount Mitchell from the Black Mountain Campground, you will pass the Camp Alice Trail Shelter near the foundations.

Return to N.C. 80 and continue in your original direction. On the left, you will see the Mount Mitchell Golf Course, open to the public. It is 3 miles from the turnoff to the Black Mountain Campground to the Carolina Hemlocks Recreation Area. Trailheads at the recreation area hook into Mount Mitchell State Park's trail system, but the real attraction is tubing on the South Toe River. During the warm summer months, tourists rent inner tubes from local grocery, gas, and convenience stores. The pastime is highly recommended. Tube in hand, just follow the squeals of laughter. The United States Forest Service has constructed an easily accessible submerged-rock stairway leading into the pool formed by the South Toe near the campground, but most people follow a well-worn path several hundred yards upriver. They then sit atop their tubes and ride the rapids down to the pool. There are docking areas farther downstream for those who want to continue past the campground, but most people prefer to simply hike back up the hill from the pool and come down again.

As you continue on N.C. 80, you will be following the South Toe River. Zeigler and Grosscup described their journey over the same route in 1883: "There are many spots of rare, sylvan beauty in the region of the upper Toe; many spots of wild and melancholy magnificence,—dells that seem the natural haunts for satyrs and fawns, and where a modern Walter Scott might weave and locate some most fascinating fictions." Perhaps they were a bit carried away, but the valley is still picturesque, especially the section lying about 4.4 miles from the Carolina Hemlocks Recreation Area, near the community of Celo. On the left at an elevation of 5,946 feet, Celo Knob (or Celo Peak) is awe-inspiring. It was the first peak Dr. Elisha Mitchell climbed in his exploration of

*Carolina Hemlocks*
*Recreation Area*

*View of the Black Mountains from Celo*

the Black Mountains. (See the Burnsville to Mars Hill Tour for more information about Dr. Mitchell and Mount Mitchell.)

It is 2.3 miles to a turnoff for the P. Mullendore Recreation Facility. Do not be misled by the official-looking directional sign; this is not a public facility, though it is a popular site for camping, swimming, and tubing. It is another 1.6 miles to Micaville. In the center of the community is an interesting structure known as the Micaville Country Store. Turn right at the store onto N.C. 80 North. It is a short distance to an intersection with U.S. 19E. Turn right.

*Mining industry*

Beginning in Micaville—as the name might suggest—and continuing through the remainder of the tour, you will witness constant evidence of the mining industry. This area can claim much of the mica and feldspar found in the United States. Ironically enough, some of the most productive mines bear evidence of work done in ancient times. From an examination of the tunnels, the shafts, and the dump piles left behind, it appears that ancient miners only sought mica that was in large, clear sheets. Zeigler and Grosscup recorded a theory about its use: "Many of the mounds in the North contain large sheets, over skeletons, from which it is inferred that it was used to cover the bodies of illustrious personages after interment, and that use may account for the zeal with which it was sought."

There were several famous local mines, including the Ray Mines near Burnsville and the Clarissa Buchanan Mine in Mitchell County. Both show evidence of prehistoric digging. The Ray Mines were considered the best in the area. Samples gathered there won a prize at an international fair in Vienna. The "Clarissey" was three hundred feet deep; the mica at that depth was said to be of as fine a grade as that from the top. The Fannie Gouge Mine near Spruce Pine was also a heavy producer. A single block of mica taken there in 1926 weighed nearly forty-four hundred pounds.

Feldspar, a by-product of the mica mines, was discarded as waste and dumped in huge piles near the mines for years. It eventually became more valuable than mica, and it is still important today. Although the mining sites do not lend much aesthetic appeal to this portion of the tour, their contribution as local employers cannot be denied.

Continuing on U.S. 19E, you will pass into Mitchell County. After 5.4 miles, you will reach the community of Estatoe, named for an Indian princess whose story is detailed in the Roan Mountain Tour. In abbreviated form, her name also survives in the Toe River.

About 0.2 mile past the Estatoe sign, turn left at the sign directing you to the Penland School. It is 2.7 miles on S.R. 1162 (Penland Road) to the small community of Penland, situated between the Toe River and the railroad tracks. Drive 0.2 mile to S.R. 1164 and turn left. It is 1.8 miles to the visitors' center for the school. You will drive through part of the 470-acre campus before reaching the visitors' center, where the pavement ends. Though the studios are not open to the public, the visitors' center is open from Tuesday through Saturday during the summer and fall. It is advisable to call ahead if you wish to visit.

The Penland School of Crafts has been described as one of the leading shapers of the American crafts movement and a producer of some of the best artisans in the country. In 1914, a man named Rufus Morgan founded the Appalachian School. Morgan wanted to include handicrafts in his program of instruction. In visiting area homes, he discovered high-quality woven articles that had been discarded when store-bought cloth became available. He convinced his sister, Miss Lucy Morgan, to return to Penland from Chicago and learn weaving from a local woman named Aunt Susan Phillips so that she could teach the skill at his school. Miss Lucy began instructing girls at the school and women in the community.

She went on to found the Penland School with the goal of perpetuating the art of weaving and providing a source of income for local people. Miss Lucy also began collecting her students' wares and selling them to the outside world. In 1928, a pottery department was added to the school. By 1929, the sale of student-made goods totaled eighteen thousand dollars.

*Visitors' center at Penland School of Crafts*

Today, the Penland School campus has fifty buildings. It is open to students during the spring, summer, and fall. Terms last from three to six weeks, and the courses vary from year to year. The curriculum usually includes work in wood, glass, fiber, clay, metal, photography, and weaving. All are studied in rustic, yet professionally equipped, studios. At peak times, the Penland School has 160 instructors and students on campus. If you browse the visitors' center, located in the first weaving cabin used by Miss Lucy, you will be impressed with the Morgans' vision in preventing the disappearance of traditional mountain crafts.

Return to U.S. 19E and turn left. It is 2.6 miles from the turnoff to the Penland School to the outskirts of Spruce Pine, a town that owes much of its prosperity to its role as the center of the mining industry. The town was founded in 1908, when the Carolina, Clinchfield, and Ohio Railroad built a station on the Toe River, making Spruce Pine a shipping center for the region's extensive logging industry.

*Spruce Pine*

Two of the earliest settlers in the area were Isaac and Alice English, who established the Old English Inn, a landmark for travelers. The Englishes' daughter is the person credited with suggesting the name Spruce Pine because of the beautiful evergreens growing along the Toe River. The only problem was one of mistaken identity—the evergreens later proved to be hemlocks.

The English family supposedly aided Union soldiers in escaping past Confederate lines during the Civil War. One of the escapees, Colonel J. M. Gere, returned after the war and joined with Isaac English in opening up the mining industry in the area. English and Gere were two of the first to mine mica and find markets for its use. Spruce Pine soon became known as the mineral capital of western North Carolina.

*Museum of
North Carolina Minerals*

For an interesting side trip, turn right at the intersection with N.C. 226 and proceed approximately 5 miles to the Museum of North Carolina Minerals, at Milepost 331 of the Blue Ridge Parkway. There, you can see some seven hundred of the state's finest mineral samples.

Continue north on U.S. 19E whether or not you

have chosen to take the side trip. Just past the stoplight is a marker that indicates you are traveling on the Overmountain Victory Trail. You will be following a route similar to the one taken by John Sevier's men for the rest of the tour.

It is 7.5 miles to a sign for the community of Ingalls, which is in Avery County. It is in Ingalls that U.S. 19E intersects N.C. 194, or Three Mile Road. An interesting character named Jacob Carpenter was born on nearby Three Mile Creek in 1833. From 1845 to 1919, "Uncle Jake" kept a record of local deaths, accompanied by brief annotations. People took to calling his notebooks the "Anthology of Death." The notebooks provide a fascinating and often amusing glimpse into the lives of local inhabitants, as seen through the eyes of Jacob Carpenter. Just to give you a flavor, here are some excerpts, with Uncle Jake's spelling and punctuation intact:

> Davis Frank ag 72 dide july 29 1842 ware fin man but mad sum brandy that warnt no good
> Abern Johnson ag 100.7 dide july 2 he war farmer and run forg to mak iron and drunk likker all his days
> Boon Pratt ag 28 dide sep 7 1906 work hard all life got rattel snak bite brandy cured it
> Frise Stamey ag 63 jan 9 1914 dide. Ware good shristen woman, She had 12 children
> Charles McKinney ag 79 dide may 1852 ware a farmer lived in blew ridge had 4 womin married 1 live in McKinney gap all went to fields to mak grane all went to crib for corn all went to smok house for meat he cild 75 to 80 hoges a year and womin never had no words bout his havin so many womin if it war thes times thar would be har pulled thare ware 42 children belongin to him they all went to prechin together nothin said he mad brandy all his lif never had no foes got along fin with everibody nod him
> Franky Davis his wife age 87 dide Sep 10 1842 she had nerve fite wolves all nite at shogar camp to save her caff throde fire chunks to save caff the camp war haf mile from home now she must have nerve to fite wolf all nite
> Joe Sing age 70 dide nove 15 1890. He robed by nite made rales by day
> Homer Hines age 28 dide july shot hisself cos of womin and whusky. Dogs run after him

*Plum Tree*

*Samuel Bright*

The last entry read, "Jacob Carpenter took down sick April 1 1919."

It is 4.4 miles farther on U.S. 19E to the community of Plum Tree. As you approach, you may notice that Plum Tree appears more scenic than some of the other towns in the area. Like its neighbors, Plum Tree grew up around mining, but it was treated to a recent refurbishing when it was chosen as a site for the film adaptation of John Ehle's novel *The Winter People*. If you have seen the movie, which stars Kelly McGillis and Kurt Russell, you will probably recognize the unusual clock, as well as the log cabin and the storefronts.

Beyond Plum Tree, the landscape opens into an expansive valley. An old Indian trail connecting the lands west of the mountains with the Yadkin and Catawba river valleys once passed through this valley.

One of the earliest settlers in the area was Samuel Bright, a rather rough and lawless man, but also a man with a reputation for kindness toward strangers passing through the valley. Another early settler was William Wiseman, who served as the local justice of the peace. The story is told that Samuel Bright's wife was brought before Wiseman. She was charged with stealing a bolt of cloth from a traveling peddler. After the lady was convicted, Wiseman passed a sentence of "thirty-nine lashes, well laid on." The only problem was that Bright was so thoroughly feared that no one could be found to carry out the sentence.

Demanding justice, the traveling peddler threatened to report the state of affairs to Judge Samuel Spencer in Salisbury. The peddler's threat apparently boded more trouble than did any scenario with Bright, so Wiseman resolved to carry out the sentence himself. Before he could do so, Bright and his family escaped over the mountains by way of the old Indian trail, which subsequently became known as Bright's Trace. The spring near the bald atop Yellow Mountain was called Bright Spring. Ironically, Wiseman eventually came to own part of Samuel Bright's original farm. It was over the same Bright's Trace that the Overmountain Men traveled past Yellow Mountain.

*Waightstill Avery*

In 1785, Waightstill Avery of neighboring Burke County took out hundreds of grants covering the entire valley. Today, the valley is still owned by the Avery family, which has become a leader in the region's venture into the Christmas-tree industry. The vigor with which local residents are pursuing the new industry is evidenced by the hundreds of acres currently in various stages of cultivation.

*John Fraser*
*and the Fraser fir*

In 1784, a Scotch botanist named John Fraser came to the area in search of rare and exotic plant life. For a short time, he joined forces with French botanist André Michaux, but there seems to have been some competition or jealousy between the two. It was Michaux who left Fraser, using the excuse that his horses had strayed and that he needed to search for them. It is hard to envision now, but the race among nations to find unusual plant species greatly resembled the space race in our own lifetimes.

Fraser was the first to discover the sturdy evergreen that now bears the name Fraser fir, a tree that has changed the economy of the mountain counties in northwestern North Carolina. The Fraser fir has recently become the Christmas tree of choice among consumers for several reasons— its sturdy branches can support heavy ornaments; it retains its needles long after it is cut; and it bounces back to its original shape after having been wrapped for shipping. The Fraser fir grows only in areas of high rainfall (seventy to ninety inches annually) at elevations above thirty-five hundred feet. With such a limited growing area, the trees bring a hefty price. Because much of northwestern North Carolina meets the criteria for growing the Fraser fir, local farmers quickly learned to plant every spare inch of their property with this lucrative crop. Driving through the valley, the extent of the new industry is obvious. Few hills have been left uncultivated. In the center of the valley, you will pass the main office of Avery Farms, one of the most established growers of Fraser firs in the area.

*View of a Fraser fir farm*

It is approximately 2 miles to an historical marker describing Yellow Mountain Road. S.R. 1132 turns off to the left and follows Roaring

Creek to the base of Yellow Mountain. It also follows Bright's Trace and the course of the Overmountain Men, though the marker would have you believe that the historic route continues on U.S. 19E. The reason for the discrepancy is that the Overmountain Victory Trail was designed as a route that could be driven, and U.S. 19E was the local road that replaced Bright's Trace in transporting people from North Carolina into Tennessee.

*Minneapolis*

It is 4.2 miles from the historical marker to Minneapolis. In the 1930s, this community was noted for having the largest deposits of amphibole asbestos in North Carolina. The material was once used in fireproofing, but it has since gained a notorious reputation as a health hazard, so the industry has died out.

*The Perkins brothers*

It is another 0.7 mile to the community of Cranberry. In 1826, Joshua, Ben, and Jake Perkins fled to North Carolina to escape arrest in Tennessee. In *A History of Watauga County*, John Preston Arthur wrote that the three brothers had been involved "in a rough play at a night feast and frolic. . . . After a log-rolling, [they] had attempted to remove the new flax shirt and trousers from Wright Moreland, and had injured him sufficiently to arouse his anger and cause him to take out a warrant for them." It was probably the luckiest thing that ever happened to the Perkins brothers.

They decided to support themselves while in North Carolina by digging for ginseng. Joshua Perkins set to work along the banks of Cranberry Creek, named for the abundance of berries in the vicinity. The Cherokees had come to the creek for centuries to collect cranberries for dye and war paint, but they had never eaten the fruit because the area was sacred to them. After the arrival of white men, the Cherokees changed their practice and began to use cranberries in their cooking.

It was iron ore—not ginseng or cranberries—that Joshua Perkins discovered. He and his brothers learned of a North Carolina statute that allowed any person who found ore on vacant land to build a tilt-hammer forge. When the person could prove that five thousand pounds of iron had been produced at his forge, the state would grant a bounty of three thousand acres covering the site. The statute was designed to encourage new mines, and it worked well.

*Cranberry Forge*

Cranberry Forge was built in 1828. Zeigler and Grosscup quoted a state geological report describing the mine: "The steep slope of the mountain and ridges, which the bed occupies are covered with blocks of ore, some weighing hundreds of pounds, and at places bare, vertical walls of massive ore, 10 to 15 feet thick, are exposed. . . . The length of the outcrop is 1500 feet, and the width, 200 to 800 feet."

The mine was eventually sold to the Dugger family. The Harden family managed it during the Civil War, when iron bars used in the manufacture of axes were hauled to Camp Vance, below Morganton.

*Peter Harden*

Peter Harden was said to be the son of a Creek Indian brought to the Harden family after the Battle of Horseshoe in 1814, though others believed him to be John Harden's illegitimate Negro son. Most months during the war, Peter Harden drove a four-horse load of iron bars to Morganton. When the mine was sold after the Civil War, he remained as caretaker. He was also the keeper of the local hotel—located near the old Cranberry High School—and he became postmaster though he could neither read nor write. His wife did all the clerical work.

It is 0.7 mile to a junction with N.C. 194. This marks the end of the tour. The old Cranberry High School is on the right. You can turn right and follow N.C. 194 South into Newland, the county seat of Avery County, or you can turn left and follow U.S. 19E/N.C. 194 North. N.C. 194 North splits off from U.S. 19E after less than 1 mile and goes to Banner Elk. U.S. 19E continues to Roan Mountain, Tennessee.

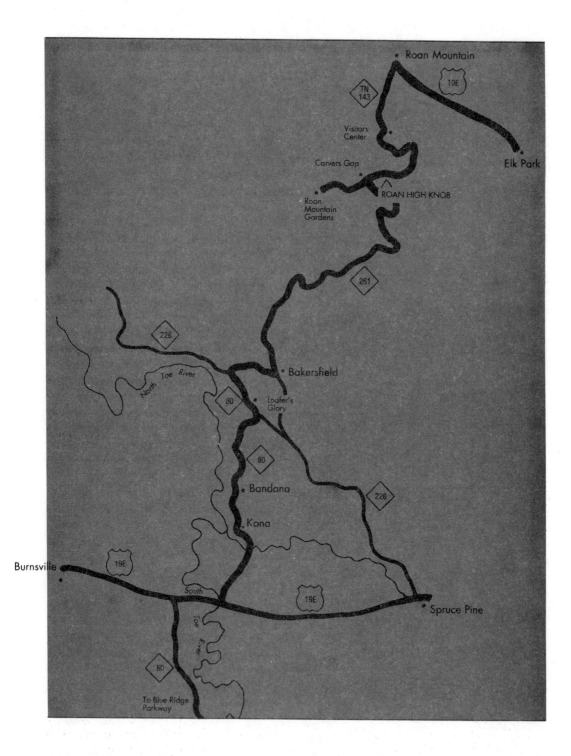

This tour begins in Elk Park, near the North Carolina–Tennessee border, and proceeds to the top of Roan Mountain. From the Roan, it travels to Bakersville, Loafer's Glory, Bandana, the Sink Hole Mine, and Kona—the home of the legendary Frankie Silver—leading ultimately to either Burnsville or Spruce Pine. Total mileage: approximately 47 miles.

▲▲▲▲▲▲▲▲▲▲▲▲▲▲▲▲▲▲▲▲▲▲▲▲▲▲▲▲▲▲▲▲▲▲▲▲▲*The Roan Mountain Tour*

To begin the tour, travel U.S. 19E heading north from Elk Park for 1.5 miles to the Tennessee state line. Continue for 4.3 miles to the community of Roan Mountain, then turn left onto Tennessee 143, heading south.

*Roan Mountain*

For centuries, the 6,285-foot "bald" peak called Roan Mountain has been an area landmark not only because of its height, but also because of the distinctive appearance of its treeless summit. Generations of scientists have tried to explain why certain mountaintops in the 2,000- to 6,000-foot range in this part of the Appalachians will not support trees. Altitude and timberline are obviously not the answer, since nearby Mount Mitchell, at almost 7,000 feet, supports tree growth all the way to the top.

*Theories explaining the "balds"*

In 1938, a professor from Louisiana State University advanced the theory that wasp eggs laid in the trees were responsible for killing them off. Unfortunately, his theory failed to explain why the infestation did not spread and why eradication of the wasps did not result in reforestation. A botanist from North Carolina State University suggested that Indians had created the balds by continually burning off the mountaintops for their settlements. But evidence from archaeologists and anthropologists showed that Indians preferred valleys near streams and never chose the tops of ridges for their villages.

As usual, when science fails, legend enters. In 1898, James Mooney recorded in his report to the Bureau of American Ethnology that the Cherokees had a mythological explanation for the origin of the balds. A Cherokee village was terrorized by a giant yellow jacket called Ulagu that swooped down, snatched up children, and quickly flew off into the distance. The ever-resourceful Cherokees posted sentinels on the tops of the mountains in order to track Ulagu to its lair, located in an inaccessible cavern. In this alternate version of the tale that appears in the Nantahala Tour, the Indians prayed to the Great Spirit for aid. Suddenly, a bolt of lightning split off the side of the mountain where Ulagu hid. The Indians then quickly fell on the monstrous insect and destroyed it.

*Ulagu, the giant yellow jacket*

According to Mooney, the Great Spirit was so pleased with the Cherokees' "initiative in uncovering [Ulagu's] hiding place, their piety in appealing for Divine aid in their extremity, and their bravery in the final combat, that it was His decree that in the future the tops of the highest mountains be bare of timber, to better serve as stations for sentries should another such visitation occur."

*The Catawba Indians' legend*

The Catawba Indians, who also frequented the area, had a different explanation. In 1849, Charles Lanman recorded in *Letters from the Alleghany Mountains,*

> There once was a time when all the nations of the earth were at war with the Catawbas, and had proclaimed their determination to conquer and possess their country. On hearing this intelligence the Catawbas became greatly enraged, and sent a challenge to all their enemies, and dared them to a fight on the summit of the Roan. The challenge was accepted, and three famous battles were fought. The streams of the entire land were red with blood, a number of tribes became extinct, and the Catawbas carried the day. Whereupon it was that the Great Spirit caused the forests to wither from the three peaks of the Roan

Mountain where the battles were fought; and wherefore it is that the flowers which grow upon this mountain are chiefly of a crimson hue, for they are nourished by the blood of the slain.

The Catawba legend is particularly accommodating because it accounts for another characteristic that helps to draw thousands of visitors to Roan Mountain each year. On the top of the Roan, there are six hundred acres of natural rhododendron gardens that put on a brilliant display of color each June.

*John Fraser*

In 1799, Scotsman John Fraser, under the patronage of the Russian government, made his third trip to the North Carolina mountains. It was during his journey up the Roan that he discovered a new plant, which he designated *Rhododendron catawbiense*. It is this plant with its crimson-colored blooms that attracts so many sightseers.

Roan Mountain also boasts an 850-acre forest of Fraser fir and spruce. The Fraser fir, named after the same John Fraser who christened the Catawba rhododendron, has become the latest rage in the domestic Christmas tree industry, spawning a whole new source of income for local landowners.

Fraser was only one of many scientists who traveled to the area. Because a number of species at Roan Mountain are rarely found outside the mountains of eastern Canada, the location offers an unusual assortment of plant life. Another famous botanist who visited the Roan was André Michaux, who was sent by the French government in 1785 to explore the United States and gather the seeds of trees, shrubs, and other vegetation for planting in the Park of Rambouillet. In 1786, Michaux established his central nursery in Charleston, South Carolina, then set about covering the entire country. He explored the area around the Roan in 1794. Some sources say that it was Michaux who actually named the peak, after the Rhone River of his native France. Though this is doubtful, he did leave his mark on the area, teaching local settlers the value of the ginseng plant and showing them how to prepare

*André Michaux*

it for the Chinese market. Still valued in the Orient for its medicinal and aphrodisiac qualities, ginseng has provided supplemental income for the people of the mountains ever since Michaux's visit.

A third well-known botanist who traveled to the Roan was Dr. Asa Gray, who visited twice in the 1840s. When Gray returned from one expedition, he called the Roan "without doubt, the most beautiful mountain east of the Rockies." While exploring the area, he discovered the unique species of lily that is still known as Gray's lily in his honor.

As you begin the route up the mountain, you will see Roan Mountain State Park's visitors' center on your left after about 1 mile on Tennessee 143. The facilities at the park are excellent. They include a swimming pool, tennis courts, and cabins with rocking chairs on their porches. Just past the visitors' center, the road begins to make its steep ascent to the summit. The route hasn't changed much since Charles Dudley Warner described it in his 1889 book, *On Horseback*: "For six miles the road runs by Doe River, here a pretty brook shaded with laurel and rhododendron, and a few cultivated patches of ground and infrequent houses. . . . We mounted slowly through splendid forests. . . . This big timber continues till within a mile and a half of the summit by the winding road. . . . Then there is a narrow belt of scrubby hardwood, moss-grown, and then large balsams, which crown the mountain."

When Charles Lanman reached the summit, he offered an observation that still rings true: "It commands an uninterrupted view of what appears to be the entire world. When I was there I observed no less than three thunderstorms performing their uproarious feats in three several valleys, while the remaining portions of the lower world were enjoying a deep blue atmosphere."

It is almost 16 miles from the visitors' center to Carver's Gap, where the crest of the ridge marks the Tennessee–North Carolina line. There is a parking area on the right. Most visitors make the climb along the section of the Appalachian Trail

*Catawba rhododendron in bloom*

*Cloudland Hotel*

*Appalachian Trail leading to the bald on top of Roan Mountain*

that leads to the top of the Roan's bald, on the left.

At the summit, there are still traces of the foundation of the Cloudland Hotel, built in 1885 by General Thomas Wilder, who owned most of the surrounding area. The Cloudland Hotel had 166 rooms. Guests could sleep in Tennessee and eat their meals in North Carolina without ever leaving the premises. The hotel was famous all over the east coast, though guests had to endure a difficult journey to the summit by stagecoach or carriage. The Cloudland even ran a hack three times a week to the railroad in Johnson City, Tennessee. In 1885–86, the hotel sent out advertisements reading, "Come up out of the sultry plains to the 'land of the sky,' magnificent views above the clouds where the rivers are born, a most extended prospect of 50,000 square miles in six different states, one hundred mountain tops, over 4,000 feet high in sight."

Many visitors at the Cloudland Hotel witnessed strange happenings atop the mountain. There were stories of ghostly music and circular rainbows. The reports grew so widespread that Henry Colton, a writer from Knoxville, Tennessee, came to investigate. Upon his return home, he reported his observations and conclusions to a Knoxville newspaper. "The sound was very plain to the ear . . . like the incessant, continuous and combined snap of two jars," he claimed, then went on to offer his explanation. Colton said that "two currents coming together in the open high plateau on the high elevation, by their friction and being on different temperatures, generated electricity. . . . The music was simply the snapping caused by this friction. . . . The heated air of the valley rises from eight in the morning until three or four in the afternoon. . . . As night comes on the current turns back into the valley, almost invariably producing a very brisk gale by three or four o'clock in the morning, which in turn dies down to a calm by seven o'clock and commences to reverse itself by nine o'clock."

Despite Colton's arguments, the hotel's mountain neighbors continued to insist that the sounds

*Mitchell County Courthouse in Bakersville*

*Loafer's Glory*

came from angels, and that the circular rainbow that frequently appeared atop the Roan after thunderstorms could only be God's halo.

After visiting the natural rhododendron gardens to the right of Carver's Gap, continue down the North Carolina side of the mountain. Tennessee 143 becomes N.C. 261. The route travels into a scenic farming valley for 13.7 miles before reaching Bakersville, the county seat of Mitchell County. This entire area was late in opening to white settlement. Content to leave the land for the Cherokees and the Catawbas, the North Carolina legislature did not officially open the territory until 1793. Mitchell County was not created until 1861.

The county seat was originally a community called Calhoun—later Childsville—but the people never liked that arrangement, so the location was switched to present-day Bakersville. Early court sessions met in a grove of trees that stood at the site of the present courthouse. A log courthouse was constructed in 1867.

Turn onto N.C. 226 North at the courthouse, heading toward Red Hill. After 2.2 miles, turn left onto N.C. 80 South. It is approximately 2 miles to an area labeled Loafer's Glory on old maps. When researchers were sent into the area by the Work Projects Administration in the 1930s, they were particularly impressed with the small community store owned by Nathan Deyton and Joe Wilson, which was located near the bridge over Cane Creek. Local men could be found at Deyton and Wilson's place on Saturdays, in the evenings, and on rainy days, as they played checkers, threw horseshoes, whittled, or just spun yarns, and it was for that reason that the store and the area came to be known as Loafer's Glory. Though the original structure is gone, there is still a small white store at the intersection where N.C. 80 takes a sharp right turn toward Burnsville. At times, local residents have put a sign reading "Loafer's Glory" on the present store, and there have even been occasional hand-lettered signs specifying the rules for loafing on the premises.

Follow N.C. 80 to the right. It is 2.5 miles on a

winding road to another country store, this one on the right and bearing a sign that reads "Bandana." The story goes that this community received its name when a railroad worker tied a bandana to a bush to mark the spot for a depot.

If you backtrack a few hundred yards, you will see the remains of the Sink Hole Mine through the trees on the opposite side of the road from the Bandana store. Some historians have theorized that this mine was first worked by the Spaniards sometime between 1540 and 1690, during their search for silver in the area. There was a tradition among the Indians that supports this theory; they told of white men coming on mules from the south during the summer and carrying off a white metal with them.

In *Western North Carolina*, John Preston Arthur described the mines as being "from sixty to eighty feet in diameter at the top. They extend along a ridge for one-third of a mile. They seem to have been a series of concentric holes. . . . Standing with their roots on some of [the] waste originally taken from these holes are several large trees nearly three feet in diameter."

In 1867, Thomas L. Clingman—United States senator, brigadier general in the Confederate army, and one of the early explorers of area mountain peaks—started mining operations on the tunnels below the old excavations. In his *Speeches and Writings*, published in 1878, he gave testimony to the great age of the previous excavations, and, by implication, to the possibility that Spaniards had mined the site: "Timber which I examined, that had grown on the earth thrown out, had been growing as long as three hundred years."

Though Clingman did not find silver at the Sink Hole Mine, a tinner named Heap took away a block of mica thinking it to be worthless, only to find a receptive market in Knoxville. Heap and a partner worked the site profitably for several years. The Sink Hole Mine was one of the first mica mines to open in the area, which soon prospered thanks to the new industry. Large pieces of the shiny, reflective metal can still be found on

*The Sink Hole Mine*

*Church near Kona*

*Frankie Silver*

the Sink Hole Mine property. A dirt road leads all the way to the top of the abandoned shafts.

It is approximately 4 miles from the mine and the Bandana store to the Kona Missionary Baptist Church, on a hillside to the right. S.R. 1176 is also to the right. It leads a short distance to the deserted community of Kona; there is a sign advising that the road is closed, so a side trip is not recommended.

Located on Deyton's Bend, where the North and South forks of the Toe River meet, Kona was once a railroad stop. It was also noted for an infamous murder committed in 1831. Frankie Silver lived in a log cabin with her husband, Charlie, and their infant daughter. Though most early versions of the tale say that she killed her husband with an ax in a jealous rage, recent research has proposed the theory that Frankie may have acted in self-defense, since Charlie frequently beat her. Because women were not allowed to testify in court at that time, Frankie never got the chance to tell her side of the story on the witness stand.

Frankie supposedly chopped the body into small pieces and burned most of it in the cabin's fireplace. Charlie's family suspected foul play and even consulted a Tennessee conjurer, who led them to the portion of the remains that Frankie had been unable to destroy. Found guilty of murder, Frankie was hanged on July 12, 1833; she remains the only woman ever legally hanged in North Carolina. A printed ballad was handed out to the crowd of witnesses at the event. Its authorship was attributed to Frankie, though there is no evidence that such was actually the case. The ballad has been preserved in its entirety in North Carolina folklore collections, insuring that the story of Frankie Silver will remain a part of the area's lore.

It is another 0.9 mile on N.C. 80 to the bridge that crosses from Mitchell County into Yancey County and spans both the railroad and the Toe River. The legend that surrounds the naming of the Toe relates that Estatoe, the daughter of an Indian chief, fell in love with the son of a rival chief. When her father refused to allow her to

*Bridge over the Toe River that forms the Yancey-Mitchell county line*

wed, Estatoe supposedly threw herself into the waters of the present-day Toe and drowned. The Indians then began calling it the Estatoe River, shortened to the Toe River by the white man. It is more probable that the name came from a well-traveled trading path that led from the South Carolina Indian village of Estatoe to the present-day Toe River. The Indians used the trail to reach mica deposits in the area. Archaeologists have discovered Indian ornaments with mica bead-work, as well as several Indian mounds containing sprinklings of mica.

It is a little over 2 miles farther to an intersection with U.S. 19E. This ends the tour. You have three choices. You can turn right onto U.S. 19E and drive 6 miles to Burnsville, or you can turn left and drive 8 miles to Spruce Pine. You might also continue on N.C. 80 until you intersect the Blue Ridge Parkway.

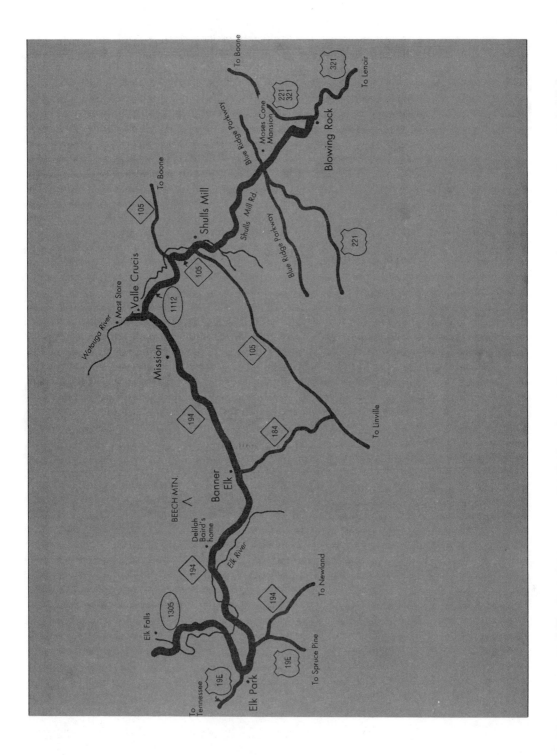

This tour begins in Blowing Rock and travels along Shulls Mill Road to the area known as Valle Crucis. It continues to Banner Elk, follows the Elk River to the town of Elk Park, and ends at scenic Elk Falls. Total mileage: approximately 35 miles.

▲▲▲▲▲▲▲▲▲▲▲▲▲▲▲▲▲▲▲▲▲▲▲▲▲▲▲▲▲▲▲▲▲▲▲▲▲▲▲▲▲*The Valle Crucis Tour*

*Moses S. Cone Memorial Park*

This tour begins in the town of Blowing Rock where U.S. 221, or the Yonahlossee Trail, heads toward Linville. Approximately 0.5 mile from Main Street on U.S. 221, there is a parking area on the right for the Moses S. Cone Memorial Park. This is actually the back section. You will notice a walking trail encircling what was once one of Mr. Cone's well-stocked trout ponds. The pond has been emptied in recent years to allow needed work on the dam. Funds have been allotted, and repairs on the two dams on the Cone Estate included in this tour are scheduled for completion by the fall of 1990. At that time, the trails will most likely experience an increase in popularity.

*Moses and Bertha Cone*

The trout ponds are just a small part of the 3,516-acre estate once owned by Moses and Bertha Cone. The eldest of thirteen children born to a Bavarian immigrant who achieved success as a dry-goods merchant, Moses Cone started out as a drummer, or traveling salesman, who solicited orders for the family business. It was on one of his sales trips that he discovered Blowing Rock. When he and younger brother Caesar switched their focus to the growing textile industry, they began to amass a sizable fortune. Moses began buying land in Blowing Rock when he was thirty-six. He continued to add to his estate for thirty-five years. Most of the acreage was purchased between 1893 and 1899.

In 1899, the Cones began construction on their Victorian, neo-Colonial manor house atop nearby Flat Top Mountain. An impressive gabled home with Tiffany windows, it now houses the Blue Ridge Parkway Craft Center. The Cones desired a self-sufficient estate, so they raised sheep, hogs, chickens, and milk cows. Their dairy was the first classified Grade A in Watauga County. The estate was so large that it supported thirty families. In an effort to introduce an alternative economy for local farmers, the Cones even experimented with apple orchards. At its height, the Cone estate had ten thousand apple trees of approximately twenty varieties.

When Moses Cone died, he left the estate to the hospital in Greensboro that now bears his name. It was specified in his will that Mrs. Cone would have use of the estate until her death. The hospital later discovered that the money set aside for upkeep was insufficient, so it arranged to donate the house and surrounding land to the federal government. In 1949, the National Park Service took over the development and maintenance of the estate as a recreation area and public park.

To tour the Cone manor house on Flat Top Mountain, simply follow the signs from U.S. 221 to the Blue Ridge Parkway turnoff, the parkway itself, and the estate's main entrance. After your visit, head back toward U.S. 221. Just before the junction, turn right onto Shulls Mill Road, which travels under the Blue Ridge Parkway. Just beyond the overpass, follow Shulls Mill Road as it forks to the left. It is less than 0.1 mile to a second trout pond, on the right. When the dams are repaired, the pond will be restored to the idyllic picnic spot it once was.

Shulls Mill Road winds and twists its way through the woods, with vistas of Grandfather Mountain sometimes visible on the left. About 2.3 miles past the trout pond, the road runs through the center of a resort development built on the former site of Camp Yonahlossee, one of the area's first summer camps for girls. Camp

*Cone manor house*

*Shulls Mill Road*

Yonahlossee began in 1922 under the direction of Dr. and Mrs. A. P. Kephart. The developers of the new resort have preserved much of the camp's original rockwork and many of its rustic buildings, including the barn, on the left, and the dam with its waterfall, around the curve on the right.

After another 1.5 miles, the first signs of the Hound Ears Club become visible. The fairways and greens of the club's golf course can be seen through the trees on the left. Shulls Mill Road leads through the center of the property. The clubhouse and hundreds of expensive summer homes cover the hills to the right. Atop one of the hills is the rock formation local residents were fond of comparing to a hound's ears before the deciduous forest grew up to cover it from view.

*Shulls Mill*

Just past the entrance to the Hound Ears Club, you will see the Shulls Mill Country Store on the left, with the Shulls Mill Baptist Church across the road. Both buildings were constructed around 1850. Along with the barn in the field on the left just past the bridge, they are all that remain of a once-prosperous community that claimed a population of more than a thousand at its peak.

Shulls Mill began around 1835, when Phillip Shull, the grandson of a German immigrant who had moved to Valle Crucis in the 1770s, built a gristmill near his farm. It was during those days that some of the community's most colorful residents began to leave their mark on area folklore.

*James Aldridge and*
*Betsy Calloway*

Around 1820, a man named James Aldridge arrived in the area and persuaded Betsy Calloway to marry him. They had seven children. All apparently went well until 1836, when another Mrs. James Aldridge appeared on the scene. It seems that Aldridge had deserted a wife and five children when he left the Big Sandy area in what is now West Virginia. It was a fur peddler passing through Watauga County who had recognized him and passed along his whereabouts. As to Betsy's reaction when her husband's first wife showed up, John Preston Arthur recorded that "she was sulky, but that [Aldridge] himself was treating both women exactly alike, and had no doubt but that Betsy would soon get over it."

Sources disagree on whether she really did "get over it." It is known that the first Mrs. Aldridge returned to the Big Sandy. Shortly thereafter, three sons and a daughter from Aldridge's first family came to live in Watauga County. Aldridge spent the next few years bouncing back and forth between Shulls Mill and the Big Sandy until both wives grew unreceptive, at which time he started living with a third woman. Betsy struggled but managed to raise her children, and occasionally the children from her husband's previous marriage as well. She died in 1900 a well-respected woman. No one even remembered much about James Aldridge by that time.

It was in 1859 that another citizen of Shulls Mill entered the history books. John Preston Arthur described David Colvert "Cobb" McCanless as "a strikingly handsome man and a well-behaved, useful citizen till he became involved with a woman not his wife, after which he fell into evil courses." Arthur didn't supply the woman's name, but other sources have identified her as Sarah Shull. Those sources also suggest that it may not have been wholly Sarah Shull's fault that McCanless turned out the way he did.

*"Cobb" McCanless*

In 1856, Cobb McCanless was elected sheriff. One of his duties was tax collection. In January 1859, he and Sarah Shull absconded with the funds he had gathered. Several months later, Mc-Canless's brother took Cobb's wife—Mary—her children, her father, her mother, and his and Cobb's sisters west to join the fugitives. How Cobb managed to balance life with Sarah Shull and Mary is not clear, but he apparently achieved some measure of success until the Civil War, when word arrived that he had been killed in Kansas.

It wasn't until 1883 that locals learned Cobb had actually been killed in a shootout with Wild Bill Hickok. The McCanless gang had allegedly been impressing horses for the Confederate cause. Hickok, known to side with the Union, disagreed with their actions. In an interview in *Harper's New Monthly Magazine*, Hickok offered a complimentary description of Cobb McCanless: "You see this M'Kandlas was the captain of a gang of desperadoes, horse-thieves, murderers, regular cutthroats, who were the terror of every body on the border. . . . I knew them all in the mountains, where they pretended to be trapping, but they were there hiding from the hangman. M'Kandlas was the biggest scoundrel and bully of them all, and was allers a-braggin of what he could do." In December 1861, a shootout occurred between ten of Cobb's boys and Wild Bill and his men. All but two of the McCanless gang were killed. Sarah Shull returned to Watauga County. She may have died knowing one of the most fascinating stories ever to have come out of this area.

Shulls Mill was a regular stop on the toll road that ran from Lincolnton, North Carolina, to Abingdon, Virginia. Between 1855 and 1861, a nine-passenger stagecoach named Old Albany made daily stops at Joseph Shull's place. But by 1893, traffic was bypassing town, and the section of the turnpike from Blowing Rock to Shulls Mill was turned over to Watauga County to be maintained as a public road. In 1914, some local citizens, dissatisfied with what they considered county neglect, established the Valle Crucis and Blowing Rock Turnpike Company. This tour follows the route of the original toll road.

_Whiting Lumber Company_

Shulls Mill began its finest hour in 1915, when William Scott Whiting, the owner of Whiting Lumber Company, selected the community as the site for a band mill. The same Shulls Mill that had listed a population of twenty-five in 1910 claimed a thousand residents by August 1917. While the town had previously boasted only a few stores (including the Shulls Mill Country Store, still standing), a hotel, and a post office, the Whiting Lumber Company helped bring a train depot for the new railroad spur, a barber shop, a movie theater, a hospital, and housing for hundreds of workers.

By 1918, the lumber company had sawed over 1.6 million feet of lumber from 1,436 acres in the area. Timber close enough to the mill to allow the company to make a profit was growing scarce by 1925, and William Scott Whiting began to move

*Mast Farm Inn*

his operation to alternate locations. He invited his workers to relocate at one of his other mills. Most accepted the offer. The flood of 1940 destroyed the majority of the buildings that remained. Inside the Shulls Mill Country Store, moved after the flood, you can still see the signs from the old depot and the post office. As you drive the bridge across the Watauga River, there is a field on the left that offers one of the most scenic views of Grandfather Mountain in the entire county. The old barn in the field is another remnant of the once-bustling community of Shulls Mill.

At the stop sign just past the bridge, turn right onto S.R. 1568, driving parallel to the Watauga River, on your right. In the summer months, this part of the river is a popular swimming hole for local residents. It is 0.8 mile to an intersection with N.C. 105. Turn right and go 0.6 mile. Just before the bridge, turn left onto S.R. 1112, heading toward Valle Crucis.

In 1883, Wilbur Zeigler and Ben Grosscup wrote in *The Heart of the Alleghanies* that "one valley in particular, by the Watauga, is of captivating loveliness. The mountains rise around it, as though placed there with no other purpose than to protect its jewel-like expanse from rough incursions of storm." Traveling this part of the tour through the valley they described, you are likely to agree with their assessment.

It is 1.9 miles to the original farm of the Shull family, the homestead established by Frederick Shull in the 1770s. The Shull home was another stagecoach stop on the route to Abingdon, Virginia. The recently renovated house standing on the right was built in 1888.

It is another 0.6 mile to the Mast Farm Inn. In *Sketches of Early Watauga*, Betty MacFarland described how this farm complex grew from its humble beginnings as a simple log cabin built by David Mast in 1812: "With this building as a nucleus, the farm illustrates the progression of an enterprising pioneer family from this rude early house on a small homestead to a larger more comfortable house, the seat of much larger landholdings. The complex includes one of the most

*The Mast Store*

complete and best-preserved groups of nineteenth century farm buildings in western North Carolina." The log house on the left in front of the large frame house is that original cabin. When the frame house was built in 1885, the log cabin was converted to a weaving house. A bedspread fashioned there was used in the White House during Woodrow Wilson's administration. Along with the barn across the road from the house, the farm consists of a wash house, a springhouse, a meat house, a woodhouse, an apple house, and a blacksmith's shop—everything necessary for a self-sustaining farm complex.

It wasn't long before the Mast Farm became recognized for the good food and hospitable lodgings it offered tourists seeking to escape the lowland heat. The tradition continues today, with the Mast Farm Inn operating as a bed-and-breakfast inn featuring a restaurant noted for its excellent food.

It is 0.1 mile to the beginning of what could be called the commercial district of Valle Crucis. On the right is the old Valle Crucis Company store, erected in 1909. It now serves as an annex for the famous Mast Store. Across the street is the Valle Crucis Methodist Church, built in 1894 on the same site as its predecessor, an 1870 log church. In the 1940 flood, the church was washed off its foundation, but it was prevented from going downstream by the large sugar maples in the churchyard. Next to the church is the building that once housed the town's bank, organized in 1914; it now serves as a private residence. These buildings and the school across the road are located on a tract of land settled in 1779 by Samuel Hix and his son-in-law, James Holtsclaw. The two men built a palisade of split logs to protect themselves from Indians and wild animals. Hix came to the wilderness to escape military service during the Revolutionary War—it is said that he sided with the British. He eventually moved on to Banner Elk, where he became a well-known character who made a living by hunting and making maple sugar. It is said that he sold his landholdings for a rifle, a dog, and a sheepskin.

*Samuel Hix and
James Holtsclaw*

*The Baird House*

<u>*Hard Taylor House*</u>

It is 0.2 mile to the well-preserved Mast Store, built in the 1880s. The store is a popular tourist attraction that has spawned several imitators in the area. Though goods touted in a 1940 advertisement included "everything from toothpicks to caskets," today's merchandise is equally eclectic. Many of the items mentioned in *Sketches of Early Watauga* can still be purchased there. "Even though it is now a general mercantile business, the store is a vivid commentary on early America in both goods and in atmosphere," Betty MacFarland wrote. "Commodities typifying by-gone days include the following items: famed penny candy, cheese and crackers, fatback; Chesterfield hats in yellowed boxes, bolts of cloth, leather goods, washboards, washtubs, cast iron pots, kerosene lamps, cherry seeders, apple peelers, sausage grinders, saddles, horseshoes, sets of harness, turning plows and cultivators." Current owner John Cooper also carries skiing and outdoor clothing and equipment reminiscent of the popular L. L. Bean store in Maine.

Diagonally across the road from the Mast Store is the Hard Taylor House, situated on a hill. The original structure was built by Henry Taylor before the Civil War. The present house, used as a gift shop, was constructed in two stages by Hardy Taylor, whose plan was to incorporate Henry's two-room brick house as a nucleus. It was the first home in the valley to have closets in every room, indoor plumbing, and central heat.

Farther down the road on the left is the W. W. Mast home, built in 1903. After another 0.5 mile, you will reach the Baird house, on the right. The original log cabin at the site was incorporated into this four-room, two-story house constructed sometime before 1873, when David and Elizabeth Baird moved in. Tradition says that this was the first home painted white in the area. The house and its picturesque barn serve as evidence of the prosperity of this farming valley.

Turn and retrace your route past the Mast Store to the school. Turn right onto N.C. 194 North and head into the most scenic part of the valley.

In *A History of Watauga County*, published in

1915, John Preston Arthur wrote, "There is, perhaps, more interest in this place and its romantic history than in any other in Watauga County. It is called the Valley of the Cross because of the fancied resemblance to that symbol of our faith caused by two creeks, each flowing from an opposite direction into Dutch Creek. . . . There is a dreamy spell which hangs over this little valley." Arthur was accurate in capturing the area's romantic overtones.

*Squire Taylor House*

After 0.9 mile on N.C. 194, you will see the Squire Taylor house on the right. Squire Taylor's first home was built in 1890 and was located where Dutch and Clark's creeks flow together on the left side of the road. The 1940 flood destroyed the original structure, as well as Squire Taylor's gristmill, but the second house, built in 1911–12, survives today as a popular bed-and-breakfast inn.

*L. Stillman Ives*

Much of the history of Valle Crucis revolves around the work of the Episcopal church. In the 1840s, L. Stillman Ives, the bishop of North Carolina, grew interested in Valle Crucis. One of the best-known men Bishop Ives brought to the area was William West Skiles, a layman who later became a deacon. In 1842, Skiles wrote,

The highland valley was magnificent in natural beauty. It lay in the elevated country between the Blue Ridge and the Alleghenies, nearly three thousand feet above the sea, while grand old mountains of successive ranges, broken into a hundred peaks, rose to nearly double the height on either hand, many so near that their distinctive features could be clearly seen, while others were only dimly outlined in the distance. These mountain ranges were peculiarly interesting, differing in some particulars from those of any other parts of the country. The vegetation was singularly rich and varied. The valley, entirely shut in by forest-clad mountains, was watered by three small, limpid streams, two of them leaping down the hillsides in foaming cascades.

By 1844, Bishop Ives had used his own money to buy two thousand acres of land and a sawmill in the area. He then began building structures of adobe brick. As the buildings were completed, young men were brought in to study for the ministry and to serve as teachers in the boarding and day school. To provide food, Ives shipped in a herd of dairy cattle and hired Skiles, an experienced farmer, to supervise the operation.

It was also about that time that Ives established the Society of the Holy Cross, the first monastic order for men in the Anglican communion since the English Reformation in the mid-1500s. By 1849, authorities in the Episcopal church were growing concerned that "the Mission at Valle Crucis had begun to drift away from the teachings of the Church, and was fast becoming a feeble and undignified imitation of the monastic institutions of the Church of Rome," as the bishops of North Carolina stated in a report. Bishop Ives resigned in 1852, and the monastic order and divinity school were disbanded. But William Skiles, so impressed by Ives's mission that he had joined the monastic order and been ordained a deacon in 1847, elected to stay in Valle Crucis, where he ran a store, practiced medicine, and taught school until his death in 1862.

In 1895, Joseph Blount Cheshire, then the bishop of North Carolina, came to the area to revive the church's work. He built a dormitory and chapel with classrooms attached. A few years later, Junius Horner, bishop of the newly created Asheville district, encouraged the school even further. In 1903, the Episcopal church bought 435 acres of the land previously owned by Bishop Ives. Apple orchards and a dairy were begun, a sawmill and a wagon factory were built, and a hydroelectric power plant was installed. The new school conducted classes from first grade through high school for both boarding and day students. A stone church, the Church of the Holy Cross, was built in 1926. Area public schools had expanded by 1936, so the mission school dropped classes for the first six grades and became a boarding school for girls only. It closed in 1943, thanks in large part to World War II. The facilities

*Bishop Ives's log cabin*

are now used as an Episcopal church conference center.

About 0.2 mile past the Squire Taylor house, you will see the mission-school buildings on the hill to the right. Rounding the curve, you will come upon the Church of the Holy Cross. Next to the church is Bishop Ives's log cabin, the only structure surviving from his era.

Follow N.C. 194 North as it climbs out of the valley. The steep, winding route may make for slow going, but the views to your left are beautiful. At the top of the ridge, N.C. 194 straightens out through a scenic valley dominated by an attractive white farmhouse. It is 6.4 miles from the mission school to the town of Banner Elk. Continue through the traffic light. Lees McRae College is on the left. Just past the campus, you will intersect N.C. 184; a right turn and a brief side trip will take you to the top of Beech Mountain, a popular resort and ski area. If you stay on N.C. 194 North, it is another 0.4 mile to the Elk River development, on the left. Beyond the entrance is the runway for the Banner Elk airport. This valley, once known as the Big Bottoms of Elk, has a colorful history.

Though it's hard to tell what is fact from what is legend, the tale of Delilah Baird still makes a good story. In 1825, Delilah, the eighteen-year-old daughter of Colonel Bedent Baird of Valle Crucis, ran off with John Holtsclaw, the husband of the former Fanny Calloway and the father of their seven children. The story goes that Holtsclaw promised to take Delilah to Kentucky, and that after their winding journey out of her home valley, she believed they had actually arrived there. After traveling from Valle Crucis to Banner Elk, you may appreciate how she was duped. Holtsclaw supposedly circled through Tennessee and returned to the valley of the Elk River, where he owned a 480-acre tract. You are now driving through that same valley.

One day, Delilah was out "sangin"—digging for ginseng—when she heard a cowbell that sounded remarkably like the one worn by her fa-

*Banner Elk*

*Delilah Baird*

ther's lead cow. Upon following the cow, she discovered how close she really was to Valle Crucis. She renewed her ties with her family but continued to live with Holtsclaw.

It wasn't long afterwards that Fanny Holtsclaw showed up asking her husband for work—she was willing to wash, weave, or do anything else to raise money to provide for her children. Holtsclaw's answer was to deed all his Elk River land to Delilah Baird. Ironically, one of Fanny's daughters, Raney, married the man who eventually came to own all of Delilah's land.

In 1881, at the age of seventy-four, Delilah learned that her eccentric ways were leading her relatives to request hearings to determine whether she was capable of handling her own affairs. She wrote to Ben Dyer, the son of a neighbor, and offered him a home and support for the rest of his life if he would come from Texas to defend her rights. "My folks are lawing me to death," Delilah put it. Ben Dyer, in his seventies himself, traveled to North Carolina the following year, only to return to Texas "loveless and forlorn" shortly thereafter. We know this last part as fact, since Dyer sued Delilah for his expenses in May 1882. A jury awarded him exactly $47.50, the price of railroad fare to and from Texas. Delilah lived until 1890 in a small log cabin that stood in front of the lovely white house overlooking the airstrip today.

It is another 5.4 miles on N.C. 194 to an intersection with U.S. 19 East. The Elk River flows beside this leg of the route much as it did in 1883, when Zeigler and Grosscup wrote,

*House overlooking the Big Bottoms of Elk where Delilah Baird lived*

> The scenery along the Elk has something decidedly romantic in its features. On one hand would be perched a moss-grown cottage on the mountain slope, with a few giant hemlocks, allowed to stand at the time of the general clearing, overshadowing it. Below, on the other hand, would lie fertile fields, watered by the noisy Elk, and enclosed on three sides by the dark and sober forests of the hemlock. The serenity of the evening was not disturbed by the farewell whistling of the quails; the rattling of the bells from the cows coming homeward across the pastures; the barking of

a dog behind the barnyard fence, and the opening cry of the whip-poor-will.

Turn right on U.S. 19 East for 1.2 miles to Elk Park. Approximately 0.2 mile past the center of Elk Park, there is a sign at the junction with S.R. 1303 directing you to the Elk River Campground. Turn right and follow the campground signs for approximately 0.3 mile. Turn left onto S.R. 1305, which travels along the Elk River through scenic farmland for 2.3 miles until the pavement ends. Continue for another 1.5 miles on the narrow, winding gravel road to the picnic area for Elk Falls. You might want to park and make the hundred-yard walk to the scenic falls.

Retrace your route to U.S. 19 East. You have three choices. A right turn will take you into Tennessee, heading toward Elizabethton and Johnson City. A left turn will take you to the junction with N.C. 194 South. There, you can follow U.S. 19E as it turns right toward Spruce Pine, or you can stay straight on N.C. 194 into Newland.

*Elk Falls*

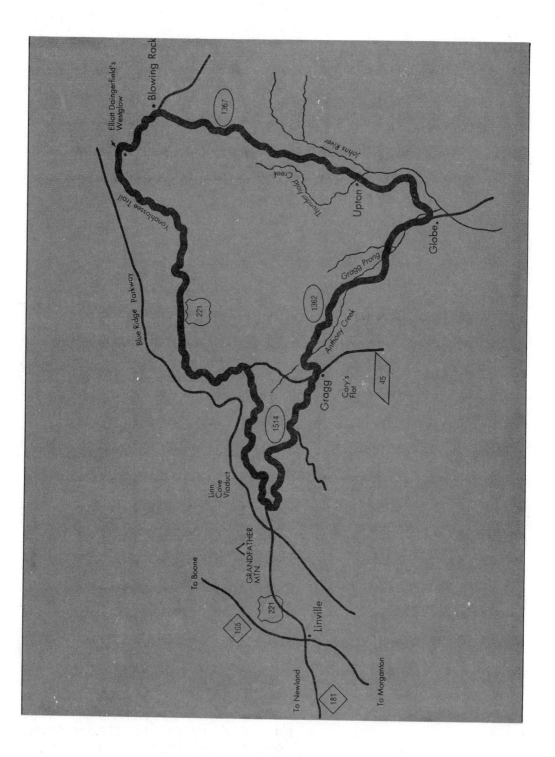

This tour begins in the town of Blowing Rock and travels almost straight downhill into a valley known locally as the Globe. It then proceeds back uphill to the foot of Grandfather Mountain and the crown jewel of the Blue Ridge Parkway, the Linn Cove Viaduct. From there, you can continue to Linville or return to Blowing Rock. Total mileage: approximately 32 miles.

▲▲▲▲▲▲▲▲▲▲▲▲▲▲▲▲▲▲▲▲▲▲▲▲▲▲▲▲▲▲▲▲▲▲*The Globe Tour*

Although this tour stops at only one of Blowing Rock's many places of interest, the town is highly recommended as a place to spend days or even weeks. Developed in the 1880s, Blowing Rock is one of the oldest resorts in the southern Appalachians. A visit to the chamber of commerce on bustling Main Street will provide you with information on several highly visible attractions.

The beginning of this little-explored route is at St. Mary's of the Hills Episcopal Church, located just down Main Street from the town park. Inside St. Mary's is an interesting painting by Elliott Daingerfield, an artist who made Blowing Rock his home for several years. Daingerfield was one of North Carolina's best-known artists, and his ecclesiastical and landscape paintings hang in many of the nation's best galleries, including the Metropolitan Museum in New York City and the National Gallery in Washington. He came to Blowing Rock in 1885 to recuperate from an illness and fell in love with the area. During his lifetime, he built three homes in the vicinity.

In 1918, William Stringfellow, a wealthy Alabaman who owned Chetola Estate in Blowing Rock, made a donation for the construction of a new Episcopal church. He asked Daingerfield to

*Elliott Daingerfield*

*St. Mary's of the Hills Episcopal Church in Blowing Rock*

contribute a painting. Daingerfield had long been fascinated with a local legend about the Madonna of the Hills; he began work at once.

Using one of his homes as a backdrop and his wife as a model, Daingerfield brought the legend of the Madonna of the Hills to canvas. Blue Ridge natives say that on the summer solstice, the Madonna walks across the hills at dawn. If her coming is attended by blue skies, there will be a rich harvest. If clouds mask the peaks and mists cling to her feet, the year will be full of sadness and want. A miracle of beauty follows in her footsteps, for wherever her feet touch the earth, there grows a carpet of daisies, lilies, and rhododendron.

It was when Daingerfield donated his creation to the church that it was decided to name the new building St. Mary's of the Hills. The painting still hangs in this picturesque mountain church for all to see.

Across from St. Mary's is the equally picturesque Rumple Presbyterian Church. A few doors down, just before the Blowing Rock Methodist Church, you will see a stop sign, with S.R. 1367 leading downhill to the right and into the Globe. The pavement ends shortly after you start your descent, and you will be on gravel roads for the rest of the route.

The first man to write a description of this area was Bishop August Gottlieb Spangenberg. Much of what he described in 1752 has remained the same. Bishop Spangenberg was sent by the Moravian church to search for desirable land for a settlement. After reading what he had to say about his ascent out of the Globe, you will probably be thankful that your tour is going downhill over the same terrain. "Here we have at length arrived after a very toilsome journey over fearful mountains and dangerous cliffs," Spangenberg wrote. "We came into a region from which there was no outlet, except by climbing up an indescribably steep mountain. Part of the way we had to crawl on hands and feet; sometimes we had to take the baggage and saddles and the horses and drag them up the mountains (for the horses were in danger of falling down backward—as we had once had an experience), and sometimes we had to pull the horses up while they trembled and quivered like leaves."

The unpaved road you are traveling does have a washboard effect in places, but at least you are in no danger of falling down backwards. Your reward comes during breaks in the foliage, when you will see a scene whose beauty has not diminished in the more than two hundred years since Spangenberg's odyssey. "Arrived at the top at last," he wrote. "We saw hundreds of mountain peaks all around us, presenting a spectacle like ocean waves in a storm."

Five miles later, you will come to the foot of the mountain, where Thunderhold Creek meets Johns River. It is also the location of the Upton community. Johns River Missionary Baptist Church, built in 1892, is just off to the right. The church and some scattered homes are about all that remain from a once-busy community. There used to be several gristmills along the route, and you can still see the cleared areas where they stood. The last remaining mill was destroyed by the flood of 1940 and was never rebuilt. The thriving business in the area today is obvious from the landscape of the valley—tree and shrub nurseries have sprung up all along the river and creeks.

At the Upton fork, bear left and continue on S.R. 1367. "We are now in a locality that has probably been seldom trodden by the foot of man since the creation of the world," wrote Spangenberg, an observation still readily appreciated by those traveling through the valley. "For 70 to 80 miles we have been traveling over terrible mountains, and along very dangerous places where there was no way at all. With respect to this place where we are encamped—one might call it a basin or kettle. It is a cove in the mountains and is very rich soil. Two creeks—one larger than the other—flow through it. Various springs of very sweet water form lovely meadow lands. . . . Our horses find abundant pasture among the buffalo haunts and grass among the springs, which they eat greedily."

*Upton*

After traveling 3 miles, you will come to the intersection of S.R. 1367 and S.R. 1362 at Globe Baptist Church, which was organized in 1797. Like Upton, this area was a thriving community at one time, even supporting an outstanding preparatory school known as the Globe Academy. The school was opened to the public in 1882, but the 1916 flood washed it away.

The region had its most exciting history during the Civil War, thanks to the exploits of L. McKesson Blalock, better known by his adopted first name, Keith. When the war broke out, Keith Blalock joined the Confederate army to avoid conscription, but he harbored the idea of deserting and joining the Union forces. His wife, Malinda, didn't want to be left behind, so she, too, joined the Twenty-sixth Regiment under Colonel Vance—only she enlisted as Sam Blalock, Keith's brother. Her disguise worked, but Keith and Sam did not get any opportunities to join the Union forces as the days rolled by. Keith finally took matters into his own hands, sneaking into some bushes and rubbing himself with poison oak. He developed such a severe rash that the doctor took it to be a more serious condition and discharged him in 1862, only one month after his enlistment.

Brother Sam soon followed. Her discharge remains in the official records. She is listed as "Mrs. L. Blaylock [*sic*]," and beside her name is the notation, "Discharged for being a woman. This lady had done a soldier's duty without a suspicion of her sex among her comrades, until her husband, L. M. Blaylock, was discharged, when she claimed the same privilege and was sent home rejoicing."

But the war was just beginning for Keith. To prevent Confederate forces from finding him when his rash was cured, he and Malinda fled and lived beneath Grandfather Mountain— "under the Grandfather," as they say locally—in a hut. The two fugitives were joined by several others trying to avoid conscription. Keith Blalock began recruiting for Unionist forces working out of Tennessee.

*Keith and Malinda Blalock*

Whenever there is guerrilla warfare between neighbors, whether a fighter is a scoundrel or a savior seems to depend on the affiliation of the observer. The mountain people were fiercely divided in their loyalties, and there were probably few areas in the country where the saying "brother against brother" was any more true than throughout the southern Appalachians. Most of the blood feuds that have survived the generations had their origins in Civil War days.

Blalock began raiding the Globe area with his band. He was frequently seen wearing a Union uniform. Southern sympathizers felt he was a traitor and a deserter, and they made their feelings known. Many of Keith's enemies lived in the Globe, so they soon found themselves the victims of constant raiding by his forces. Malinda was wounded in one raid and Keith lost an eye in another, but they managed to inflict more than their share of injury, to be sure.

The Southern forces retaliated by killing Keith's stepfather, which only inspired Blalock to increase his raids on the people of the Globe. After the war, he ambushed and killed the man he felt was responsible for the murder of his stepfather. He was subsequently pardoned by the governor, a Union sympathizer. Keith Blalock's name is still remembered around these parts, and how it is remembered often depends on which side people's ancestors took in the war. Blalock's grave lies in Montezuma Cemetery, a few miles from Linville. Ironically, it is marked by a large tombstone erected to honor him as a Confederate veteran.

Turn right at Globe Baptist Church and follow S.R. 1362. For the next 6 miles, you will be climbing steadily back up the mountain and traveling alongside Gragg Prong, and later Anthony Creek. There are beautiful cascades and small waterfalls all along the route. Visitors have fashioned a number of turnouts along the roadside—the turnouts usually indicate scenic spots. At the top of the mountain, turn right onto S.R. 1514. You are now in the community of Gragg. This flat area is also known locally as Cary's Flat. It is a

*"Keith" Blalock's grave in the Montezuma Cemetery*

spot from which you can look straight up into the face of Grandfather Mountain.

Stay on S.R. 1514 as it runs past a general store and New Hopewell Baptist Church—you will be heading straight toward the Grandfather. Said to be over 140 million years old, Grandfather Mountain dominates the landscape of the entire area. In 1794, it affected French botanist André Michaux so profoundly that he wrote, "Climbed to the summit of the highest mountain of all North America with my guide, and sang the Marseillaise Hymn, and cried, 'Long live America and the French Republic! Long live liberty!'" Many people who hike to the top of Grandfather today feel the same kind of exhilaration, though they no doubt express it in humbler terms.

A little over 1 mile past New Hopewell Baptist Church, you will come to a fork in the road. Stay on S.R. 1514, which goes to the left. Driving this route, you will see both Grandfather Mountain and the Linn Cove Viaduct, on the Blue Ridge Parkway, straight ahead. The mammoth, S-shaped Linn Cove Viaduct is one of the most complicated structures of its kind in the world. Its opening in 1987 completed the 470-mile Blue Ridge Parkway. For years, motorists had been forced to leave the parkway when they approached Grandfather Mountain and take a 14-mile detour. The delay in construction was caused by battles over rights of way and funding, as well as environmental concerns. After long years of hammering out a compromise, it took another four years and $10 million to complete the viaduct. But the wait was well worth it, because this section of the parkway is now proving to be one of the most popular.

Almost 5 miles past Gragg, you will see what remains of a rock quarry just below the viaduct; 0.5 mile later, you will come to N.C. 221. You have three options in completing the tour. You can turn left onto N.C. 221, go 0.4 mile to an intersection with the Blue Ridge Parkway, and head north on the parkway. A short drive will bring you to the viaduct and its incredible view. This route also takes you past Price Lake and the

*View of Grandfather Mountain
from Gragg*

Moses Cone Estate en route to Blowing Rock. For more information on these attractions, write the Blue Ridge Parkway office (see Appendix). If you exercise your second option by turning left and staying straight on N.C. 221, you will pass the entrance to Grandfather Mountain. There is an admission charge. The town of Linville is just a few miles past Grandfather's entrance on N.C. 221. Your third option is to turn right at the intersection of S.R. 1514 and N.C. 221 and follow N.C. 221 back to Blowing Rock.

*Yonahlossee Trail*

N.C. 221 has quite an interesting history of its own. The road serves as testimony to how far our techniques in building mountain roads have progressed in this century. Also known as the Yonahlossee Trail—which translates from the Cherokee as "trail of the black bear"—N.C. 221 looks like the surveyors must have been tracking a bear when they laid out its course. Built by Hugh MacRae in 1889, it was originally a toll road designed to open MacRae's isolated resort of Linville to visitors in the Blowing Rock area.

MacRae ordered one of the last coaches ever made by the Wells Fargo Company and used it to transport tourists from Blowing Rock to Linville. The coach was to be called Awahili, meaning eagle in Cherokee, but the imprinter misread the instructions and the coach came back with Awahili Cherokee printed on its door. The stage held up to eighteen people and made one trip a day, charging two dollars a head. MacRae also charged twenty-five cents for a two-horse wagon traveling his road and ten cents for a rider on horseback. The toll road operated until 1920, when it became a public road.

*View of the Linn Cove Viaduct and Grandfather Mountain*

Unlike the $24 million spent on the final 8 miles of the Blue Ridge Parkway, MacRae's road cost only $18,000 to build. Ironically, his is the route that served as the detour while all the controversy surrounding the building of the final stretch of the parkway was being resolved. The Yonahlossee Trail took two years to build, and more than three hundred men worked on it. The task was accomplished by bush crews, log crews, and shovel and mattock crews, in contrast to the

*Elliott Daingerfield's home, Westglow*

heavy machinery that built the parkway now running above the old road. Although it takes a lot longer than the scenic parkway, N.C. 221 may be your choice if you have already traveled the parkway and are looking for a change of scenery. If you choose a right turn off S.R. 1514, it is approximately 12 miles back to Blowing Rock along this route.

Near Blowing Rock on N.C. 221 is Westglow, one of the homes built by Elliott Daingerfield. This white Colonial mansion is the one that provided the background for his *Madonna of the Hills*. The two-story Grecian columns at the front of the house were imported from Italy. They were floated by river barge and hauled up the mountain by oxen. The stairwell and banister inside the house were designed by a French architect. The home was filled with antiques and oriental rugs. It was completed in 1917 for a reputed cost of twenty thousand dollars. With a glimpse of Daingerfield's summer home in Blowing Rock, you will have come full circle.

*The Globe*

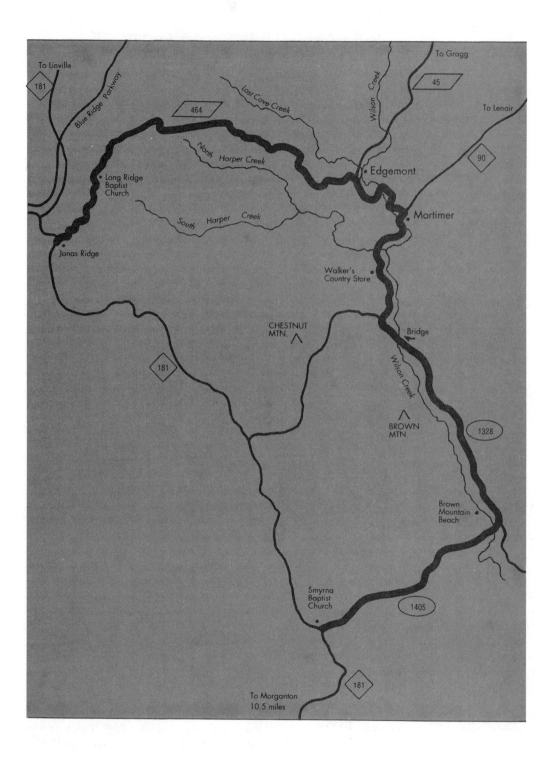

This tour travels along the foot of Brown Mountain, a ridge famous for the mysterious lights that have been spotted for generations. The tour also parallels scenic Wilson Creek, passes the virtual ghost town of Mortimer and the community of Edgemont, climbs through the proposed wilderness areas of Harper Creek and Lost Cove, and ends at the community of Jonas Ridge. Total mileage: approximately 26 miles.

▲▲▲▲▲▲▲▲▲▲▲▲▲▲▲▲▲▲▲▲▲▲▲▲▲▲▲▲▲▲▲▲▲▲▲ *The Brown Mountain Tour*

*Wilson Creek*

The tour begins 10.5 miles north of Morganton on N.C. 181. As you round a sharp curve, you will see the white clapboard Smyrna Baptist Church. Turn right onto S.R. 1405, following the signs to Brown Mountain Beach. Go 5 miles to S.R. 1328, turning left just past a bridge. There is a United States Forest Service sign indicating that the Mortimer Recreation Area is 8.5 miles away. Almost all the area covered in the rest of this tour is part of the Grandfather Ranger District of Pisgah National Forest.

Prior to 1750, this entire area was used primarily as an Indian summer hunting ground. Today, it is stocked with bear and wild turkey and is once again a prime hunting area. The region has a large deer herd, as well as plentiful squirrel and grouse. There are also several miles of streams that have been designated trophy, native, or general trout waters.

Approximately 1 mile from where you turned off S.R. 1405, you will see Brown Mountain Beach on the left. The unusual rock buildings visible from the road serve as clues that this campground was in operation long before modern, full-hookup facilities came into being. The creek running alongside the campground is Wilson Creek. In 1916, the entire area was devastated by a major flood. That July, torrential rains fell for thirty-six hours. The Catawba River, fed by Wilson Creek, was said to have risen forty-five feet. Because one of the main industries of the region was the clearing of timber, the heavy rains falling on the recently deforested hills caused landslides along Wilson Creek. The natural dams created by the landslides didn't last long, and their demise sent a violent rush of water deeper into the valley. Along with the water went buildings, bridges, railroad trestles, lumber, and huge boulders. A great deal of the debris landed at the present site of Brown Mountain Beach.

A summer resort was constructed on the land scooped out by the disastrous flood. It has been a camping and recreation spot since the 1920s. Today, Brown Mountain Beach is a modern facility that rents both campsites and cottages. A small dam protects a sandy beach and a swimming area. Traveling past, you may be able to see the huge boulders that line the campground's drives. They are remnants of the 1916 flood.

Past the campground on S.R. 1328, you will enter Pisgah National Forest. This is where the paved part of the tour ends. For the next 4.5 miles, you will be traveling along a gravel road with occasional cliffs on one side and Wilson Creek's gorge on the other. There are designated parking areas all along the route. This part of the tour is a popular summer hangout for people from the surrounding counties because of its numerous natural swimming holes. It might be advisable to drive this part of the tour early in the morning, before the sunbathing, beer-drinking crowds arrive. Most of the designated parking areas have trails that lead down to the rocky creek. Some have steps or railings, but most of the paths are still treacherous. You will probably notice a great many fishermen, swimmers, and sunbathers along this part of the route.

You are also traveling parallel to the ridge

*Brown Mountain Beach*
*after the 1940 flood*

known as Brown Mountain, the supposed location of the renowned Brown Mountain Lights. Ask anyone who lives in the area about the lights and they will probably have a story to tell. Most will probably claim to have seen them. The only problem is that no two people seem to describe the same thing. Some say the lights are red at first, then change colors before they fade to pale blue. Some say they are white, while others say they are like big, shining stars. Some say they appear in groups of three, each light ascending, hovering for a brief period, and then vanishing. Despite the variations in description, there doesn't seem to be much doubt that there are lights on or near the mountain, the cause of which has yet to be explained.

In 1771, Gerard de Brahm, a German engineer and the first white man to explore the region, recorded his account of the lights. He wrote that "the mountain emits nitrous vapors, which are borne by the wind, and when the laden winds meet each other the nitre inflames, sulphurates, and deteriorates. This causes the lights to inflame." If Gerard de Brahm's version sounds a bit far-fetched, rest assured that it's no worse than some of the later theories.

The Reverend C. E. Gregory of New York is credited in some sources as being the first to bring the lights to the world's attention. In 1910, he built a cottage south of the mountain and soon told all his friends about the mysterious lights that he could see from his home. By October 1913, popular interest had grown so strong that the United States Geological Survey sent D. B. Sarrette to make a study of the lights. Sarrette quickly concluded that they were simply the headlights of locomotives on the railway in the Catawba Valley below. Although many old-timers claimed that the lights had been seen since Civil War times—before the railroad was built—Sarrette's theory was accepted by most of the educated public. Then came the flood of 1916, wiping out all railroad transportation that summer. No one could explain why the lights continued to make their appearance in the absence of railroad activity.

During the next few years, numerous individuals conducted independent studies, each emerging with a different conclusion. The theories attributed the lights to will-o'-the-wisp, foxfire, St. Elmo's fire, Andes lights, and even radium emanations. In 1922, the United States Geological Survey tried again. The new investigator, George Rogers Mansfield, took his assignment very seriously. The first thing he did was set about refuting the theories advanced by the independent investigators. Then, armed with a battery of surveying instruments, cameras, and topographical maps of the region, he spent two weeks observing the lights and mapping their approximate origin. He reported that of the twenty-three lights he observed, seven were caused by locomotive headlights, since their time and location coincided with those of passing trains; ten by automobile headlights; two or three by stationary lights in towns; and the remainder by brush fires.

*Mansfield investigation*

The 1916 flood may have washed out the railroad and temporarily eliminated it as a possible cause of the lights, but Mansfield dismissed that as an irrelevant point, since the lights witnessed during the period following the flood were probably caused by automobiles. The fact that there was very little automobile travel in the area before the flood didn't seem to sway him. Though his findings may have accounted for some of the sightings, there were still a great many that he did not explain. And Mansfield still hadn't answered the question of why the lights only appeared in one particular location. He did concede that although the lights originated from artificial sources, "they were given a supernatural aspect by reason of the particular and unique atmospheric conditions in the area."

There is no shortage of legendary explanations for the lights, either.

*Legends of the
Brown Mountain Lights*

According to Cherokee legend, the lights existed as far back as the year 1200, when the Cherokee and Catawba Indians fought atop Brown Mountain. The Cherokee version attributes the lights to the widows of the fallen braves, widows who are still searching for their lost husbands today.

Lafayette Wiseman, a Civil War veteran who served under Robert E. Lee, is credited with transmitting the tale that the lights were the ghost of an old slave searching for his low-country master, who had disappeared in the mountains while on a hunting expedition. Wiseman's great-nephew Scotty grew up to become a popular star at the Grand Ole Opry, and he used the story to write the "Legend of the Brown Mountain Lights." Recorded by country-music star Tommy Faile, the song became a popular ballad in the early 1960s.

*The legend of Belinda*

One favorite is the story of Belinda, as recorded by famous folklore collector Frank C. Brown. According to the legend, a man named Jim was the husband of Belinda and the father of her child. He had, however, been seeing another woman, named Susie. When Belinda and her child mysteriously disappeared one day, many local people suspected foul play but couldn't refute Jim's claim that Belinda had just "put on her old bonnet and left the other day and she hasn't come back yet."

Soon after Belinda's disappearance, the mysterious lights began. Some area residents finally decided to follow them to their source. They were led to a cliff, where they discovered what appeared to be the bodies of Belinda and her child. One witness to the discovery was the narrator of the version recorded by Frank C. Brown. That narrator remarked, "You know folks say the skulls of murdered people never decay, and I have heard all my life that if you ever took the skull of a murdered person and got it over the head of the person who murdered the one who was murdered, and asked them about it they couldn't tell a lie; they would have to tell the truth."

Jim was put to the test. He supposedly turned white as a sheet and began to tremble, but he wouldn't admit to murdering his wife and child. From then on, things went downhill for Jim. He began to lose his mind, constantly beating at the air and screaming for Belinda to "get away." He died a short time later, but it is said that Belinda's soul still roams the ridge in the form of the mysterious Brown Mountain Lights.

Perhaps the moral to be gleaned from all these versions—whether grounded in science or folklore—is that the cause of the lights doesn't really matter. Most people like to conjure up visions of spirits and ghosts when they are sitting alone on a darkened mountain, anyway. Perhaps the more versions, the deeper and better the legend.

Shortly after passing Brown Mountain, you will cross the Wilson Creek bridge and come to a fork in the road. Proceed to the right on S.R. 1328, following the signs for the town of Mortimer and Walker's Country Store. Walker's will be on your left. A visit with Arnold Walker will reveal a great deal about the history of this area. The valley where his store is located was once the community of Hut Burrow, but the flood ended that town's existence, as it did so many others. After traveling 3.5 miles past the Wilson Creek bridge, you will begin to see the remains of the once-bustling community of Mortimer.

*Walker's Country Store*

"Mortimer sprung up almost in a night and has flourished like the green bay tree. There are more than 100 houses in the place and some of them are as pretty as a fellow would find in a day's journey. I cannot imagine a better location for a little town than the one on which Mortimer is built." So wrote an admirer in 1905. In 1904, the Ritter Lumber Company had bought area land for its timber and developed the town of Mortimer to process lumber. In addition to buildings for its lumber operation, Ritter constructed a company store, a blacksmith's shop, a church, a school, a hotel, and numerous houses. With the arrival of the Carolina and Northwestern Railroad in September 1905, there was even a depot.

*Mortimer*

Some reports suggest that as many as eight hundred people were employed by Ritter and that the company had five engines bringing logs from the mountainside to the mill in the village. Things were becoming so civilized that by 1906 Mortimer had two churches, a motion-picture facility, and the Laurel Inn, which attracted visitors for weekend stays. Teddy Roosevelt himself reportedly visited Mortimer and danced with Mrs. Bill Mortimer in the ballroom of the Laurel Inn. The Carolina and Northwestern added passenger service by 1910, bringing as many as thirty passengers a day.

*Flood of 1916*

But disaster struck with the flood of July 1916. Much of the lumber company's operation was destroyed, along with many homes. Though more than ten million feet of lumber remained, most of it was badly damaged. Ritter Lumber Company supplied the manpower that restored the rail service so vital to its operation, and the trains were running again as soon as August 29. Unfortunately, most of the virgin timber had already been cut, so Ritter began to slow its operation, staying only long enough to process the lumber on hand.

It appeared Mortimer was doomed, but the erection of a cotton mill about a mile below the village in 1922 made it a thriving community once again. The revitalization was short lived. A fall in demand for the coarse yarn produced by the mill led its owners to close up shop in 1928.

Another burst of activity came in 1933, when the Civilian Conservation Corps (CCC) built a camp for three hundred men engaged in constructing trails and roads and repairing many of the buildings in the village. In 1934, the old mill was reopened for the production of hosiery. The owner, O. P. Lutz, imported German-made machinery and even hired German technicians to run some of it, but his enterprise never really got off the ground. By 1938, the railroad closed. The final blow came in 1940 with a second devastating flood.

*Lutz's hosiery mill*

*Flood of 1940*

The 1940 flood was caused by a hurricane that poured three days of rain on the area from August 12–14. Highway officials estimated that 90 percent of the bridges in Caldwell County were washed away. Wilson Creek reportedly reached a record flood stage of ninety-four feet.

Few buildings in Mortimer survived, though the CCC camp somehow managed to escape destruction. The men of the camp stayed on through the early 1940s. One of their tasks was to take up the railroad tracks, which were reportedly shipped off for use in making war materials. The old railroad bed is now the road on which you are traveling.

Approaching Mortimer on S.R. 1328, you will see the remains of the hosiery mill stretching for about 0.1 mile on your right—eerily overgrown, but still impressive in its size. Before crossing the small bridge, you can see the hill where the Laurel Inn used to stand. The hill, on the left, overlooks the creek. The inn collapsed from neglect, but there is still evidence of where it stood. The village of Mortimer has been replaced by small cabins and trailers leased by fishermen and campers from the heirs of hosier O. P. Lutz.

On the left just past the congested area of cabins and trailers is what remains of a bridge abutment. Mortimer's old school used to stand near this location, but it was burned as a precaution after it was used to house patients during a smallpox epidemic. The old depot once stood in the field near the present general store, but it was moved to greener pastures as an exhibit at Frontier Village in Kentucky.

The only two buildings that survived the 1940 flood are, on your right, the general store, and across the road, the white ranger station built by the United States Forest Service—the structure seems to be guarding the entrance to the campground area. The three different signs hanging on the outside of the building serve as evidence that the store has undergone numerous name changes. Today, at least, it is called the Sipes Store, and it continues to serve the area.

At the Sipes Store, turn left onto N.C. 90, pass the Mortimer Recreation Area and its camping facilities, and head up the mountain to Edgemont. Because Edgemont escaped the brunt of the floods that hit Mortimer, there is greater evidence of past prosperity here. On the left 2 miles past Mortimer, you may see a big white building with green shutters almost completely hidden by large evergreens. Closer to the roadside is a small white building that is a bit more visible. The larger of the two is the old Edgemont railroad depot. It has

*Old Edgemont railroad depot*
*(now a private residence)*

*Edgemont Hotel*

*Edgemont Baptist Church*

been restored and now serves as a private residence. The smaller building, once the baggage house, is now a guesthouse. Since Edgemont was the end of the railway line coming up from Chester, South Carolina, it also became the rendezvous point for the hired carriages and wagons sent down from resorts in Linville and Blowing Rock to transport tourists. During the week of the Fourth of July, there were even special excursion trains running from South Carolina.

Edgemont turned into something of a resort area itself with the opening of a large hotel known as the Edgemont Hotel or the Rainbow Lodge. As you continue on N.C. 90, you will cross a creek just past the old depot. Turn right at the sign directing you to Edgemont Baptist Church; you will soon see the picturesque white church built in 1916 sitting atop a small hill. Turn right again just before reaching the church to see the Edgemont Hotel. The former grandeur of the old lodge can easily be envisioned, though it appears neglect will soon claim another victim. In the hotel's glory days, there were even cabins for Camp Rainbow, a summer camp for girls run by the Order of the Eastern Star. The camp was located in the large field in front of the hotel.

If you return to N.C. 90 and turn right, you will soon approach Coffey's General Store, the focal point of what remains of the village of Edgemont. The store is well worth a stop. It seems to have changed little since it was built in the early 1900s. Unlike many of the "restored" general stores that are cropping up for tourists in the mountains, Coffey's is the real McCoy. The store was originally located on the other side of the creek, but when the flood of 1916 changed the creek's course and necessitated the relocation of the road, the store's owner decided to move it to the side where it now stands. The store was actually placed up the road several hundred yards from its present location, but the floodwaters of 1940 moved it a second time. As Archie Coffey, who ran the store and the Edgemont post office for over forty years, put it in a 1977 newspaper interview, the flood "picked up this store building and washed it up against a big tree. I didn't lose but about five or six cans off the shelves, but I never did get it level again. That's why the floor is buckled." Buckled floor or not, the store still stands. Coffey's, like the Sipes Store in Mortimer and Walker's Country Store earlier in the tour, is a working store that still serves its community. All three are recommended stops for travelers to sit a spell and ask questions about the history of the area. Both the Sipes Store and Coffey's have old photographs showing the effects of the two major floods.

When you have seen Edgemont, turn around and drive back past the old depot. Just after the depot is F.R. 464. Turn right onto this "narrow winding road with turnouts," as the sign correctly describes it. The road is steeply graded as it travels through the proposed wilderness areas of Lost Cove and Harper Creek. The area abounds with intersecting hiking trails. Because they are in proposed wilderness areas, most of them are not obviously marked, so it is suggested that you purchase a United States Forest Service Wilson Creek Area Trail Map, a detailed topographical trail map that will prove vital if you decide to partake of the hiking facilities. You can write the district ranger for a copy (see Appendix for address), or you can purchase one at Coffey's General Store in Edgemont. Incidentally, you can purchase fishing licenses and hunting permits at Coffey's as well.

With the dramatic drops in altitude in the area, many of the twenty-five trails around Wilson Creek offer hikers stunning waterfalls. Some of the most impressive are the two-hundred-foot falls and cascades known as South Harper Creek Falls, the exceptionally beautiful North Harper Creek Falls, the three-tiered Hunt Fish Falls, and the several sets of scenic falls along Gragg Prong Creek. As you proceed up F.R. 464, you will see trailheads all along the road.

About 6 miles past Edgemont, the profile of Grandfather Mountain begins to break through the gaps in the forest on the right. If you look above the road to the left, you will also notice a sheer rock wall that is known as Little Lost

*Coffey's General Store in Edgemont*

*Harper Creek*

*Little Lost Cove Cliffs*

*Big Lost Cove Cliffs*

*Jonas Ridge*

Cove Cliffs. On the left is a trailhead for a hike up the cliffs. The elevation at the top of Little Lost Cove Cliffs is 3,400 feet, and there is an excellent view of the mountain range dominated by Grandfather.

It is 0.9 mile farther down F.R. 464 to a primitive campsite on the right. Just past the campsite, again on your right, is the trailhead for a hike leading to Big Lost Cove Cliffs. A prime vantage point on the Blue Ridge Parkway for viewing the Brown Mountain Lights is the Lost Cove Cliffs Overlook, which stares right into the face of these cliffs.

Past the trailhead for Big Lost Cove Cliffs, just around another curve on F.R. 464, you will see Long Ridge Baptist Church on the right. Turn left onto the dirt road directly across from the church. About 0.5 mile up that road is Pittman Gap Church. Turn left and go 2.1 miles to the Jonas Ridge post office, housed in a trailer on your left. The naming of the community of Jonas Ridge is an interesting bit of trivia. Its namesake, Jonas Braswell, did not own land, reside, or farm here. He did not even discover the place. His name has been stamped on this ridge because it was here that Jonas Braswell froze to death. Caught in a snowstorm while on a camping trip in the 1800s, Jonas became ill and was forced to spend the night camped under a rock on a high ridge. The next day, he was carried to a nearby house, but he was too far gone to be saved. The evolution of the name from Jonas's Ridge to Jonas Ridge was a slow but logical one.

Now that you have reached "Jonas's" Ridge, you have also concluded the tour. You are at the intersection with N.C. 181. An intersection with the Blue Ridge Parkway is a few miles to your right. A left turn will take you down N.C. 181 to Morganton.

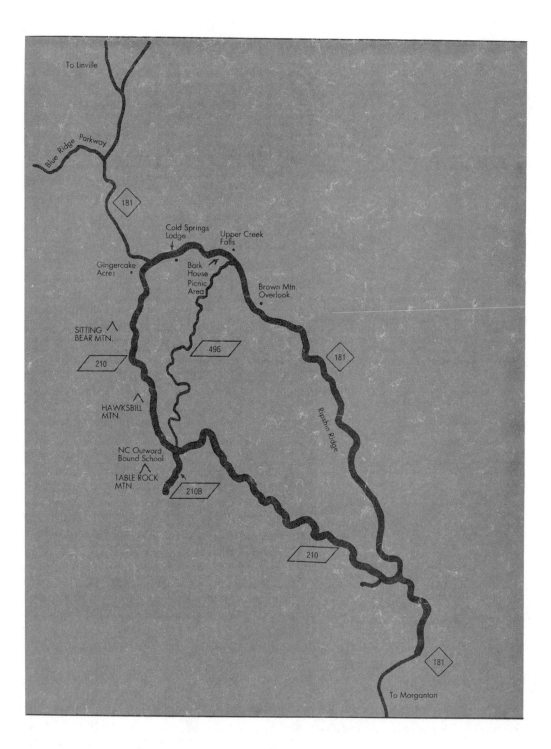

This tour travels into the heart of the Linville Gorge Wilderness Area. At points, it parallels the ridge that features Table Rock and Hawksbill mountains, both prominent peaks. The tour then turns onto a United States Forest Service road that travels past Hawksbill and to the top of Table Rock. There are several recommended short hikes on trails with moderate grades, but this tour also allows you to enjoy an abundance of remarkable scenery without ever leaving your car. Total mileage: approximately 50 miles.

# ▲▲▲▲▲▲▲▲▲▲▲▲▲▲▲▲▲▲▲▲▲▲▲▲▲▲*The Table Rock Tour*

*Table Rock*

The tour begins by heading west out of Morganton on N.C. 181. The highway roughly parallels a toll road built by Anderson Loven in 1889. Called the Turnpike Road by locals, it ran from Joy, a small community outside Morganton, to the community of Pineola, at the top of the ridge. Building the road through native rock was no small feat, and Loven soon learned to pour boiling water over the rocks to crack them and make them easier to move. He did such a good job of road building that his toll road existed until 1927.

Traveling up N.C. 181, you will be aware of two uniquely shaped peaks dominating the landscape. When the ascent begins to level off, you will be on Ripshin Ridge. You will also see Table Rock and Hawksbill mountains so close on the left that you will feel as if you could reach out and touch them. The areas on both sides of N.C. 181 and Ripshin Ridge are part of Pisgah National Forest. The forest is divided into four ranger districts—this tour travels through the Grandfather District. Between Ripshin Ridge and the ridge that includes Table Rock and Hawksbill is

*Linville Gorge*
Photo by Clay Nolen
Courtesy of N.C. Division of Travel & Tourism

*Jules Verne's*
*Great Eyrie*

the deep river valley called Linville Gorge. The Linville River and the 10,975 acres that make up the gorge have been declared a wilderness area. Wilderness status carries with it regulations concerning road building and tree cutting, among other things, and it should insure that this tour remains a backroad for some time to come.

The Linville River descends 2,000 feet in a 14-mile stretch. The whole gorge abounds in plant and animal life. There are five species of rare plants, four species of rhododendron, and even virgin forests tucked in the rugged coves. Deer, bears, squirrels, raccoons, hawks, and owls, as well as copperheads and timber rattlers, can all be found in the forest.

Travelers in the area have long recorded their impressions, most of them focusing on the magnificence of Table Rock and Hawksbill. One such visitor was French novelist Jules Verne, who found Table Rock so memorable that he made it the setting for mysterious happenings in his novel *The Master of the World*. Published in 1904, one year before Verne's own death, the novel opens with a description of a place called Great Eyrie, but there is little doubt that Verne was actually writing of Table Rock: "There, deep amid the Blueridge [*sic*] Mountains rises the crest called the Great Eyrie. Its huge rounded form is distinctly seen from the little town of Morganton on the Catawba River. . . . It rises rocky and grim and inaccessible, and under certain atmospheric conditions has a peculiarly blue and distant effect." Though there are no dastardly deeds going on inside Table Rock like there were in Verne's Great Eyrie, traveling alongside the mountain certainly gives you an idea of why he found it the perfect vehicle for his plot.

Another visitor, Charles Lanman, toured the area on horseback in 1849. He was more impressed with Hawksbill than with Table Rock. In his *Letters from the Alleghany Mountains*, Lanman wrote, "The prominent pictorial feature of the North Cove is of a mountain called the Hawk's Bill, on account of its resemblance to the beak of a mammoth bird, the length of the bill being about fifteen hundred feet. It is visible from nearly every part of the valley, and to my fancy is a more

*Upper Creek Falls*

*The Bark House*

picturesque object than the Table Mountain, which is too regular at the sides and top to satisfy the eye. The table part of this mountain, however, is twenty-five hundred feet high, and therefore worthy of its fame." Actually, Table Rock measures 3,909 feet and Hawksbill 4,020. After the tour, you can select your own personal preference.

Approximately 18 miles from Morganton, you will see an overlook on the right, one of the recommended vantage points for the Brown Mountain Lights. (A detailed discussion of the mysterious lights is in the Brown Mountain Tour.) Looking into the valley, Brown Mountain is the ridge to the right.

Just past the overlook, again on the right, is a sign designating Upper Creek and Greentown trails. Both are good hiking trails, but they do not offer short hikes. The Grandfather District has 200 miles of trails, most of them unmarked. The trails are usually obvious, but a United States Forest Service topographical map is recommended to help solve dilemmas when they arise.

About 0.5 mile farther on N.C. 181 is the Bark House Picnic Area, on the left. This picnic area, sheltered by trees and rhododendron, has an interesting history of its own. The name Bark House lingers from a home that stood for many years on the opposite side of what is now N.C. 181. The house was built by the same Anderson Loven of toll-road fame for a rich New Yorker named Kirkby. Legend has it that Kirkby decked his place out with the best of furniture, silver, linens, and crystal, all for the benefit of his English bride. Upon being brought to the Bark House—so named because it was weatherboarded with bark—Mrs. Kirkby was not duly impressed with either the surrounding scenery or the isolation. The house was deeded to her mother in New York, but it was inhabited solely by caretakers until it and a hundred acres of surrounding land were sold to the United States Forest Service. The house was torn down, but the name somehow found its way to this scenic picnic ground.

As you drive N.C. 181 near the Bark House Picnic Area, you must negotiate a series of steeply banked curves. The mountain you are circling is Winding Stair Knob. Believe it or not, N.C. 181 was completely closed for several years while the road was "straightened" to its present form. There can be little doubt about how the mountain received its name.

The land around Winding Stair Knob and the Bark House Picnic Area was also the scene of a Civil War skirmish that left local people calling the area Kirk's Battle Ground. There were both Union and Confederate supporters in the mountains of North Carolina, a state of affairs that led to frequent dissension. In 1864, eastern Tennessee was captured by Union forces under Captain George Kirk, who proceeded to conduct raids throughout Tennessee and western North Carolina. On June 29, Kirk made one of his most daring moves with a raid on Camp Vance, located near Morganton. Approximately 130 of his men marched into the camp under a flag of truce and tricked the lieutenant in charge into surrendering. Kirk's men immediately violated the terms of the agreement by burning every building except the hospital, whose kinder fate was attributed to the "blarney and ingenious persuasion" of the camp's surgeons. Some 279 prisoners were supposedly taken, including 240 unarmed and unorganized junior reserves.

After stripping the camp, Kirk and his men retreated up the mountain. The Burke County Home Guard, in hot pursuit, caught up with them at Winding Stair Knob. According to one source, Kirk left only twenty-five men—including twelve Cherokee Indians—to engage the Confederates, since the Union position was so strong. The Burke County Home Guard had to march straight up the narrow road into a dense fog. They were strung out for 1 mile or more down the mountain, with no space to form except in the road. Kirk's men fired on the advance guard, killing William Waightstill Avery, one of Burke County's leading citizens. When the home guard retired, Kirk retreated into eastern Tennessee. Some local people say that for many years bullets from the skirmish could be found lodged in the surrounding trees. Whether the action at Camp Vance constituted a strategic Union victory depends entirely on which

*Kirk's Battle Ground*

*Mountain Laurel*

*Upper Creek Falls*

*The Loven Hotel
(now a private residence)*

*Sitting Bear Rock*

side you believe.

Continuing 1.3 miles up N.C. 181, you will see a sign directing you to the Upper Creek Parking Area, from which you can take a moderately difficult trail to Upper Creek Falls. The round-trip distance is 1.6 miles and the estimated hiking time one hour. The trail crosses the creek and ascends to the base of the falls. It is a nice side trip and might prove a welcome respite from traveling in the car. To find the unmarked trailhead, just walk to the edge of the parking area nearest the woods and follow the sound of rushing water. You should see a well-trodden path.

At the crest of a ridge on N.C. 181 less than 1 mile past the Upper Creek Parking Area, you will notice a white building on the left. It stands where Anderson Loven built his lodge at the height of his toll-road business. Even after the days of the toll road, the Loven Hotel remained successful as a summer resort and a bear-hunter's paradise. It passed through several owners and a name change—Cold Springs Lodge—before fire destroyed it in 1950. A new building was erected and attempts were made to run it as a lodge, but that structure was eventually turned into the private residence you see today.

On the left 0.3 mile past the site of the former lodge is the entrance to Gingercake Acres (Old Gingercake Road or S.R. 1264). There is also a sign directing you to the Table Rock Picnic Area. Turn left onto this road, which will take you through a residential area. At 0.3 mile, turn left at the first fork onto Gingercake Acres Road (S.R. 1265), which becomes F.R. 210 when the pavement ends. The rest of the tour will be on gravel roads.

It is 1.5 miles from the end of the paved portion of the road to the trailhead for Sitting Bear Trail. A hike of approximately thirty minutes will take you to Sitting Bear Rock. This strange formation consists of a huge boulder thirty-two feet long and about eight feet thick balanced precariously on a pyramid-shaped stone thirty feet high. It is called Sitting Bear Rock because of its resemblance to a bear on its haunches. Though the resemblance isn't perfect, you'll at least concede that it looks more like a bear than it does a slice of

*Sitting Bear Rock*

Culgee Watson

ginger cake. Early settlers in the area apparently thought differently, calling it Gingercake Rock. Gingercake Mountain was thus named for the singular pile of rock perched on its extreme summit. Charles Lanman wrote in 1849 that the "appearance of this rocky wonder is exceedingly tottleish, and though we may be assured that it has stood upon that eminence perhaps for a thousand years, yet it is impossible to tarry within its shadow without a feeling of insecurity." Lanman's observation still rings true.

Maybe one explanation for why the original name seems out of place is that the perceptions of the character credited with naming the rock were a bit distorted. That character was a hermit known as Culgee Watson who lived in the gap between Gingercake and Hawksbill mountains. Watson died in 1816 and is supposedly buried somewhere in the area. It is said that he moved to this isolated spot because of a disappointment in love. That would go a long way toward explaining his aversion to the female sex, an aversion so extreme that he burned the rail of any fence a female touched and covered with dirt any place a female sat. Watson was also well known in the area because he raised peacocks and used their feathers to trim his clothing. For some unknown reason, he called his suit covered with peacock feathers his "culgee," so he became known as Culgee Watson. You probably won't see any peacocks, but a hike to Sitting Bear Rock is definitely worth your time nonetheless.

It is an additional 1 mile on F.R. 210 to the trailhead for Hawksbill Mountain Trail. If you are in the mood for another hike, park you car, cross the road, and tackle the steep ascent of Lettered Rock Ridge. At 0.5 mile (after about fifteen minutes of hiking), you will come to a trail junction marked only by a post in the middle of the trail. The marker may be misleading, but if you look back over your left shoulder you will see the side trail you want ascending straight up the mountain. After 0.7 mile and another fifteen minutes or so, the side trail reaches the summit of Hawksbill. It is worth every step, because you are on top of the world, with a 360-degree view of the area that features Table Rock, Linville Gorge, Lake

James at the end of the gorge, and Grandfather Mountain on the opposite side. The round-trip hike will probably take around an hour, depending on how you take to climbing steep trails, but it is highly recommended.

A right turn off F.R. 210 about 2 miles past the parking area for Hawksbill Mountain Trail will take you to the Table Rock Picnic Area. You will be turning onto F.R. 210B. Before reaching the picnic area, you will pass a mildly confusing turn at the sign describing the North Carolina Outward Bound School. The camp is 0.5 mile to the right, but you should follow the sign to the Table Rock summit and parking lot, which are 2.5 miles ahead. The last mile is a steep climb up a poor road, but the view from Table Rock is well worth the effort. The parking area offers limited space. From it, you can see the beginning of a 1-mile trail described on a sign as "hazardous cliff, rocky trail" leading to the top of Table Rock. Hiking time to the summit is approximately thirty minutes.

The fact that the parking area is frequently filled on weekends also means that the number of hikers who can make the trek to the summit is limited. Hikers are often rewarded with rappelling demonstrations. The United States Army brings some of its soldiers to Linville Gorge for wilderness-training exercises. They and students from the North Carolina Outward Bound School often rappel down the sheer face of Table Rock. But even if you find no action on the rocks, the view is the perfect culmination of this tour.

You have a few options in returning to civilization. One course is to backtrack to the intersection of Old Gingercake Road (S.R. 1264) and N.C. 181; the Blue Ridge Parkway and the town of Linville are only a few miles to your left. Or you may choose to retrace the tour all the way back to Morganton, where you can pick up I-40. If you want to continue exploring new territory, you can make a circle back to Morganton by turning right at the intersection of F.R. 210B and F.R. 210. This route takes you 9 miles downhill over a gravel road. The drive takes approximately forty-five minutes. When you reach pavement, turn left. It is 0.3 mile to an intersection with N.C. 181 approximately 10 miles west of Morganton.

*The top of Hawksbill Mountain*

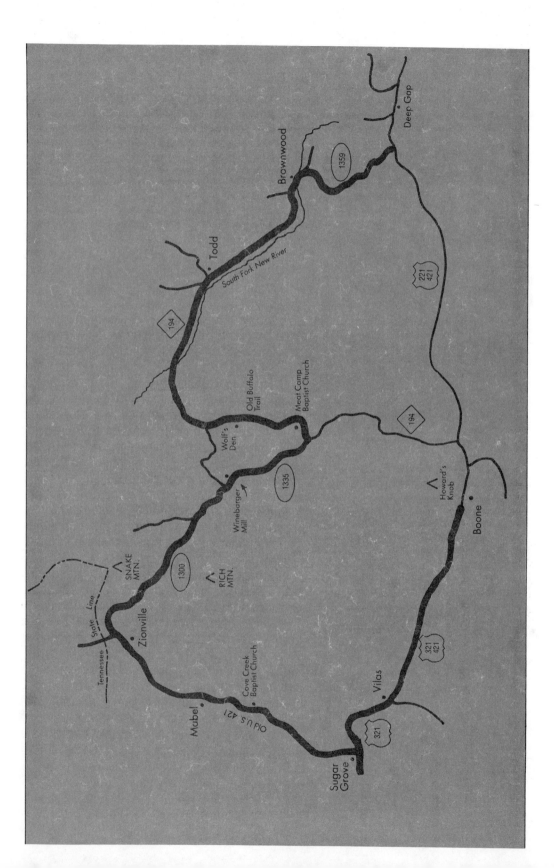

This tour follows the South Fork of the New River to the community of Todd. From there, it weaves along the ridges of a trail originally cut by herds of buffalo. It passes by the site of a Revolutionary War skirmish, by an old hunters' camp called Meat Camp, and through the Rich Mountain Gap to Zionville, near the Tennessee state line. It continues to Cove Creek before ending at the town of Boone. Total mileage: approximately 44 miles.

# ▲▲▲▲▲▲▲▲▲▲▲▲▲▲▲▲▲▲▲▲▲▲▲▲▲▲▲▲▲▲▲▲▲▲▲▲*The Old Buffalo Trail Tour*

*South Fork of the New River*

The tour starts on U.S. 421 near Deep Gap, approximately 6 miles east of Boone. At Brownwood Road (S.R. 1359), there is a large sign directing you to Todd's General Store, 8 miles up the road. Turn onto Brownwood Road and follow the creek through scenic farmland and rolling hills cleared for pasture. After 2 miles on Brownwood Road, you will come to a sign marking the boundary between Watauga and Ashe counties. The actual border is the South Fork of the New River, on your left. Follow the river through the scenic valley and drive over the bridge that crosses the New. At the stop sign, turn left, continuing to follow the signs to Todd's General Store. You will still be traveling alongside the New River as you come into the community of Todd.

In 1914, the Norfolk and Western Railroad decided to lay tracks from Abingdon, Virginia, to Todd, and the arrival of passenger, mail, and express trains made Todd a center of activity. All the interest in Todd centered around the timber business; the railroad was built to enable timber companies to export the area's lumber. At one point in its history, Todd boasted two hotels, nine stores, a bank, four doctors, a dentist, a druggist, a Masonic lodge, an Odd Fellows' hall, a post office, a mill, and even a rent-a-buggy service for hotel guests who wanted to venture into the community.

Entering present-day Todd, the first building you will see is a stately, white house on your left. Over a hundred years old, the building was once an elegant hotel. It is said that a huge turntable was built into the kitchen wall to allow the cooks to place food on a table and then rotate it into the dining room. That feature and a private power generator insured that guests were treated in fine style.

Across the road from the old hotel is Todd's General Store, established in 1914. Although the store now caters mainly to the tourist trade, it still manages to suggest the prosperity that its community once experienced.

Farther down the road on the left is the old railroad depot, next to the post office. Until the railroad was built, the town was known as Elkland or Elks Crossroads. It was the railroad company that changed the name to Todd, in honor of Captain J. W. Todd, an eminent lawyer and leading citizen of Ashe County. The sign on the depot today, however, still shows the old name of Elkland.

In 1933, the timber ran out, and the railroad pulled up its tracks and left, taking most of the area's businesses with it. Besides the depot, the only evidence left of the railroad is a restored caboose sitting next to the depot. The area in front of the depot is supposedly the place where three strong men using a turntable rotated the train each day for its 5:00 A.M. departure back to Virginia.

Thanks to John Preston Arthur's *History of Watauga County*, written in 1915, we have some interesting tales about Peggy Clawson, one of Todd's most colorful characters. There is no record of her husband's name. "Her evident inclination was to have him simply the 'husband' of Peggy Clawson," Arthur wrote. Domestic tranquility was apparently an unknown commodity

*Todd's General Store*

Peggy Clawson

in the Clawson household. As Arthur delicately put it, "Tradition says, in a most friendly spirit, that they occasionally 'fell out and kissed again with tears.'" Arthur also related that Peggy was excommunicated from Three Forks Baptist Church in July 1832 for "beating her son." But the following October, she "made open acknowledgment for her transgression and was restored to full membership."

Personal life aside, Peggy left her mark on regional folklore for an incident that occurred while she was in the woods making maple sugar (some sources say she was gathering ginseng) on a cliff overlooking the New. Arthur wrote that "a dog chased a bear into the river, and [Peggy] got into the canoe tied near by, poled out to the bear swimming in a deep hole at the base of the cliff, and drowned it by holding its head under the water with the canoe pole. After this exploit, it being Saturday, she walked down to the Old Fields Baptist Church in time for morning service." This was definitely a woman who could take care of herself, and she left such an impression that the story is still told in the vicinity.

Leaving Todd, the road ends at the stop sign at N.C. 194. Turn left, heading south. Approximately 5.2 miles down the road, immediately after you crest a hill, you will see an abandoned farmhouse and barn on your right. In the woods behind the farmhouse is a rock cave known as Wolf's Den. Though Wolf's Den is overgrown by the encroaching forest today, people who grew up in the area can still remember playing inside the large cave.

During the late 1700s, members of the Lewis family were well-known local wolf hunters. At that time, the county was paying $2.50 for each wolf scalp brought in by bounty hunters. Since a scalp from a cub brought the same bounty as that from a mature wolf, the Lewises followed the same female to her lair each year, took her six to ten cubs, and allowed her to escape. When asked why he never killed the mother wolf, Gideon Lewis answered, "Would you expect a man to kill his milch-cow?" Because the cave inhabited by their favorite female wolf proved so lucrative for the Lewis family, it became known as Wolf's Den.

*Abandoned farmhouse near Wolf's Den*

The site is also that of the only military engagement during the Revolutionary War that took place within present-day Watauga County. The Patriots, or Whigs, were the revolutionaries of their time, of course, while the Loyalists, or Tories, were the conservatives or traditionalists. The Patriots of the area around Wolf's Den had already organized their own militia to fight the British by the time actual fighting broke out. Between 1770 and 1780, there were also a number of British sympathizers living in the mountains who secretly organized their own Tory militia. Small-scale skirmishes between mountain people who were longtime neighbors were the result.

One of the earliest Patriot militia groups was led by Colonel Benjamin Cleveland, a man who was preceded by his reputation. Before the Revolutionary War broke out, the local militia spent most of its time defending frontier settlements against Indian attacks. On one foray into Indian country, Cleveland and his men had been attacked and robbed of their horses and most of their belongings. Unlike most men in similar situations, Cleveland possessed the fortitude to return to the scene of the attack, where he regained his possessions and even managed to wangle an apology from one of the Cherokee chiefs.

A strong performance at the battle of Kings Mountain followed. Cleveland then turned his attention to Tory activity in the mountains. Historian Lyman Draper wrote that "Colonel Cleveland was active at this period in sending out strong scouting parties to scour the mountain regions, and, if possible, utterly break up the Tory bands still infesting the frontiers."

Cleveland had also established a reputation for being inhumanly cruel. One legendary punishment came after Cleveland captured two men described as "Tory horse-thieves." He hanged the first man without any semblance of a trial. He then turned to the second and offered him the kinder fate of cutting off his own ears. The second man chose self-mutilation over hanging, and the legend of Cleveland's cruelty grew.

In April 1781, when local Tory leaders learned that the infamous Colonel Cleveland was in Ashe County visiting his New River farmlands, they

*Benjamin Cleveland*

could not resist the temptation to capture him and take him to South Carolina, where they knew the British would pay a handsome reward.

Led by Captain William Riddle, the Tory group caught up with Cleveland at the Perkins farm. They stole his horses and set up an ambush, knowing he would follow. Draper described the scene: "Cleveland from his great weight—fully three hundred pounds knew he could not run any great distance, and only be too prominent a mark for Tory bullets, dodged into the house with several Tories at his heels." When one of the attackers seemed to find the thought of killing Cleveland on the spot more enticing than the promise of a future reward, the resourceful Cleveland "instantly seized Abigail Walters, who was present, and by dint of his great strength, and under a high state of excitement, dextrously [*sic*] handled her as a puppet, keeping her between him and his would be assassin." At that point, Captain Riddle intervened and assured Cleveland that he would not be harmed if he surrendered peacefully.

After traveling up the New River with their captive, Riddle and his men decided to camp for the night at Wolf's Den. According to Draper, the next morning found Cleveland "sitting on a large fallen tree, engaged, under compulsion, in writing passes for the several members of Captain Riddle's party, certifying that each was a good Whig to be used, when in a tight place." Cleveland harbored a strong suspicion that his usefulness would run out as soon as all the passes were written, so "naturally but a poor penman, he purposely retarded his task as much as possible, hoping to gain time for the expected relief, apologizing for his blunders." His stall tactics worked—his rescue party was soon at hand. When "the Whigs rushed up, yelling their loudest yells, Colonel Cleveland, comprehending the situation, tumbled off the prostrate tree, on the side opposite to his friends, lest their balls might accidentally hit him."

Riddle and his men fled, and Cleveland was saved. Some sources say that Cleveland eventually caught up with Riddle and hanged him on the famous "hanging oak" that still stands in

*Meat Camp Baptist Church*

Wilkes County. The mountain where Wolf's Den is located is called Riddle's Knob to this day, while the creek flowing past is still known as Riddle's Fork.

Cleveland went on to lose his North Carolina lands and move to South Carolina. He apparently ballooned to 450 pounds and died at age sixty-nine while sitting at his breakfast table.

Leaving Wolf's Den, travel downhill for 2 miles on N.C. 194. On the left, you will see a marker stating that this is the location of the Old Buffalo Trail of Watauga County. There is evidence that hundreds of years before the arrival of Columbus, large herds of buffalo roamed east of the Mississippi. The herds supposedly wintered on the Atlantic coast and migrated westward across the Appalachians for the summer. Some of the buffalo passed through Watauga County and left distinctive trails that can still be seen today.

Relics found along the Old Buffalo Trail attest to the fact that Indians hunting in the vicinity also used the well-defined trail. As white settlers moved closer to the area, groups of men known as long hunters came into the mountains to hunt for extended periods. We know that they used the Old Buffalo Trail because there are records of a camp—Meat Camp—erected in the area before the Revolutionary War.

Meat Camp supposedly derived its name from its status as a primitive packing house. Hunters stored their dressed animal carcasses there until they were ready to return to their homes in the lowlands. The location became so well known that the community is still known as Meat Camp.

Between 1790 and 1800, the main road from the Yadkin River Valley near Wilkesboro to Taylorsville, Tennessee, followed the Old Buffalo Trail. Buffalo tended to avoid the swamps and the laurel thickets that grew along the creeks, usually following the mountain ridges instead. They often laid out steep grades on dry land. When the road to Tennessee was plotted, such grades were avoided. Where the buffalo had established a good trail along the crests and sides of the mountains, the road followed exactly the same course.

As you journey on N.C. 194, you will see Meat Camp Baptist Church on a hill on your right 1.1

miles past the Old Buffalo Trail marker. The church was organized in 1851, and it and the service station 0.4 mile farther down the road serve as the center of the Meat Camp community today.

At the service station, you will see S.R. 1335 to the right. Turn right and follow Meat Camp Creek for 1.8 miles. Through the trees on your right, you will see what appears to be a group of abandoned buildings. There is a gravel road to the right that leads to the largest building, an old gristmill built by Jacob Winebarger in 1873. On the mill is a sign that instructs interested parties to see the miller in the white house on the hill behind the building. The mill is functional, and the present Mr. Winebarger still grinds corn on occasion. At one time, similar mills were all over the mountain region, but this is the only one still operating in Watauga County.

You have two choices at this point in the tour. You can return to S.R. 1335, turn left, and drive back to the Meat Camp service station; at the intersection with N.C. 194, you can then turn right and continue a few miles into Boone to complete the tour.

On the other hand, if you are an adventuresome sort and don't mind riding over a bumpy, little-used gravel road, you can turn right onto S.R. 1335 when you leave the Winebarger Mill. After 1.7 miles of paved road, you will see the Meat Camp Assembly of God Church on your left and a Methodist church on your right. Across from the Methodist church is a gravel road marked S.R. 1300. Turn left and begin your ascent to Rich Mountain Gap. For the next 4.8 miles, you will be traveling on a very bumpy, steeply graded road. The drive can be undertaken without a four-wheel-drive vehicle, but you might feel uncomfortable in a new Cadillac.

It's 1.7 miles to the top of the ridge. You will probably begin to think you are following a herd of buffalo—a breed not known for its general intelligence—but the view from the top of the gap is incredible. On the right is Snake Mountain, with an elevation of 5,574 feet. On the left is Rich Mountain, standing 5,372 feet. Both are void of large trees, due largely to the fact that they have

*Winebarger Mill*

*Rich Mountain Gap*

been used as pasture for cattle for decades. The ridges now resemble natural balds and boast beautiful stands of rhododendron and laurel in late June.

It may be hard to believe, but this road was used as a turnpike for travelers crossing the mountains into Tennessee as late as 1902. Thanks to the prosperity of Boone, the main road comes up from that town today.

After crossing the crest, you will be headed straight downhill for the 3.3 miles until you hit U.S. 421. At the junction, a huge billboard announces your arrival in the state of Tennessee, on your right. Across the road is Zionville Baptist Church, which can be reached by turning right onto U.S. 421 and then making an immediate left onto Old 421 (as it is identified on the road signs) for the short distance into Zionville.

In Zionville, the Daughters of the American Revolution (DAR) erected one of a series of monuments marking the trail Daniel Boone followed in the 1700s when he cut across the mountains on his way to the fabled land of Kentucky. It is 0.2 mile from the church on Old 421 to an abandoned store, on the left. Turn left onto S.R. 1302, which runs beside the store. The marker is on a hill behind the store, in the front yard of a brick house.

Continue on Old 421 through the communities of Mabel and Mast. It is 5.8 miles from Zionville to the community of Amantha. The road curves around Henson's Chapel Methodist Church, organized in 1858. The present building was erected in 1926.

It is only 0.8 mile farther to the Cove Creek Baptist Church, formed in 1799. It is 0.6 mile to the Western Watauga Community Center, on the right. Ahead, you can see the stone Cove Creek School, built by Work Projects Administration laborers in 1937. Between the community center and the school, on the right, is a stone monument, another of the DAR markers set out to designate Daniel Boone's trail, which you have been following since Zionville.

The Cove Creek marker, however, is different

## Zionville

## Cove Creek

*Marker designating the Old Buffalo Trail and Daniel Boone's trail*

Benjamin Howard

from the other DAR markers. It shows Daniel sitting down with his gun. His dog is nearby. Below Daniel's plaque is a plaque of a buffalo. The DAR apparently realized that the Old Buffalo Trail and Boone's trail intersected. Unfortunately, whoever installed the markers in 1913 put the marker that should be in Zionville at the Cove Creek location. All things considered, it doesn't really matter, since you can still have your photograph made in front of the monument no matter where it is.

It is almost 2 miles past the school to the center of Cove Creek. The names on the buildings may lead to some confusion. The Cove Creek Volunteer Fire Department is near the Sugar Grove post office. The explanation is that the first post office for Cove Creek was located in an area known locally as Sugar Grove because of its sugar maples. The Sugar Grove post office thus became a permanent part of the Cove Creek community.

Turn left onto U.S. 321. It is 1.2 miles to an intersection with U.S. 421. Turn right. As you travel the 6-mile segment into Boone, you will begin to see Howard's Knob on the left. At 4,451 feet, the mountain towers above Boone. Its name comes from Benjamin Howard, a man who fled to a cave at the base of a low cliff 0.25 mile north of the knob when American Patriots pressed too hotly for his assistance during the Revolutionary War. Accounts say that he sheltered himself in his cave rather than join the fighting. It is also said that his daughter, Sallie, was the real heroine, because she was willing to endure a severe switching rather than reveal her father's hiding place. Howard finally took the oath of allegiance in 1778, but his hideout retained his name. In addition to serving as an area landmark, Howard's Knob was the site of energy experiments designed to assess the potential of giant, wind-powered generators.

Upon reaching Boone, the home of Appalachian State University and the commercial mecca for the entire region that bills itself the High Country, you should be able to find the modern conveniences that you may have missed while traveling the Old Buffalo Trail.

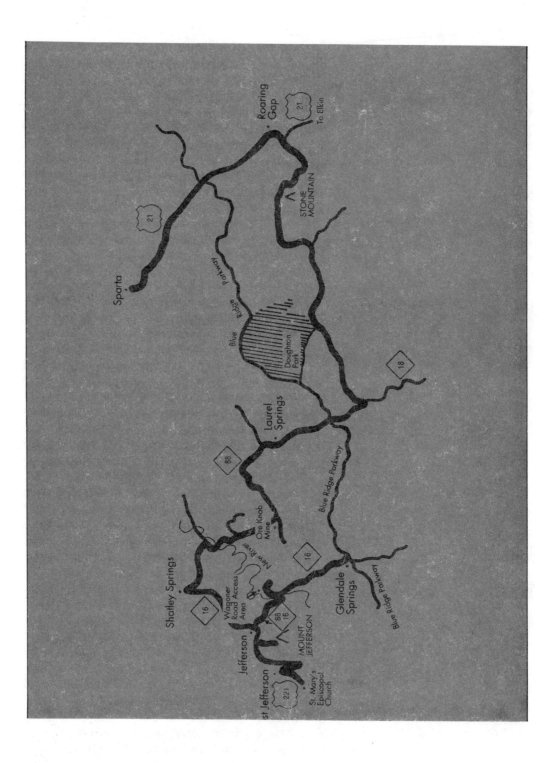

This tour begins near Sparta and goes to Roaring Gap, Stone Mountain State Park, the Ore Knob Mine, Shatley Springs, Mount Jefferson State Park, and West Jefferson. It then visits the frescoes at Beaver Creek, travels to New River State Park, and ends at the frescoes in Glendale Springs. Total mileage: approximately 88 miles.

▲▲▲▲▲▲▲▲▲▲▲▲▲▲▲▲▲▲▲▲▲▲▲▲▲▲▲▲▲▲▲▲▲▲▲▲▲▲▲▲▲▲▲▲ *The New River Tour*

The tour begins where the Blue Ridge Parkway intersects U.S. 21 about 7 miles south of Sparta, the county seat of Alleghany County. Head south on U.S. 21.

*The Lost Provinces*

The area encompassed by this tour has been known as the Lost Provinces historically. When the earliest settlers in Ashe, Alleghany, and Watauga counties were building roads and railroads, the most practical routes took them into southwestern Virginia. While Ashe and Alleghany counties were officially a part of North Carolina, many of their trade and business connections were with Virginia and Tennessee.

*The New River*

The unusual features of the New River also contributed to the unique development of the area. The New is the only river in the eastern United States that flows northward to the Midwest. Development proceeded in the same direction. The fact that the path of commerce was westward instead of eastward created a growth pattern different from that of the rest of the North Carolina mountains.

The New is the oldest river in America. At one time, it held the headwaters of the mighty Teays River; hard to believe as it is, scientists tell us that the Ohio and Mississippi rivers were once tributaries of the prehistoric Teays. Scientists also tell us that the New has changed little since it was first seen by settlers, a claim that seems to be supported by the writings of Bishop August Spangenburg, an early traveler sent by the Moravian church to find land for a settlement. In his account of his journey, Bishop Spangenburg recorded his impression of a river that was undoubtedly the New. His December 14, 1752, entry states, "We were completely lost and whichever way we turned we were walled in. . . . We crossed only dry mountains and dry valleys and when for several days we followed the river in the hope that it would lead us out, we found ourselves only deeper in the wilderness, for the river ran now north, now south, now east, now west, in short to all points of the compass! Finally we decided to leave the river and take a course between east and south, crossing the mountains as best we could." Bishop Spangenburg's remarks ring true to anyone who has ever traveled the backroads along the New.

Many of the original settlers along the river were Revolutionary War soldiers who were given land grants. Much of the land in the area still remains in the hands of the descendants of those early grantees. As a result, the region has had one of the most stable populations in North Carolina for two hundred years. Only recently have real estate developers and land speculators invaded this section of the mountains as they have the rest of western North Carolina. The relative isolation that existed until recent decades enabled the land to retain its charm. A day spent along the New provides a refreshing glimpse of what the rest of western North Carolina looked like only a few years ago. On the other hand, visitors may end up wishing they could stop the inevitable march of progress.

After 4 miles on U.S. 21, you will reach the town of Roaring Gap and the Roaring Gap Store, which houses the local post office. Across the street is the entrance to the Roaring Gap summer resort community, one of the oldest in the moun-

*Absolam Smith*

*Stone Mountain*

tains. Because of the town's proximity to the Piedmont cities of Winston-Salem and Greensboro, many wealthy industrialists and businessmen chose to build summer homes in Roaring Gap. Since the late 1890s, the cool summer days have attracted the Reynolds and Hanes families, among others.

Oral tradition tells that the first settlers in Roaring Gap came for a different reason. A man named Absolam Smith left England for America in 1775. Because he could not afford his passage, he labored as an indentured servant for a rich planter near Norfolk, Virginia. While working off his seven-year obligation, Absolam fell in love with the planter's daughter, Agatha. Knowing that her father would never approve of the relationship, Agatha eloped with Absolam to the mountains. It is said that they were accompanied by a horse and an old Negro servant who had been with Agatha for many years. Along their journey, they escaped an Indian attack, perhaps only because the Indians were too thoroughly amazed at the sight before them to pursue in earnest—Absolam was swimming the Yadkin River leading Agatha on the horse, with the Negro servant, who could not swim, clinging desperately to the horse's tail. The Smiths built a home in Roaring Gap, where they lived out their lives. Their graves are nearby in the cemetery at Antioch Church. It seems fitting that Roaring Gap, born of such romantic beginnings, should have proven a prosperous community.

Continue south on U.S. 21. After 2 miles, you will see signs for Liberty Knob Baptist Church and the John P. Frank Parkway. Turn right onto S.R. 1100 just past the sign marking the eastern continental divide (elevation 2,972). The turn comes up quickly, so be alert. The pavement ends a little over 1 mile down S.R. 1100. On the right is Liberty Knob Baptist Church, formed in 1884. After approximately 3 miles on S.R. 1100, you will reach Elk Knob Baptist Church and the intersection with the John P. Frank Parkway. Turn right into the entrance to Stone Mountain State Park. You can pick up a park map at the office, on the

*Farmhouse near
Doughton Park's trailheads*

right at the entrance. It is 3 miles to the main parking area. Visitors who arrive early in the day can park closer to the base of Stone Mountain than those who arrive later, but even if you have to use the lower lot and walk up, it is worth the hike.

Stone Mountain, elevation 2,305, is a dome-shaped granite mass that rises 600 feet from base to summit. Since most of the surrounding valleys have elevations of 1,400 to 1,600 feet, the huge, sheer wall seems even more impressive. The circumference at the base of Stone Mountain is nearly 4 miles. Permanent trail maps are located at the base of the mountain. The valley at the base is an excellent vantage point from which to watch rock climbers negotiating such colorfully named routes up the rock as Electric Boobs, Grand Funk Railroad, and Rainy Day Women. It seems that the routes must have been named during the late 1960s or early 1970s.

Once you have viewed Stone Mountain, take a left out of the bottom parking lot and continue on the gravel road. It is 0.9 mile to a marker for Widows Creek Trail, on the right. The hike to a small, sheltered waterfall is a relatively short one, but be forewarned if you decide to cross the stream—the slippery rocks may be the reason it's called Widows Creek.

It is another 2.1 miles to an intersection with S.R. 1737. Turn right. It is 2.6 miles to the Double Creek Baptist Church, on the left. The pavement ends after another 0.5 mile. You will enter a scenic, pastoral valley that has recently been auctioned off—you can see indications of where developers have surveyed lots. A beautiful, well-maintained, late-nineteenth-century white farmhouse with two-tiered porches and decorative woodwork dominates the valley. It is the centerpiece of Basin Creek Farm, which raises and boards quarter horses. It is to be hoped that the present owners will keep the valley's pastures intact for grazing.

You will see a trail entrance for Doughton Park on the right 1 mile from the farmhouse. Doughton Park is one of the most popular attractions on the

*Sign outside the Laurel Springs General Store*

Blue Ridge Parkway, though most visitors see only the upper part of its six thousand acres. The trail entrance provides access to the lower half by way of several of Doughton Park's hiking trails. You can enjoy short hikes up some relatively deserted routes or plan a longer hike that takes advantage of the loops throughout the park. There are even primitive back-country camping areas. Interested visitors should check with park officials to reserve one of the popular campsites.

From the parking area for the hiking trails, continue on the gravel road for another 2.2 miles. Bear right when you reach pavement. It is 4.3 miles on the paved road to an intersection with N.C. 18. Turn right, heading north. It is 6.2 miles to an intersection with the Blue Ridge Parkway, then another 0.2 mile on N.C. 18 to the Laurel Springs General Store, on the right.

A visit to the Laurel Springs General Store is highly recommended. You will notice from the rather unusual items on display outside that it is not your typical general store. A hearse usually sits out front awaiting renters. The annex at the side houses an array of mannequins and stuffed animals dressed and displayed in unusual combinations. Most of the mannequins have tongue-in-cheek biographical information attached to them—if you count yourself among those people who believe everything they read, you'll come away convinced that the dummies are the ancestors of the store's owner, Linda Woodie. As you enter the store, be sure to notice the rubber spiders and other insects nailed to the railing. Visitors are usually greeted by music from a player piano or an old phonograph record. In addition to browsing the unusual collection of knickknacks and antiques, you can purchase beer, soda, and ice cream.

Continue north on N.C. 18. After 2 miles, you will see the Laurel Springs post office on the right. Turn left onto N.C. 88. You will pass an agricultural research station that looks like an advertisement for the perfect mountain farm. After 4.3 miles on N.C. 88, you will see an historical marker for Ore Knob Mine on the right. Just past the marker, turn right onto S.R. 1595. After a little less than 1 mile, you may still be able to see the remains of the famous Ore Knob Mine on the left. The area is overgrown, and the shafts have been closed down and fenced off, but you may be able to glimpse the mound of earth still there.

*Ore Knob Mine*

The Ore Knob Mine had a rather inauspicious beginning. In 1800, a French mining engineer came to Ashe County in search of iron. Though his undertaking was quite successful, his judgment failed him where the three hundred acres at Ore Knob were concerned. He bought the tract thinking it showed promise of bearing iron, only to abandon it after determining that whatever iron was there was so badly adulterated by copper as to be virtually worthless. The property was sold, and after his taxes were paid, the Frenchman was left with a balance of eleven dollars, which was split equally among his eleven children. In 1870, two capitalists from Baltimore purchased the tract and began to make a huge profit once copper started bringing a high price.

In January 1982, news of a sensational murder involving the notorious Outlaws motorcycle gang hit the media. An undercover informant told police that in December 1981, he had unwillingly participated in the murder of a man whose body was thrown into a deserted two-hundred-foot shaft at the Ore Knob Mine. A second body was also believed to be in the shaft. Investigators examined the vicinity but were unable to corroborate the informant's story. It was proposed that someone be lowered into the hole for a closer look, but mining officials judged the shaft to be too unstable.

*The Nashville Flame*

In one of those cases where fact is stranger than fiction, it just so happened that a man who called himself the Nashville Flame learned of the dilemma while watching television in a motel. The Flame was performing as a stunt man on a local thrill-show circuit. Finding himself in the right place at the right time, he offered his climbing talents to the authorities, who eventually accepted his offer. One of his quirks was that he allowed the media to photograph him only when

*South Fork of the New River*

*Martin Shatley*

his face was covered by a helmet or a ski mask.

When the Flame really did find the two bodies at the bottom of the shaft, one of the most sensational series of murder trials in the history of western North Carolina was launched. It ended with the murder conviction of four men, including the original informant. The Flame continued to insist that there were more bodies in the mine, but the attorney general of North Carolina made the wise decision to permanently seal the dangerous shaft, and the final chapter in the saga of the Ore Knob Mine was officially closed.

Continue on S.R. 1595 for 2.8 miles, then turn left onto S.R. 1599 for a quick 0.3 mile. Just before the bridge, turn right onto S.R. 1601, a gravel road that parallels the South Fork of the New River. This is a scenic route, with the New River frequently only a few feet from the road. It is on this part of the tour that you will see the beauty of the New up close—so close that you'll almost feel like you're canoeing the river.

You will pass the Yellow Knife Ranch, on the right. After 3 miles, you will come upon a dead-end sign, but don't panic. Follow the main road as it makes a ninety-degree turn and crosses what resembles a pontoon bridge. The bridge is safe. For the next 2 miles, you will be driving directly beside the New. Turn left onto U.S. 221, heading south. Just past a small bridge 1.5 miles down U.S. 221, turn right onto Shatley Springs Road (S.R. 1571). When the road forks 1 mile later, bear left onto Tom Fowler Road (S.R. 1572). After less than 0.5 mile, turn right onto N.C. 16, heading north. It is 0.5 mile to a sign on the left announcing the entrance to Shatley Springs Inn.

Though the family-style country cooking served at the inn is the primary attraction at Shatley Springs today, the healing waters that once drew people from near and far are still bubbling. In the 1880s, a chronic sufferer named Martin Shatley wheezed into the area dragging his considerable ailments like a ton of bricks. Shatley was long-winded and graphic in describing his condition, but a brief sampling should suffice to establish that he was not a well man. "I

*Shatley Springs Inn*

*Mount Jefferson*

first broke out with pimples," he wrote. "Soon my skin got scaly, when I rubbed my hand briefly over my skin I could see hundreds of scales fly off my skin. . . . My eyes were most of the time red and swollen. Sometimes I had to hold my eyelids up with my hands to see my way to walk."

Shatley's long search for a cure ended when he bought a farm in Ashe County. One day when he was out walking, he stopped to bathe his irritated face in a cool spring. Within an hour, his condition was so markedly improved that he returned and immersed his whole body. Within three days, the man the doctors had given up on was completely healed. Needless to say, word of Shatley's miraculous cure swept the countryside, and a resort was established at the site. Countless gallons of spring water have since been carried away by people who believe in its curative powers. Regardless of whether the water has healing power, it certainly does taste good. Visitors can either buy three plastic gallon jugs for a dollar or bring their own and fill them for free.

Refreshed by the miracle water, return to N.C. 16 and turn right, heading south. After 4 miles, U.S. 221 joins N.C. 16, and the two run conjunctively for 1.3 miles before U.S. 221 splits off to join N.C. 88. Turn right and follow U.S. 221/N.C. 88, heading west. The huge mountain on the left is Mount Jefferson. After 3.6 miles, a sign on the left directs you to Mount Jefferson State Park. Follow Mount Jefferson Road (S.R. 1149) for 1 mile, then S.R. 1152 for 2.1 miles to the summit.

In 1827, Dr. Elisha Mitchell climbed Mount Jefferson and recorded in his diary that he had never seen anything more beautiful than the view from the big rock near the summit. For more than a hundred years after Mitchell's visit, the summit remained inaccessible except by difficult trails, but when the federal Work Projects Administration came to Ashe County in the 1930s, local citizens hoping to attract tourists proposed that a road be built. When supporters of the project learned that federal funds could not be used to build a road to private property, they set out to acquire the twenty-six acres at the top for use as a public park. The land was donated and the road then built. Due to a lack of maintenance funds, it soon fell into disrepair. In 1941, local citizens petitioned the North Carolina government to accept the acreage as a state park. The effort was unsuccessful at first, but the group finally convinced the government to designate the Mount Jefferson land a state recreation area. When North Carolina later passed a law requiring a minimum four hundred acres for state-supported parks, local citizens once again set out to meet the challenge. Once they secured financial contributions and land donations of the necessary acreage, Mount Jefferson State Park was born.

Even the naming of the mountain was the subject of longstanding controversy. Until fairly recently, Mount Jefferson was known locally as Nigger Mountain or Negro Mountain. In his book *Ashe County: A History*, Arthur Fletcher credited tourism, not racial enlightenment, for the change. He stated that the members of various committees were afraid that hosts of potential visitors would get the idea that the new park was for blacks only and stay away. It was finally suggested that the mountain be named for the two towns at its base, which were themselves named for a great president, and the issue was resolved.

The reason for the original name is also a subject of debate. Most sources say that the mountain served as a station on the underground railroad during the Civil War and that it was named for the runaway slaves who hid there. Historians have discredited that view, since land grants predating the Civil War carried references to Negro Mountain. The most likely explanation for the name comes from the fact that the mountain is a solid black color during the winter. Because of the high elevation, most of its trees are stunted. When their foliage is off, the bare black rocks are all that can be seen.

Return to U.S. 221/N.C. 88 and turn left, heading toward West Jefferson. It is 1.3 miles to an intersection with N.C. 163/194 at a stoplight. Turn right and head into West Jefferson. It is 1.5

*Mount Jefferson*

miles to the center of town. Turn right at the corner of Main and Fourth streets. The Ashe County Cheese Company's factory and outlet store are located half a block down Fourth Street. A tour of the factory reveals how cheese is made. Freshly made samples are available at the outlet store.

In the early 1900s, Ashe County farmers learned that raising dairy herds could be a profitable industry in the mountains. With the increase of milk-producing herds in the area, the North Carolina Department of Agriculture promoted the establishment of cheese factories. Cheesemaking demonstrations were met with enthusiasm. The first factory opened in 1915. Soon, there were small operations throughout the county. Unfortunately, the widely scattered locations of the factories and the poor mountain roads prevented cheesemakers from reaping much of a profit. All but one of the plants is closed now. The Ashe County Cheese Company carries on the long-standing tradition alone.

Retrace your route to N.C. 163/194. Just before the intersection with U.S. 221/N.C. 88, there is a McDonald's on the right. A sign indicates the route to the "Church of the Frescoes." Turn right onto Beaver Creek Road, following the signs for the frescoes. It is 0.8 mile to St. Mary's Episcopal Church.

Though this small, picturesque mountain church houses one of the area's main tourist attractions, it was not always the focus of community pride. Milnor Jones was an Episcopal minister and active missionary who organized the first Episcopal church in Ashe County, the Church of St. Simon the Zealot. On June 21, 1896, Bishop Joseph Blount Cheshire came from Raleigh to conduct services. He was met at the church by an unexpected greeting committee. He wrote, "I was assaulted and forcibly prevented from entering this building by a mob of between fifty and one hundred men which had been gotten together for the express purpose of preventing our service that day. And the reason they gave for this action was that they 'did not like Mr. Jones' doctrine' and they understood that I taught the same doctrine."

Cheshire further noted that he "met with the most violent opposition, accompanied with bitter abuse from Methodists and Baptists, especially the latter." Milnor Jones went on to organize a school at Beaver Creek. His quaint Church of St. Simon the Zealot was later renamed St. Mary's. It was eventually abandoned for lack of funds until a different sort of notoriety came its way.

*Ben Long and the frescoes*

In the summer of 1980, artist Ben Long returned to the United States to train others in a dying art form. For seven years, he had studied fresco painting in Italy with a master of Renaissance technique. Long relocated to Ashe County, where he took on as many as twenty apprentices at one time and used two Episcopal churches in the area as his studios.

Fresco painting is a tedious and complicated process, which explains its rarity in today's world. Natural ground pigment is mixed with distilled water, thinned with lime, and painted onto damp plaster. As the plaster dries, the lime and pigment bind chemically, so that the wall literally becomes the painting. This unusual technique produces an interesting effect—many say that fresco walls seem to glow. The drawback is that the pigment is absorbed the moment brush touches plaster, so a mistake can necessitate the removal of an entire section of wall.

Long imported lime from the same site in Florence, Italy, that Michelangelo used when working on the Sistine Chapel. He mixed the lime with North Carolina sand to make his plaster. Local people served as models for the characters in his frescoes; Long himself took the role of Doubting Thomas. The results are so impressive that over two hundred thousand people a year visit the out-of-the-way chapels to view Long's frescoes. *Mary, Great with Child; John the Baptist;* and *The Mystery of Faith* are featured at St. Mary's. Despite the possibility of encountering a busload of tourists, St. Mary's is a worthwhile stop.

Retrace your route past Mount Jefferson State Park, but continue straight when the road becomes N.C. 88, heading south. Approximately 8 miles from St. Mary's, you will cross the North

Fork of the New River. Turn right onto N.C. 16. You will immediately see a sign for the Wagoner Road Access Area, which is one of the canoe access areas in New River State Park. Turn right onto Wagoner Road (S.R. 1588), a gravel road that passes under the bridge you just crossed. The 2.1-mile scenic drive along the New that follows is well worth the short detour. At the top of the hill, turn left onto S.R. 1590 to reach the Wagoner Road Access Area and the park office.

In 1965, the Appalachian Power Company applied for a license to dam the New and build reservoirs in Virginia and North Carolina. What followed was a case study in the organization of grass-roots opposition—citizens' groups, environmentalists, federal agencies, and the states of North Carolina and West Virginia joined forces to lobby against the proposed damming. In 1975, North Carolina declared the 26.5-mile stretch of the New from its confluence with Dog Creek (near the Wagoner Road Access Area) to the Virginia line a state scenic river. In 1976, it became part of the National Wild and Scenic River System, and the New remains free-flowing today. The Wagoner Road Access Area is the only section of New River State Park that can be reached by automobile at present. If you feel adventurous, renting a canoe will provide you an opportunity to see the river from an entirely different perspective.

From the park office, retrace S.R. 1590 past Wagoner Road (the number changes from 1590 to 1591 at the intersection) and continue straight for 0.6 mile to the junction with N.C. 16/88. Turn right. The road splits after 1.6 miles; follow N.C. 16. About 3.6 miles after you pass the other end of Wagoner Road—where this short side trip began—you will start to see a new set of "Church of the Frescoes" signs. Turn right onto S.R. 1631.

On your left, you will see the Church of the Holy Trinity, the second Episcopal church housing examples of Ben Long's frescoes. Long's interpretation of the Last Supper occupies the entire front wall. Another interesting, if unrelated, characteristic of the church is the columbarium, located downstairs. If you've ever contemplated

*New River State Park*

*Church of the Holy Trinity in Glendale Springs*

*Church of the Holy Trinity
in Glendale Springs*

having your remains cremated but couldn't decide what should be done with your ashes, the columbarium at the Church of the Holy Trinity provides one unusual alternative.

Continue on S.R. 1631 for 0.1 mile to the intersection with S.R. 1632. Straight ahead, you will see the historic Glendale Springs Inn, a well-known inn and restaurant. The tour ends here. If you turn left onto S.R. 1632 and follow it past N.C. 16, it is only 0.3 mile to an intersection with the Blue Ridge Parkway at the Northwest Trading Post.

# Appendix

## Federal Agencies

Andrews Pickens Ranger District
(Sumter National Forest)
USFS
Star Route
Walhalla, S.C. 29691
803-638-9568

Blue Ridge Parkway
Headquarters Office
700 Northwestern Bank Building
Asheville, N.C. 28801
704-259-0779

Cradle of Forestry Interpretive Association
1002 Pisgah Highway
Pisgah Forest, N.C. 28768
704-884-5713

Great Smoky Mountains National Park
District Ranger Office
Box 4, Park Circle
Cherokee, N.C. 28719
704-497-9147

Great Smoky Mountains National Park
Headquarters Office
Gatlinburg, Tenn. 37738
615-448-6222

Nantahala National Forest

> Cheoah Ranger District
> USFS
> Route 1, Box 16-A
> Robbinsville, N.C. 28711
> 704-479-6431

> Highlands Ranger District
> USFS
> Route 2, Box 385
> Highlands, N.C. 28741
> 704-526-3765

Tusquitee Ranger District
USFS
201 Woodland Drive
Murphy, N.C. 28906
704-837-5152

Wayah Ranger District
USFS
Route 10, Box 210
Franklin, N.C. 28734
704-524-4410

National Forests of North Carolina
Post and Otis Streets
P.O. Box 2750
Asheville, N.C. 28802
704-257-4200

Pisgah National Forest

French Broad Ranger District
USFS
P.O. Box 128
Hot Springs, N.C. 28743
704-622-3202

Grandfather Ranger District
USFS
P.O. Box 519
Marion, N.C. 28752
704-652-2144

Pisgah Ranger District
USFS
1001 Pisgah Highway
Pisgah Forest, N.C. 28768
704-877-3350

Toecane Ranger District
USFS
P.O. Box 128
Burnsville, N.C. 28714
704-682-6146

## North Carolina agencies

Division of Travel and Tourism
North Carolina Department of Commerce
430 N. Salisbury Street
Raleigh, N.C. 27611
919-733-4171
800-847-4862 (outside Raleigh)

Division of Parks and Recreation
P.O. Box 27687
512 N. Salisbury Street
Raleigh, N.C. 27611
919-733-7275

Superintendent
Mount Mitchell State Park
Route 5, Box 700
Burnsville, N.C. 28714
704-675-4611

Superintendent
Stone Mountain State Park
Star Route 1, Box 15
Roaring Gap, N.C. 28668
919-957-8185

## Chambers of Commerce and Other Tourist Agencies

Alleghany County Chamber of Commerce
P.O. Box 1237
Sparta, N.C. 28675
919-372-5473

Ashe County Chamber of Commerce
P.O. Box 31
West Jefferson, N.C. 28694
919-246-9550

Avery County Chamber of Commerce
P.O. Box 700
Newland, N.C. 28657
704-733-4737

Banner Elk Chamber of Commerce
P.O. Box 335
Banner Elk, N.C. 28604
704-898-5605

Beech Mountain Chamber of Commerce
608 Beech Mountain Parkway
Banner Elk, N.C. 28604
704-387-9283

Blowing Rock Chamber of Commerce
P.O. Box 406
Blowing Rock, N.C. 28605
704-295-7951

Boone Chamber of Commerce
350 Blowing Rock Road
Boone, N.C. 28607
704-264-2225

Brevard Chamber of Commerce
P.O. Box 589
Brevard, N.C. 28712
704-883-3700

Cherokee County Chamber of Commerce
104 Valley River Avenue
Murphy, N.C. 28906
704-837-2242

Clay County Chamber of Commerce
P.O. Box 88
Hayesville, N.C. 28904
704-389-3704

Franklin Area Chamber of Commerce
180 Porter Street
Franklin, N.C. 28734
704-524-3161

Graham County Friends
Travel and Tourism Authority
P.O. Box 1206
Robbinsville, N.C. 28771
704-479-3790

Greater Haywood County Chamber of Commerce
P.O. Box 125
Waynesville, N.C. 28786
704-456-3021

Greater Hendersonville Chamber of Commerce
330 N. King Street
Hendersonville, N.C. 28739
704-692-1413

Highlands Chamber of Commerce
Highlands, N.C. 28741
704-525-2112

High Country Host
701 Blowing Rock Road
Boone, N.C. 28607
704-264-1299 (in Watauga County)
800-222-7515 (in North Carolina)
800-438-7500

Jackson County Chamber of Commerce
18 North Central
Sylva, N.C. 28779
704-586-2155
704-586-2336

Mitchell County Chamber of Commerce
Route 1, Box 796
Spruce Pine, N.C. 28777
704-765-9483,

New River Country Travel Association
Route 1, Box 13
Scottville, N.C. 28672
919-982-9414

Swain County Chamber of Commerce
P.O. Box 509
Bryson City, N.C. 28713
704-488-3681

Tryon Chamber of Commerce
401 N. Trade Street
Tryon, N.C. 28782
704-859-6236

Yancey County Chamber of Commerce
Burnsville, N.C. 28714
704-682-7413

## Outfitters

French Broad Rafting Company
Route 5, Box 372
Marshall, N.C. 28753
704-649-3574

High Country Outfitters
P.O. Drawer J
Bryson City, N.C. 28713
704-488-3153

Nantahala Outdoor Center
U.S. 19W, Box 41
Bryson City, N.C. 28713
704-488-2175

Nantahala Rafts
U.S. 19W, Box 45
Bryson City, N.C. 28713
704-488-2325

New River Outfitters
P.O. Box 433
Jefferson, N.C. 28640
919-246-7711

Rolling Thunder River Company
P.O. Box 88
Almond, N.C. 28702
704-488-2030

Smoky Mountain River Expeditions
P.O. Box 398
Hot Springs, N.C. 28743
704-622-7260

Southern Whitewater Expeditions
P.O. Box 29
Walnut Rural Station
Marshall, N.C. 28753
704-649-3679

Zaloo's Canoes
Route 1, Box 85Z
Jefferson, N.C. 28640
919-246-3066


## Others

Appalachian Trail Conference
P.O. Box 807
Harpers Ferry, W.Va. 25425
304-535-6331

Cherokee County Historical Museum
205 Peachtree Street
Murphy, N.C. 28906
704-837-6792

Fontana Village
Fontana Dam, N.C. 28733
704-498-2211

Historic Flat Rock
P.O. Box 295
Flat Rock, N.C. 28731

John C. Campbell Folk School
Brasstown, N.C. 28902
704-837-2775

Oconee State Park
Star Route
Walhalla, S.C. 29691
803-638-5553

Penland School of Crafts
Penland, N.C. 28765
704-765-2359

Roan Mountain State Park
Route 1, Box 50
Roan Mountain, Tenn. 37687
615-772-3303

# Bibliography

Alderman, Pat. *In the Shadow of Big Bald.* Mars Hill, N.C.: Bald Mountain Development Corp., 1972.

Alexander, Nancy. *Here Will I Dwell: The Story of Caldwell County.* By the author, 1956.

Allen, Martha Norburn. *Asheville and Land of the Sky.* Charlotte, N.C.: Heritage House, 1960.

Alley, Judge Felix E. *Random Thoughts and Musings of a Mountaineer.* Salisbury, N.C.: Rowan Printing Company, 1941.

Appalachian State University. *Forever Alive: Mountain People, Mountain Land.* 1978.

Arthur, John Preston. *A History of Watauga County, North Carolina.* Richmond, Va.: Everett Waddy Company, 1915.

———. *Western North Carolina: A History from 1730 to 1913.* Raleigh, N.C.: Edwards and Broughton Printing Company, 1914.

Ashe County Heritage Book Committee. *The Heritage of Ashe County, North Carolina.* Vol. 1. Winston-Salem, N.C.: Hunter Publishing Company, 1984.

Blackmun, Ora. *Western North Carolina: Its Mountains and Its People to 1880.* Boone, N.C.: Appalachian Consortium Press, 1977.

Bradley, Jeff. *A Traveler's Guide to the Smoky Mountains Region.* Boston, Mass.: Harvard Common Press, 1985.

Burke County Historical Society. *The Heritage of Burke County, 1981.* Winston-Salem, N.C.: Hunter Publishing Company, 1981.

Buxton, Barry M. *A Village Tapestry: The History of Blowing Rock.* Boone, N.C.: Appalachian Consortium Press, 1989.

Caldwell County Heritage Book Committee. *The Heritage of Caldwell County, North Carolina.* Vol. 1. Edited by E. Carl Anderson, Jr. Winston-Salem, N.C.: Hunter Publishing Company, 1983.

Carpenter, Cal. *The Walton War and Tales of the Great Smoky Mountains.* Lakemont, Ga.: Copple House Books, 1979.

Cherokee County Historical Museum. *The Heritage of Cherokee County, North Carolina.* Vol. 1. Edited by Alice D. White. Winston-Salem, N.C.: Hunter Publishing Company, 1987.

———. *Marble and Log: The History and Architecture of Cherokee County, North Carolina.* Edited by Dr. Carl Dockery. Murphy, N.C.: Cherokee County Historical Museum, 1984.

Colton, Henry E. *Mountain Scenery: The Scenery of the Mountains of Western North Carolina and Northwestern South Carolina.* Raleigh, N.C.: W. L. Pomeroy, 1859.

Cooper, Horton. *History of Avery County, North Carolina.* Asheville, N.C.: Biltmore Press, 1964.

———. *North Carolina Mountain Folklore and Miscellaney.* Murfreesboro, N.C.: Johnson Publishing Company, 1972.

de Hart, Allen. *North Carolina Hiking Trails.* 2d ed. Boston, Mass.: Appalachian Mountain Club Books, 1982, 1988.

Dykeman, Wilma. *The French Broad.* Knoxville: University of Tennessee Press, 1955.

Federal Writers' Project of the Federal Works Agency Work Projects Administration. *North Carolina: A Guide to the Old North State.* Chapel Hill: University of North Carolina Press, 1939.

FitzSimons, Frank L. *From the Banks of the Oklawaha*. 3 vols. Hendersonville, N.C.: Golden Glow Publishing Company, 1976-79.

Fletcher, Arthur L. *Ashe County: A History*. Jefferson, N.C.: Ashe County Research Association, Inc., 1963.

Fossett, Mildred B. *History of McDowell County*. Marion, N.C.: McDowell County American Revolution Bicentennial Commission Heritage Committee, 1976.

Freel, Margaret Walker. *Our Heritage: The People of Cherokee County, North Carolina, 1540–1955*. Asheville, N.C.: Miller Printing Company, 1956.

Frome, Michael. *Strangers in High Places*. New York: Doubleday and Company, 1966.

Genealogical Society of Watauga County. *The Heritage of Watauga County, North Carolina*. Vol. 1. Winston-Salem, N.C.: Hunter Publishing Company, 1984.

Graham County Centennial 1972, Inc. *Graham County Centennial 1872–1972*. 1972.

Griffin, Clarence W. *The History of Old Tryon and Rutherford Counties: 1730–1936*. Spartanburg, S.C.: Reprint Company, Publishers, 1977.

———. *Western North Carolina Sketches*. Forest City, N.C.: Forest City Courier, 1941.

Hannum, Alberta Pierson. *Look Back with Love: A Recollection of the Blue Ridge*. New York: Vanguard Press, 1969.

Henderson County Genealogical and Historical Society. *The Heritage of Henderson County, North Carolina*. Vol. 1. Edited by George Alexander Jones. Winston-Salem, N.C.: Hunter Publishing Company, 1985.

Jackson County Historical Association. *The History of Jackson County*. Edited by Max R. Williams. Sylva, N.C.: Jackson County Historical Association, 1987.

Johnson, Earline. *Jonas Ridge History*. Banner Elk, N.C.: Pudding Stone Press, 1974.

*Journal of Cherokee Studies* 4 (Fall 1979).

Kephart, Horace. *Our Southern Highlanders*. 1913. Reprint. New York: MacMillan Company, 1957.

Lanman, Charles. *Letters from the Alleghany Mountains*. New York: G. P. Putnam's Sons, 1849.

Macon County Historical Society, Inc. *The Heritage of Macon County, North Carolina, 1987*. Edited by Jessie Sutton. Winston-Salem, N.C.: Hunter Publishing Company, 1987.

Marsh, Blanche. *Historic Flat Rock: Where the Old South Lingers*. Asheville, N.C.: Biltmore Press, 1961.

McIntosh, Gert. *Highlands, North Carolina . . . A Walk into the Past*. Highlands: By the author, 1983.

Medford, W. Clark. *The Early History of Haywood County*. Asheville, N.C.: Miller Printing Company, 1961.

———. *Haywood's Heritage and Finest Hour*. Asheville, N.C.: Daniels Graphics, 1971.

———. *Land o' the Sky: History, Stories, Sketches*. Waynesville, N.C.: By the author, 1965.

———. *The Middle History of Haywood County*. Asheville, N.C.: Miller Printing Company, 1968.

Miller, Clyde C. *The Old Buffalo Trail of Watauga County, North Carolina Bicentennial, 1976*.

Mooney, James. *Myths of the Cherokee*. Washington, D.C.: Government Printing Office, 1900. (One of several papers accompanying the Nineteenth Annual Report of the United States Bureau of American Ethnology to the Secretary of the Smithsonian Institution in 1897–98.) Reprint. New York: Johnson Reprint Corp., 1970.

Morgan, Lucy, with LeGette Blythe. *Gift from the Hills*. New York: Bobbs-Merrill, 1958.

Morgan, Robert Lindsay. *The Lure of the Great Smokies*. Boston, Mass., and New York: Houghton, Mifflin and Company, 1927.

Morley, Margaret W. *The Carolina Mountains*. Boston and New York: Houghton, Mifflin and Company, 1913.

Mull, J. Alex. *Mountain Yarns*. Banner Elk, N.C.: Pudding Stone Press.

Padgett, Guy. *A History of Clay County, North Carolina*.

Parris, John. *Mountain Bred*. Asheville, N.C.: Citizen-Times Publishing Company, 1967.

———. *My Mountains, My People*. Asheville, N.C.: Citizen-Times Publishing Company, 1957.

———. *Roaming the Mountains*. Asheville, N.C.: Citizen-Times Publishing Company, 1955.

———. *These Storied Mountains*. Asheville, N.C.: Citizen-Times Publishing Company, 1972.

Patton, Sadie Smathers. *A Condensed History of Flat Rock*. Asheville, N.C.: Church Printing Company, 1961.

———. *Sketches of Polk County History*. Spartanburg, S.C.: Reprint Company, Publishers, 1976.

———. *The Story of Henderson County*. Asheville, N.C.: Miller Printing Company, 1947.

Peattie, Donald Culross. *Pearson's Falls Glen: Its Story, Its Flora, Its Birds*. Tryon, N.C.: Tryon Garden Club, 1962.

Peattie, Roderick, ed. *The Great Smokies and the Blue Ridge: The Story of the Southern Appalachians*. New York: Vanguard Press, 1943.

Phifer, Edward W., Jr. *Burke: The History of a North Carolina County, 1777–1920*. Morganton, N.C.: By the author, 1977.

Polk County Historical Association, Inc. *Polk County History*. Edited by D. William Bennett. Dallas, Tex.: Taylor Publishing Company, 1983.

Reeves, Eleanor Baker. *A Factual History of Early Ashe County, North Carolina: Its People, Places and Events*. West Jefferson, N.C.: By the author, 1986.

Reid, Christian [Frances Christine Fisher Tiernan]. *"The Land of Sky"; Or, Adventures in Mountain Byways*. New York: D. Appleton and Company, 1876.

Reynolds, T. W. *Born of the Mountains*. 1913.

———. *Highlands*. 1964.

Rights, Douglas L. *The American Indian in North Carolina*. 1947. Reprint. Winston-Salem, N.C.: John F. Blair, Publisher, 1957.

Schenck, Carl Alwin. *The Birth of Forestry in America, Biltmore Forest School 1898–1913*. Santa Cruz, Calif.: Forest History Society and the Appalachian Consortium, 1974.

Schwarzkopf, S. Kent. *A History of Mt. Mitchell and the Black Mountains: Exploration, Development, and Preservation*. Raleigh: North Carolina Department of Cultural Resources, Division of Archives and History, 1985.

Southern Appalachian Historical Association. *The Heritage of Watauga County, North Carolina*. Vol. 1. Edited by Curtis Smalling. Boone, N.C.: Hunter Publishing Company, 1987.

Street, Julia Montgomery. *Judaculla's Handprint and Other Mysterious Tales from North Carolina*. Chapel Hill, N.C.: Briar Patch Press, 1975.

Swain County Genealogical and Historical Society. *The Heritage of Swain County, North Carolina, 1988*. Winston-Salem, N.C.: Hunter Publishing Company, 1988.

Teacher Training Class of Burnsville, 1930. *History and Geography of Yancey County*. 1930.

Thomasson, Lillian Franklin. *Swain County: Early History and Educational Development*. Bryson City, N.C.: 1965.

Tinsley, Jim Bob. *The Land of Waterfalls: Transylvania County, North Carolina*. Brevard, N.C.: J. B. and Dottie Tinsley, 1988.

Van Noppen, Ina W., and John J. Van Noppen. *Western North Carolina Since the Civil War*. Boone, N.C.: Appalachian Consortium Press, 1973.

Walser, Richard. *North Carolina Legends*. Raleigh: North Carolina Department of Cultural Resources, Division of Archives and History, 1980.

Warner, Charles Dudley. *On Horseback: A Tour in Virginia, North Carolina, and Tennessee*. Boston, Mass., and New York: Houghton, Mifflin and Company, 1889.

Wellman, Manly Wade. *The Kingdom of Madison: A Southern Mountain Fastness and Its People*. Chapel Hill: University of North Carolina Press, 1973.

Wheeler, John H. *Reminiscences and Memoirs of North Carolina and Eminent North Carolinians*. Columbus Printing Works, 1884. Reprint. Baltimore, Md.: Genealogical Pubishing Company, 1966.

White, Newman Ivey, ed. *The Frank C. Brown Collection of North Carolina Folklore*. 5 vols. Durham, N.C.: Duke University Press, 1952.

Zeigler, Wilbur G., and Ben S. Grosscup. *The Heart of the Alleghanies or Western North Carolina*. Raleigh, N.C.: Alfred Williams and Company, 1883.

# INDEX

Work Projects Administration (WPA), 212, 268, 278

Yadkin River, 273
Yale, Charlotte, 141
Yancey County, 179–80
Yellow Mountain, 202, 204

Yonaguska, Chief (Drowning Bear), 3–4
Yonahlossee Trail, 237–38
Young's Fort, 139, 140, 144
Yunwi Tsunsdi. *See* Little People

Zionville, 268
Zionville Baptist Church, 268